HOW THE NAVY WON THE WAR

By the same author
Advertising on Trial
Erskine Childers
How the English Made the Alps
We Come Unseen
Riviera
Storming the Eagle's Nest
Queen's Ransom

HOW THE NAVY
WON THE WAR

The Real Instrument of Victory 1914–1918

Jim Ring

Foreword by Rear Admiral Chris Parry

Seaforth
PUBLISHING

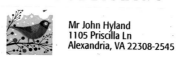

For Michael John Tapper
'Justice is truth in action'

British Library Cataloguing in Publication Data

A catalogue record for this book is available from the British Library

ISBN 978 1 4738 9718 2 (hardback)
ISBN 978 1 4738 9720 5 (epub)
ISBN 978 1 4738 9719 9 (kindle)

Pen & Sword Books Limited incorporates the imprints of Atlas,
Archaeology, Aviation, Discovery, Family History, Fiction, History, Maritime,
Military, Military Classics, Politics, Select, Transport, True Crime, Air World,
Frontline Publishing, Leo Cooper, Remember When, Seaforth Publishing,
The Praetorian Press, Wharncliffe Local History, Wharncliffe Transport,
Wharncliffe True Crime and White Owl.

Typeset and designed by MATS Typesetting, Leigh-on-Sea, Essex SS9 5EB
Printed and bound in Great Britain by TJ International Ltd, Padstow

Contents

Foreword   vi
Preface   x
Introduction   xii

 1 Curtains   1
 2 By Naval Action Alone   14
 3 The Ides of August   36
 4 Lord Kitchener Intervenes   53
 5 Culture and Anarchy   73
 6 Lord Fisher's Modest Proposal   81
 7 The Squadron Which Could Win Us the War   92
 8 Independence Day   107
 9 The Kaiser Plays Macbeth   129
10 The Plague Bacillus   142
11 Lloyd George's *Coup de Théâtre*   150
12 Don't Do It Again   166
13 One Flew Over the Cuckoo's Nest   178
14 Freedom and Bread   193
Epilogue: Pictures at an Exhibition   205

Sources and Acknowledgements   218
Select Bibliography   220
Index   227

Plate section between pages 72 and 73

Foreword

The title of this book might seem a radical, even provocative, way of describing the Royal Navy's role in the First World War, especially as British public perception, folk memory and the vast output of documentation, memoirs, letters and poetry from four million soldiers (in comparison to 450,000 naval personnel) have tended to favour the decisive role of land forces in the defeat of the Central Powers. This view has also been firmly entrenched because of the persistent but erroneous belief that all wars have to be won, almost by definition, on land with 'boots on the ground', whereas, in reality, it is the *effects* of war on land (where people live) that are decisive. In many cases, these effects are indeed realised by forces on the ground, but not always, as when a population is starved, bombarded from the air or blockaded into submission.

It is also difficult for the public to connect emotionally and physically with war at sea; battlefield tours and re-enactments are evidently problematic, there are no landscapes to wander over, few mass graves and, until recent decades, precious few relics to be recovered.[1] This detachment is reinforced by the public notion, born of a tradition of famous sea fights characterised by Nelson's three glorious victories, that success in sea warfare is only about battles. The Royal Navy itself contributed to this misunderstanding of its role and achievement in the First World War. The instincts of its officers and men were to replicate the tactical feats of daring and derring-do that they so admired in their Nelsonian forebears. Every battle had been a missed opportunity, especially Jutland. Lord Chatfield, writing of the end of the war, lamented that 'the crowning feat of British arms, the destruction in battle of the German Fleet, had been denied the navy'.

However, Chatfield and his colleagues missed the point by confusing strategic and tactical effect. British strategy for a war against Germany and its allies envisaged the imposition of a tight sea blockade that would deprive both enemy military forces and populations of the will and means to continue a war: 'in a protracted war, the wheels of our sea power (though they would grind the German population slowly perhaps) would grind them exceedingly small – grass would sooner or later grow in the streets of Hamburg and wide-spread dearth and ruin would be inflicted'. The criterion for strategic success would be the imposition of a stranglehold on the Central Powers' maritime communications by 'far distant, storm-beaten [predominantly British] ships'[2] of the Allies and the suppression of Germany's attempts to break that stranglehold, while Allied armies, once the battle-lines had stabilised, fixed the enemy in position, as modern doctrinal thinking has it, until enough fighting power was available to drive the enemy from France and Belgium.

As will be seen, the blockade's effectiveness restricted the main theatre of war to Europe and allowed the Entente powers to dominate the sea-lanes of the world. It largely confined Germany's High Seas Fleet to port, despite the attempt at Jutland to reduce significantly the substantial margin of British naval superiority.[3] More importantly, it caused the progressive erosion of the political and public will in the Central Powers from 1916 in the face of severe shortages of raw materials and food. Admiral Scheer (the commander of the High Seas Fleet) admitted as early as late summer of 1916 that: 'the enemy's vast material superiority cannot be coped with to such a degree as to make us masters of the blockade inflicted on us'.[4]

The result was that Germany resorted to instituting its own blockade of Britain by attempting 'the crushing of English economic life through U-boat action against English commerce' (Scheer[5]) through a resumption of unrestricted submarine warfare in February 1917. As a result, the first six months of 1917 were a critically dangerous time for Britain and its allies,[6] leading Fisher to ask, 'Can the Army win the war before the Navy loses it?'[7] Beatty also entirely understood the strategic issue: 'Our armies might advance a mile a day and slay the Hun in the thousands, but the real crux lies in whether we blockade the enemy to his knees or whether he does the same to us'.[8]

However, the catastrophic effect of the German decision was to bring the United States into the war on the side of the Allies and the deployment of two million troops to Europe, with unrestricted submarine warfare thwarted by the (belated) introduction of convoy techniques and the considerable destroyer and minelaying reinforcement provided by the United States Navy.[9] Meanwhile, the remorseless effects of the blockade provoked continuing unrest, severely depleted military supply chains, malnutrition and, from 1917 onwards, mutiny, starvation and revolution.

Contemporary opinion was in no doubt about what had brought Germany and its allies to defeat. Sir Walter Runciman wrote to Jellicoe on 14 November 1918:

> Throughout these four years every sane Englishman's mind has rested in confidence on the Navy, and now the end has come the British Navy is more clearly than ever both the saviour of the country and the destroyer of the Central Powers. How true it is and how often forgotten that the final collapse is the direct inevitable result of our command of the seas![10]

In Germany, Erich Raeder,[11] reflected that 'we were in the end defeated by sea power, which deprived us of our food and raw materials, and slowly throttled by the blockade'.

This book will enlighten readers about the Royal Navy's decisive weakening of the fighting capacity of the Central Powers and the collective will of their populations. It will also show how the final Allied land offensive that began on 18 June 1918 would scarcely have been possible without the vast amount of war material and reinforcements that had been successfully carried to Europe from America and the wider world. There will still be doubters about the Navy's importance in the First World War; the folk memory and public sentiment, fixed as they are on trenches, war poetry, pals' battalions and re-enactors, remain too strong. Nevertheless, in encouraging the reader to look at the war through the other end of the telescope, so to speak, the book should restore some balance to assessments about how the Allies managed to prevail. Not for nothing was the 2014 London commemoration of the dead of the war entitled 'Blood Swept Lands *and* Seas of Red'.[12]

Rear Admiral Dr Chris Parry CBE PhD

1 In the book, *The History of the First World War in 100 Objects* by John Hughes-Wilson, the war at sea attracted a mere ten objects.
2 The famous expression of Alfred Thayer Mahan, writing of the British blockading ships in the war against Napoleon.
3 In the memorable words of an American journalist, 'The German fleet has assaulted its jailer, but it is still in jail'. Geoffrey Bennett, *Naval Battles of the First World War* (London: Batsford, 1968), p246.
4 Reinhard Scheer, *Germany's High Seas Fleet in World War One* (London: Cassell, 1919), pp168–9.
5 Ibid.
6 Monthly losses of shipping to U-boats in the first six months of 1917 varied between 600,000 and 860,000 tons.
7 Arthur Marder, *1917: Year of Crisis* (London: OUP, 1969), pp1 –13.
8 Ibid, p40.
9 The United States not only contributed a battle squadron (the 6th) to the Grand Fleet, but also, just as importantly, destroyers to add substantial anti-submarine capacity and minelaying assets to block access routes for German submarines and surface raiders in the North Sea and Channel.
10 A Temple Patterson (ed), *The Jellicoe Papers Volume II* (London: Navy Record Society, 1968), p281.
11 The former chief of staff to Admiral Franz Hipper. He later became, as a Grand Admiral, the head of the Kriegsmarine 1928–1943.
12 Between July and November 2014, the moat of the Tower of London was filled by 888,246 ceramic poppies by artists Paul Cummins and Tom Pipe.

Preface

I had not thought of writing anything about the Great War.

At the time the idea was first put to me, I was just preparing a novel for the press and had already published a clutch of works of non-fiction. If asked, I sometimes said they all had a common theme of the British Empire in its less formal expressions: as it were, on holiday. A book about the English in the Alps, a sequel about the Alps at war, the tale of the French Riviera under unofficial English rule, the story of Britain's Cold War submariners, and a biography of Erskine Childers, he of *The Riddle of the Sands*. Frankly, it was rather difficult to make the cap fit. Still, the books had given me some appreciation of that wondrous thing, the cloud-capped towers of the British Empire at the zenith of its majesty, grace and power; and they had given me an interest in the one organisation that made the Empire possible: the Royal Navy; and in working on Childers I had come across Commodore Reginald Tyrwhitt, under whom the martyr to the Irish cause served in the Great War.

Tyrwhitt, hawk-nosed and keen of eye, was one of the forgotten naval heroes of the war. Wherever there was trouble in the North Sea, Tyrwhitt's Harwich Force of light cruisers and destroyers was sure to be there. Heligoland Bight, Dogger Bank and a score of lesser-known actions gave him the reputation of 'creating the right atmosphere' to discourage the pretensions of Kaiser Wilhelm's stripling Kaiserliche Marine, the Imperial Germany Navy. Childers adored him. On returning to harbour one day in his flagship HMS *Arethusa*, Tyrwhitt was gainsaid. 'The Commodore was slightly annoyed at our stern persisting in swinging to windward. He does not like nature to defy him!' I was more than happy to be asked to write a new biography of the man who became Admiral of the Fleet Sir Reginald Yorke Tyrwhitt, 1st Baronet GCB DSO, the only senior naval officer to emerge from the Great War with a reputation beyond reproach.

On reading about Tyrwhitt and his background, it immediately became apparent that he slipped into the black hole of the unjustly neglected. In his time, a household name to be bandied about with the Beattys, Beresfords, Fishers, Jacksons and Jellicoes of the naval world, Tyrwhitt is now a name associated with shirts. Yet as soon became equally clear, it was not just Tyrwhitt who had been forgotten. It was the whole of the Royal Navy and its work during the war – with the unfortunate exception of the battle of Jutland, a scab always being picked. In *The Riddle of the Sands*, Childers had written in 1903 what he called 'a novel with a purpose', warning his readers of the lamentable complacency of the Admiralty and 'those blockheads of statesmen' in the face of the growing power and ambition of Wilhelmine Germany and the Imperial German Navy. All in all, here was an opportunity too good to miss. I might explore the extent to which Childers' 'clarion call' to action had been answered; judge whether his concerns had been justified and – accordingly – whether Tyrwhitt and the Royal Navy's story were justly forgotten. This is the book I have written.

Introduction

This book corrects a misconception, sets the record straight, rights a wrong: quite an important wrong, too, some might feel.

As a nation we sometimes seem to have a peculiarly powerful yet myopic view of the Great War. It's short-sighted because of the extent to which a global conflict has been reduced and narrowed to the fields of Flanders and plains of Picardy, the trenches of the Western Front where the members of the British Expeditionary Force died in their hundreds of thousands. This is the war that still lingers in folk memory, the bells that toll the great names of Bapaume, Cambrai, Loos, Mons, Passchendaele, Vimy, Ypres and above all of the Somme; of the Last Post at the Menin Gate, of those known unto God in cemeteries from Arras to Zeebrugge. Sombre names, redolent of senseless, futile, wholesale slaughter; of armies sent apparently aimlessly across the Channel to – in Churchill's graphic phrase – 'chew barbed wire in Flanders'. This is the war of Vera Brittain, Robert Graves, Isaac Rosenberg, Wilfred Owen, Siegfried Sassoon, Charles Sorley and Edward Thomas. It is the war of C R W Nevinson, John Singer Sargent, David Bomberg, Eric Kennington, John Nash and Percy Wyndham Lewis.

Yet although in some respects the truth, this reading is something of a caricature – even a travesty – of the war that was to end European supremacy, to see the fall of the Habsburg, Ottoman, Tsarist and German empires, the slaughter of 10 million combatants, the birth of totalitarianism and the end of utopian ideas about the ever-increasing perfection of the human race – the one in Europe, anyway. As Paul Fussell pointed out in *The Great War and Modern Memory*, such views are in many respects a function of the force of literature and of the written word over historical, political and economic fact. It is a consequence of the evergreen poetry and prose of that war, of 'Strange Meeting', 'Anthem for Doomed Youth', 'Dulce et Decorum Est', *Memoirs of an Infantry Officer, Goodbye to All That* and *Testament of Youth* that we see the war the way we do. All's quiet on the Western

Front. No matter the six other theatres of war so designated by the Triple Entente: the Balkans, Russia, Egypt, Africa, Asia and Australasia. Say nothing of Togoland. This is the war of Flanders fields and the poppies of the annual commemoration of Armistice Day, of the eleventh hour of the eleventh day of the eleventh month. This is the story of Tommy Atkins, of the long, long way to Tipperary, of the Maxim gun, of the Minenwerfer, and of Laurence Binyon's fine words:

> They shall grow not old, as we that are left grow old:
> Age shall not weary them, nor the years condemn.
> At the going down of the sun and in the morning,
> We will remember them.

If a single image can capture that view of the Great War, it is of a bedraggled Tommy in a sodden trench in that dreary, rain-drenched expanse of northern France and southern Belgium called Flanders.

This is a misconstruction for somewhere like Great Britain, removed as we are from the rest of the world, a pattern of islands off the European continental shelf. Ours is the sceptred isle, the fortress built by nature for herself against infection and the hand of war. We are an island race. As a consequence we are – or at least we were – a sea power. In 1914 by far and away the greatest of all such powers. A sea power, the power that rules the waves, and through the waves the world.

Sir Edward Grey was the foreign secretary who told the *Westminster Gazette* in August 1914 that the lamps were going out all over Europe. He also said that 'The British Army should be a projectile fired by the British Navy'. He made the simple yet quite easily neglected point that, as an island nation, we could mount no direct campaign against our inconvenient, uncivilised, intransigent and often belligerent European neighbours unless and until the Royal Navy ferried the Army across the Channel, the North Sea, or over the great waters beyond to the theatres of war of the Empire further afield. Without the Navy, the Army could not even be used against the Irish. By implication, he said more. He made the point that Great Britain was what Winston Churchill would later call 'the great amphibian'. It had the ability to move its army anywhere in the world to where its force might be most effectively used.

In the Great War, the Navy was – secondly – far more than the Army's ferryman, shepherding troops and hurrying shells, victuals, letters to the rich and letters to the poor to the Western Front and other places as remote as Samoa, Pelew Island and Manila, vital though this work was. Its very existence acted as a deterrent to the invasion foretold in the 'literature of warning', now best recalled by Erskine Childers' *The Riddle of the Sands*. This was a venture which the Deutsches Heer or Imperial German Army certainly contemplated. Yet no invasion fleet of troop transports could risk decimation in the seas around our islands which the Royal Navy commanded. As was once said, the British Isles were lumps of land surrounded by the Navy. Woe betide the invader!

Thirdly, it was the Grand Fleet of revolutionary dreadnought battleships, the lineal – albeit distant – descendants of Nelson's *Victory* that kept its German counterpart, the Hochseeflotte or High Seas Fleet, at bay. For the first half of the war the Grand Fleet kept the seas open to the British mercantile shipping, on which our livelihood, our ability to make war, and indeed our very existence as a nation depended; as a corollary it kept those same seas closed to the German mercantile fleet and denied her the resources of the world open to Britain and her Allies. In the second half of the war we owe to the Navy the defeat of the so-called 'unrestricted' or illegal U-boat warfare that would have seen the country starved.

Finally, it was the Navy's own blockade of Germany that helped bring that country to her knees and precipitated the revolution that saw the Armistice of November 1918, the abdication of the Kaiser, the establishment of a republic, and the peace settlement of Versailles in 1919. By closing the two western approaches to Germany through the Channel and the North Sea and thus denying Germany access to – and from – the Atlantic, the Navy gradually starved the Kaiser's nation of war materiel and food, just as the U-boat campaign had attempted on Great Britain. The difference was that the British blockade – though not in itself – brought the dividend of victory.

These naval achievements were the five pillars of victory, the blockade most of all. Said David Lloyd George, who successively as chancellor, minister of munitions, secretary of state for war and prime minister did as much as any one man to win the war, 'Germany has been broken almost as much by blockade as by military methods.' It was Churchill who said that the commander of the Grand Fleet, Admiral Sir John Jellicoe, was the one man who could lose the war in an afternoon. He did not say that his was also the service which – over an altogether longer period – could play a major part in winning it. For John Buchan the Navy was 'The weapon on which all others depended'. In 2016 Professor Sir Hew Strachan in his inaugural Rothermere American Institute lecture brought this up to date by saying that 'So much of our understanding of the First World War focuses on the conflict on land and yet the nation who controlled the seas also controlled the flow of resources, so critical in such a long and attritional war.' 'Naval power', he concluded, was 'critical to the outcome.'

This story, by no means unfamiliar to naval and military historians, is one which has never captured the public's imagination or, indeed, attention. This is for a number of reasons, not least because the British were deeply disappointed by what they saw as the failure of the Royal Navy during the Great War.

In the nineteenth and early years of the twentieth century the Navy played a part in national consciousness difficult to appreciate today. It was by far and away the most powerful naval force in the world, its magisterial ships were revered as symbols of Great Britain's status as the world's greatest power; Nelson, its most famous son, was the nation's first and foremost national hero; it had been given doctrinal credibility – as if it needed that – by Captain Alfred Thayer Mahan's astonishing bestseller, *The Influence of Sea Power upon History, 1660–1783*; it was the country's talisman on which expectations, sterling and dreadnoughts had been lavished in almost equal quantities; it was the country's principal armed service, the Senior Service, the backbone of the defence of the realm. Jan Morris wrote:

The Royal Navy was the very heart and pride of Empire. Upon it, as everyone knew, the security of the realm rested and around it there grew, like a cloud of reassuring signals, an accretion of legends and

victorious memories, mellowed by age, gun-smoke and salt-spray ...
The British had absolute confidence in their Navy. It was supreme.
It had always won.

'Britannia rules the waves' was the necessary sequitur to 'Rule
Britannia'.

In the early months of the war the Navy was expected on an almost
daily basis to deliver what Lloyd George later called 'the knock-out
blow' that would see an armistice before Christmas. As the days
stretched into weeks, the weeks into months and the months into
years, as the engagements of Heligoland Bight and Dogger Bank were
forgotten and the German naval bombardments of east-coast towns
like Scarborough, Hartlepool, Yarmouth, Whitby and Lowestoft were
remembered or seemed soon to be repeated, people recalled the words
of the coroner at Scarborough. He had called an inquest to deliberate
on the unchallenged Hochseeflotte attack of 16 December 1914 that
had left 424 wounded and eighty-six dead in his home town. It fell to
him to ask the question on everyone's lips, 'Where was the Navy?'

When, at long last, on 31 May 1916 around 250 vessels, twenty-five
admirals and 100,000 men of the two great fleets finally gave battle off
the Danish peninsula of Jutland – at that time the greatest naval battle
ever fought – the Navy lost more than twice the tonnage of the
Hochseeflotte and more than twice as many men. Said the commander
of the Battle Cruiser Squadron, Admiral Sir David Beatty, 'There seems
to be something wrong with our bloody ships today.' Said the Kaiser,
'The spell of Trafalgar has been broken.' No matter that Admiral
Reinhard Scheer's crippled fleet fled the battlefield twice with its tail
between its legs; no matter that it rarely ventured out again from its
Wilhelmshaven bases; no matter that the strategy of the piecemeal
destruction of Jellicoe's Grand Fleet was abandoned, to be replaced by
the unrestricted U-boat warfare that would bring the United States
into the war and precipitate Germany's defeat.

The reality was that Jutland was a strategic victory for Jellicoe and
the country, yet it did not feel so at the time. So many hopes had been
pinned on the spellbinding, majestic, pugnacious leviathans of the
Grand Fleet, such great expectations. With stalemate on the Western
Front and the catastrophe of the Somme unfolding over the summer

of 1916, the Navy seemed to have failed the country in her hour of greatest need. To their utter astonishment, the ship's company of Beatty's flagship *Lion* was booed and jeered by dockyard workers when the battlecruiser limped into Rosyth in the aftermath of the battle; other crews were hissed on the streets of Edinburgh. In 1923 Churchill could write in *The World Crisis*, 'The disappointment of all ranks was deep; and immediately there arose reproaches and recriminations, continued to this day.' A generation later, Captain Donald Macintyre's 1957 account had at its heart 'the old question, *Who won at Jutland?*' Another forty years on and John Keegan could write that, 'the inconclusiveness of the event has continued to haunt the mind of the Royal Navy ever since.' The centenary of the battle in 2016 saw yet more books and – now – television programmes revisiting the old conundrum. After all, in 1916 the German newspaper headlines really had screamed, 'Great Victory at Sea'.

Beyond the exploits of the Grand Fleet itself, the public also found – or was offered – no very convincing answer to the coroner's question. After the revenge of Coronel at the Falklands in December 1914, and the relatively modest actions of Heligoland Bight and Dogger Bank, the escapades of Commodore Reginald Tyrwhitt of the Harwich Force of light cruisers and destroyers caught the public's eye. These were on a small scale, tactical rather than strategic, dashing though they were. Almost by definition, few knew about the underwater exploits of the nascent submarine flotilla; its motto was, after all, 'We Come Unseen'; its remarkable achievements in the Baltic and the Dardanelles attracted little publicity. As the naval historian Andrew Lambert has remarked, much of the other vital but routine work of the Navy, particularly the blockade, was 'grindingly dull and essentially attritional, as naval wars have invariably been.' The squalor, the futility, the tragedy and the sheer scale of the slaughter in the trenches that so struck the war poets and artists had no equivalent in the war at sea. 'Public perceptions,' continues Lambert, 'were dominated by the horrific business of trenches, gas, machine-guns, high explosive, and death on an unprecedented scale. Sea power and dreadnoughts seemed irrelevant'. Neither did the war at sea attract such gifted memorialists. Churchill, something of the Navy's architect as First Lord of the Admiralty from late 1911 to May 1915 found a few words in 1940 to deify the fighter pilots of the RAF and to immortalise their exploits. He found no such lapidary phrases after Jutland, even though he drafted the press release. Nor did anyone else.

It has been suggested that this was a consequence of the relatively small numbers serving in the Navy by comparison with the Army; and – worse still – because the war at sea was neither intrinsically important nor of great significance to the final outcome; and that whereas Kitchener's armies attracted those articulate members of the middle classes who would never normally have enlisted – Sassoon, Blunden, Thomas, Graves – the Navy continued to draw from its traditional wellsprings. These men, it is said, were handier with the sword than the pen. So 'Taffrail' (Captain Henry Taprell Dorling) was a serving officer and a vivid writer who wrote powerfully enough about the destroyers at Jutland, but he was no Nicholas Monsarrat, C S Forester or Patrick O'Brian, let alone a Robert Graves or Erich Maria Remarque. Of the poetry, Shane Leslie's *Jutland: a fragment of epic* is about as good as it gets, and that is not very good at all. A few of Francis Ledwidge's surviving poems concern the sea war. Others include Ronald Hopwood, Rudyard Kipling (*The Fringes of the Fleet*), Constance Renshaw, Cicely Fox Smith, Editha Jenkinson, Wilfred Gibson and Edward Hilton Young. With the exception of Kipling it is not a greatly distinguished list. An anthology of the sea war was published during the war, but soon fell out of print. Who remembers a single poem about the war at sea?

In any case, the wound was left to fester. Although the Navy had its defenders, no pen really exonerated, let alone celebrated, the service; and an opinion once it has crystallised is extremely difficult to dissolve. Three years ago a naval historian – Robert Maltser – could write that until quite recently, 'It was common belief in Britain that the Royal Navy played only a minor part in the war, the Grand Fleet spending most of its time at anchor in Scapa Flow or Cromarty Firth waiting for the German High Seas Fleet to emerge from its bases, and that only one battle, Jutland, was fought in the North Sea.' For Churchill's biographer Martin Gilbert, 'The war at sea was in many ways the forgotten war.' Gary Mead, a recent biographer of Beatty's military counterpart, Field Marshal Sir Douglas Haig, would echo, 'For the general public ... the victory in 1918 was a British-led victory, won by the biggest British Army ever to take part in a continental war.' Sea power – or indeed the French, Russians or the Americans – played no part.

This is the travesty, and it is one to which there are plenty of parallels. Sir Herbert Maxwell told his Edwardian contemporaries that, 'Nine English out of ten think of Waterloo as a purely British victory in which the army of the King of Prussia figures, if it figures at all, as a merely subsidiary factor'; contrary to the implications of *Saving Private Ryan*, a film that has informed the cadre of millennials, the Normandy D-Day in landings in 1944 were far from an exclusively American venture, bravely though GIs fought on Omaha and Utah beaches. I suppose everyone knows about Hiroshima; Nagasaki is rarely mentioned. Stalin's efforts to exterminate his critics on the most ambitious of scales belittle – at least in numerical terms – those of Hitler's endeavours in Auschwitz, Belzec, Chelmno, Majdanek, Sobibor, Treblinka and Trostenets. There is no equivalent to Holocaust Day.

This is all thoroughly regrettable. It is the more so because, in reality, the Navy's story is such a good one.

I have outlined the pivotal contribution the service made to victory. Of the men behind it, Admiral 'Jacky' Fisher, creator of the dreadnoughts and the Edwardian navy at large, was one of the Senior Service's greatest characters and greatest servants who – if he had lived today – would have been the best ever contestant on *Strictly Come Dancing*. Dazzlingly opinionated, astonishingly prescient and remarkably light on his feet, in 1908 he predicted that European war would break out in September 1914. The tale of his relationship with Churchill, who brought the ageing admiral back into harness as First Sea Lord – professional head of the Navy – in October 1914, has all the overtones of tragedy. The First Lord of the Admiralty himself performed miracles in the two and a half years up until the outbreak of war in August 1914. Thereafter, the political head of the Navy – the man who in 1940 became the saviour of the nation – over-reached himself in a series of gaffes and misjudgements that culminated in the catastrophe of Gallipoli and his dismissal by Prime Minister Herbert Asquith. Churchill's wife Clementine wrote, 'I thought he would never get over the Dardanelles. I thought he would die of grief.' Admiral Sir John Jellicoe and Admiral Sir David Beatty, respectively commanding the battleship and battlecruiser fleets under the overall command of the former, provide a wonderful study in contrasting character and method. The one – Jellicoe – a stickler for rules, procedures and the punctilious Grand Fleet Battle Orders which he wrote himself, these being 'the tactics to be pursued by the different units of the Fleet in action under all conceivable conditions.' What need twenty-five admirals? What need one? The other a man of dash and brio, flair and daring, a swashbuckling huntsman who was as much at home with the Quorn as in *Lion's* wardroom. Detail he abhorred. A cartoonist might have cast them as Jekyll and Hyde or Punch and Judy. Among the public they shared the blame for Jutland, and the long-sighted may discover in Trafalgar Square two remarkably small busts of the pair, cowering under the shadow of Nelson. Was someone making a point?

Among their underlings, Roger Keyes and Reginald Tyrwhitt might have walked straight from the pages of *Stirring Deeds of Britain's Sea-Dogs.* At a rather low point in the war, of which there were many, the Fourth Sea Lord proposed that all the British admirals ('princes of the sea') should be dismissed and Tyrwhitt promoted commander-in-chief. The commander of the Harwich Force, responsible among other things for keeping the Hochseeflotte out of the southern part of the North Sea, was almost alone of his senior naval or military contemporaries in retaining his command throughout the war. He was not found wanting. A household name, he was the hero of the battles of Heligoland Bight and Dogger Bank that have largely eluded public memory. An Admiralty misjudgement kept him from Jutland. A young lieutenant on one of the flotilla destroyers at the battle wrote, 'The destroyer business in the night at Jutland was an awful mess-up. If only they allowed Com. T [Tyrwhitt] to be there ... things might have been very different.'

Tyrwhitt's friend Roger Keyes was a splendidly aggressive officer, pioneer of the submarine flotilla and the man behind the spectacular Zeebrugge Raid of April 1918. Instigator of the Heligoland Bight raid of August 1914, he was also one the few to emerge with any credit from the Dardanelles, not least because of the work of Martin Dunbar-Nasmith in the submarine *E11*. Similarly tireless and unsung were officers and men who crewed the ships of the blockade, the 10th Cruiser Squadron, successively under Rear Admiral Dudley de Chair and Vice Admiral Reginald Tupper. These were the contemporary counterparts of the real heroes of the Napoleonic wars, of Mahan's 'far distant, storm-beaten ships, upon which the Grand Army never looked, [but which] stood between it and the dominion of the world.' In 1915 Maurice Hankey, secretary to Asquith's war committee and much else besides, told the prime minister that 'when the psychological moment arrives and the cumulative effects [of blockade] reach their maximum and are perhaps combined with crushing defeats of the enemy, the results may not be merely material, but decisive'.

By comparison the commanders of the land war were for some – though by no means all historians – rather less competent. Field Marshals Kitchener (as Secretary of State for War), French and especially Haig were pre-eminent among those whose repeated and repetitive bloodlettings meant they lived to inspire a good book with an even better title, *On the Psychology of Military Incompetence*. For more than three years they sought and failed to break the deadlock of the trenches that ran from the Alps to the North Sea. In so doing they eventually expended around three-quarters of a million British and Empire lives, rightly called the flower of the nation. Their work was crowned on the Somme, the battle which – for John Keegan – 'marked the end of an age of vital optimism in British life which has never been recovered.' Only in 1917 when the collapse of Tsarist Russia into the mire of Bolshevism was counterbalanced by the entry of the United States into the war were there many signs of hope. When the land war in the west culminated in the great German offensives of the spring and early summer of 1918, the Allied generals under the choreography of Generalissimo Ferdinand Foch stemmed the tide by means of a headlong retreat towards Paris and the Channel ports; the subsequent Hundred Days Offensive drove the Deutsches Heer back towards its own borders. This was undoubtedly a great Allied achievement and the contribution made by the Kitchener armies to victory from 1916 onwards was pivotal – in many respects despite of, rather than because of, its senior leadership. As Niall Ferguson asserts, 'Without the armies raised by Kitchener, Germany would have won the land war.' Yet it was the sailors of the Germany navy who sparked the revolution that brought the final collapse of their country. They refused to man their ships to execute Admiral Reinhard Scheer's suicidal plan of 24 October 1918 for one last sortie against what had had become an overwhelmingly superior Grand Fleet. Armistice followed.

These are the facts, these the people, this the argument.

I have, though, no inclination to add to the lofty pile of narrative histories of the Great War. There is a splendid scene in *The Riddle of the Sands*, when it occurs to the novel's heroes Davies and Carruthers that their yacht's library may betray their purpose of espionage in the German Frisian Islands. 'Then there were the naval books [amongst them, of course, Alfred Thayer Mahan]. Davies scanned them with a look I knew well. "'There are too many of them," he said, in the tone of a cook fixing the fate of superfluous kittens. "Let's throw them overboard."' In general, British readers have certainly been well served by historians of the Great War. A spacious library could be stocked using such sources alone. John Buchan broke the ground with his magisterial and hugely influential history of the war. He was followed by a quire of great writers and historians ranging from Churchill, Arthur Bryant and Basil Liddell Hart to A J P Taylor and John Keegan. More are now making or burnishing their reputations. It is also remarkable how often, so long after the event, that writers of fiction turn to the Great War for inspiration, Pat Barker, William Boyd and Sebastian Faulks just amongst the best. Then there are the books on the war at sea itself, with more than five hundred accounts of Jutland alone – many of which consider how many angels can dance on the head of a pin; or at least dwell in great detail on a battle that lasted not much more than twelve hours.

So there are, indeed, too many; it would be presumptuous of me try to emulate such writers; and in any case yet another narrative history does not necessarily seem the best way of making my point in a fresh and accessible way for those without a professional interest in the Great War.

Rather, I have chosen within a broadly chronological structure that alludes to rather than recounts in any detail the story of the conflict, to dramatise the turning-points and milestones of the war that play to my particular argument. For instance, it was the abandonment of the Imperial German Navy's ambition for a decisive naval surface battle that was at least as important as Jutland itself; it was Lloyd George's imposition of the convoy system on a reluctant Admiralty that turned the battle against the U-boats; it was the submarine, the mine, the newfangled flying machines and the tank that turned the course of the war almost as much as Haig's infantry offensives on the Western Front; the Germans dug their own grave when they bankrolled Lenin's return from exile in the famous sealed train; it was – as I have remarked – as much the revolt and mutiny amongst the men of the Imperial Navy at Kiel as the events on the battlefield that finally forced Wilhelmine Germany to the agree the terms of the Armistice; and so on. These epiphanies, snapshots and vignettes may or may not be less eye-catching than the more spectacular failures and successes of the War Cabinet and its attendant admirals and generals. They are the more intriguing because, ultimately, they were decisive. They were the days, hours and even moments during which the war was won.

Clearly, a very fair number of these could be identified. With a bow to President Woodrow Wilson of the United States, he of the famous Fourteen Points, I have chosen that number. In so doing, I have written what amounts neither to a general account of the war nor a history of the war at sea. I have rather tried to show the different ways in which the two services contributed towards victory. My aim in so doing has not been to belittle the considerable achievements of the Army – not least of the men themselves – but to do justice to the Navy.

A century after the catastrophic events of the Great War, in the midst of a time at which the country is once again pondering its own identity – indeed is undergoing an existential crisis that is surely the envy of the shades of Simone de Beauvoir and Jean-Paul Sartre – this story seems worth telling.

'War. What is it good for? Absolutely nothing.' Perhaps the American singer Edwin Starr was right in his lyrical diatribe about the war in Vietnam. Yet we have an apparently inexhaustible and unquenchable thirst and appetite for accounts of conflict, especially of the two world wars. This is perhaps because battle brings to the fore some of the most remarkable qualities of humankind: heroism, unparalleled courage, devotion to duty, comradeship, ingenuity, endurance, collective effort and self-sacrifice; as well as some of the most deplorable, despicable, vicious, brutal, barbarous and, indeed, inhuman. War displays human nature at its most extreme. Personally, I find it difficult to deny Churchill's proposal that the country's stand against Hitler in 1940 was her finest hour; impossible to take issue with his speech to the boys at his old school, Harrow, a year later. 'These are not dark days: these are great days – the greatest days our country has ever lived.' Whether we like it or not, we owe much of our sense of identity as a nation to our naval and military record; much as Canadians, Australians and New Zealanders feel that their national identities were forged in the fires of Vimy Ridge and the Gallipoli peninsula; much as Germans owe a good deal of their sense of self to their own rather less happy chronicle. 'The Germans,' noted John Keegan, 'cannot decently mourn their four million dead of the Second World War, compromised as the Wehrmacht was by the atrocities of the Nazi state.' Such is the hand of history that lies on their shoulder. As A J P Taylor once remarked, 'War has been throughout history the curse and inspiration of mankind.'

That said, we owe it not only to the past, but to the present and to the future to have a proper understanding of the essentials of our own record. The Great War might have been fought on land, but it was won at sea. Not so, but this is much closer to the truth than is widely believed and understood. In 1988 Keegan could write that 'no Briton of my generation, raised on food brought through the U-boat packs in the battle of the Atlantic, can ever ignore the narrowness of the margin by which sea-power separates survival from starvation in the islands he inhabits.' Keegan's generation has gone the way of all flesh, and the millennials who in due course will hold the fate of the country in their hands have not yet had the sort of experiences that would give them the opportunity to ignore or to forget. At least in some respects, they should. As George Santayana said, 'Those who cannot remember the past are condemned to repeat it.'

So my wife – who certainly says she studied under Professor Sir Lawrence Freedman at London's Kings College Department of War Studies – suggested as a title for this work *Where Was the Navy?* Feeling that something marginally more nuanced might be fitting, I have settled for *How the Navy Won the War*. This is the statement I hope this book will be found to explain.

1

Curtains

'The war which is now on the threshold of coming to an end, has been won by sea power ... Military successes have been great. Military victories have been achieved under circumstances which have produced difficulties all of which have been overcome by the greatest gallantry, devotion to duty and sacrifice. But all that would have been of no value without the sea power of England.'

Admiral Sir David Beatty, 24 November 1918

It is Picardy in November 1918, Picardy between Paris and the English Channel, the Picardy of grey uplands and hedgeless roads, of unfenced fields, lines of stiff trees, and here and there the shallow valley of a stream; it is a landscape of sodden vistas, of the dreary waterlogged plain of Albert, Arras, Vimy Ridge and the Somme. Here the night falls early on the countless unmarked graves of Frenchmen, Englishmen and Germans alike. This is the epicentre of the Western Front, the last resting-place of perhaps half a million unlived lives. It is a godforsaken place. Here, in the trenches, in the shell-holes, in the dugouts, in no man's land, here in the entanglements of barbed wire, in the pillboxes, on the fire-steps, on the stretchers, in the casualty-clearing stations, here in the makeshift operating theatres, here is where hope died for friend and foe alike. Wilfred Owen wrote:

'Strange friend,' I said, 'here is no cause to mourn.'
'None,' said that other, 'save the undone years,
The hopelessness. Whatever hope is yours,
Was my life also; I went hunting wild
After the wildest beauty in the world,
Which lies not calm in eyes, or braided hair,
But mocks the steady running of the hour,

1

And if it grieves, grieves richlier than here.
For by my glee might many men have laughed,
And of my weeping something had been left,
Which must die now. I mean the truth untold,
The pity of war, the pity war distilled.'

Through a stygian gloom, through darkness visible, the German party pushed its way gingerly south towards the French lines, the sharp air dank in their nostrils, the rank smell compounded of wet clay, latrines, cordite and rotting human flesh, the carbide lamps on the cars picking out a road – if road it was – cratered by mortar and shellfire. The men had been directed to approach the French picket lines on the roadway that ran due west from Chimay via Formies and La Capelle to Guise. It skirted the Franco-Belgian border where the curtain rose on the European apocalypse four years and three months earlier, in August 1914. The Germans heralded their approach with white flags and a bugler sounding his trumpet. One. Two. Three. Four. The shrill blasts pierced the dark air, where who knows what treachery stirs, for this was indeed no man's land.

Among the Kaiser's men was Matthias Erzberger. He was the 43-year-old Secretary of State whose son had died three weeks earlier in the Rhineland, in Karlsruhe. Not of wounds, but as a victim of the influenza epidemic that was sweeping the whole of the world. In the golden morning it was Erzberger, as one of the leaders of the Catholic Centre Party and secretary of the country's Military Affairs Committee, who had formulated a memorandum on Germany's War Aims. It was presented to the Reichstag, Imperial Germany's parliament in Berlin, on 2 September 1914. The purpose of victory, he noted, was to gain control of the European continent 'for all time'. The three conditions necessary for the success of this proposal were 'the abolition of neutral states on Germany's borders', the dismemberment of the Russian titan, and the end of 'England's intolerable hegemony in world affairs'. He shared with some of today's politicians the characteristic that he had 'no convictions, only appetites'. Now these plans lay in ruins and Erzberger bore on his shoulders the realisation that with the failure of Ludendorff's great spring offensives and with revolution erupting at home, the war was utterly lost. He remembered, 'My feelings on the journey to Karlsruhe were no more depressed than at the present moment.' In the whirligig of the collapsing German state, he had been charged by the new chancellor, Prince Maximilian of Baden, to do what he could with the Allies. 'Obtain what mercy you can, Matthias,' the prince had instructed as the delegation left Berlin on Wednesday, 6 November 1918, 'but for God's sake bring peace.'

At around 10pm the following day, some one hundred and fifty yards beyond the German lines, Erzberger spotted the first of the *poilus*, elements of the French 171st Infantry Battalion. The chancellor's men were expected. Asked one young soldier tentatively: '*Finie la guerre?*' After 1567 days, after the slaughter of 10 million combatants, perhaps four times that number in all, it seemed impossible. Formally, curtly, the bugler was replaced by his French opposite number, and an escort of French headquarters' staff assembled. The five-car motorcade edged southwest down the broken road towards the railhead at Tergnier, due south of St Quentin, a halting journey through a landscape ravished by war, a world of swamp, duckboards, of the amputated stumps of trees, of rubble and of ruin. Of Tergnier itself, once a flourishing township, little still seemed to exist beyond the railway, its metals withering away into the night. Here stood a special train: a locomotive with steam up, a dining car, a sleeping car and a special coach. This had been chosen with forethought and care. It was upholstered in a rich green satin, embroidered with a bold 'N'. Once it had belonged to Napoleon III, the French emperor from whom the Prussians had seized the Rhineland provinces of Alsace and Lorraine in 1870. Touché!

The delegation, the German Armistice Commission, was ushered on board. The doors were locked and the blinds drawn down. Already it was two in the morning. The men dozed uneasily as they clanked their way slowly southwest towards a destination unknown. Around dawn, not much before 0800 at this time of year, the train drew to a halt close to Rethondes. This was forty miles northeast of Paris in the forest of Compiègne. The blinds were raised and the chancellor's men found themselves in a forest clearing. Drawn up just feet away was a train the mirror image of their own: a locomotive, a dining car, a wagon-lit and a saloon car. At around 0900 they were ushered into the dining car, a railway wagon numbered 2419. It had been set out with table and chairs for a conference yet had something of the air of a stage-set. There were little lamps under pink shades, maps of the front line, hand-cranked telephones and – on each side of the table – the place names of the participants in the making of history.

There was a setting for Erzberger himself as leader of the delegation, for the foreign minister Count Alfred von Oberndorff; for Major General Detlof von Winterfeldt of the army; for the navy, Admiral Ernst Vanselow. Their opposite numbers were Marshal of France Ferdinand Foch, the Allied supreme commander; General Maxime Weygand, Foch's chief of staff; and three British naval officers: the First Sea Lord Admiral Sir Rosslyn Wemyss, his deputy Rear Admiral George Hope, and his assistant Captain Jack Marriott. The British Army, Field Marshal Haig himself, the commander-in-chief of the British armies on the Western Front, was represented by the Frenchman Foch, commander-in-chief of the Allied armies as a whole. The Marshal of France, a wizened little figure looking rather more than his sixty-seven years, established the credentials of the Kaiser's party, not that there could be much doubt. Satisfied, and addressing the party through an interpreter, Foch posed a rhetorical question. 'Ask these gentlemen what they want.' Erzberger replied, 'We have come to inquire into the terms of an armistice, to be concluded on land, on sea and in the air.' It was a statement for which the world had been waiting for more than four years, and for which Great Britain and her Empire and her great Allies of Russia, France and – later – the United States, had sacrificed so many lives. Foch was prepared. Under the direction of Prime Minister David Lloyd George in England and his counterpart Georges Clemenceau in France, and under the influence of President Wilson's Fourteen Points, he had himself largely drafted the terms of the Armistice.

General Weygand read out the thirty-four clauses in French, the interpreter repeating them in German. They were uncompromising. Evacuation of all the invaded countries including Alsace-Lorraine, seized from France in 1871; the evacuation of the west bank of the Rhine and the strategic bridgeheads on the east bank at Cologne, Coblenz and Maine; surrender of 5000 heavy guns, 25,000 machine guns, 3000 *Minenwerfer* ('mine-launchers', or mortars), 2000 aircraft; the surrender of 5000 locomotives, 150,000 wagons and 5000 motor lorries. Erzrberger and his colleagues listened dumbfounded at the ever-growing list. Their eyes wandered over to the First Sea Lord, Admiral Rosslyn Wemyss, nicely rendered by the economist Maynard Keynes as 'A comical, quizzical face and a single eye-glass ... pleasure-loving, experienced, lazy.' Wemyss returned their stares. 'A common-looking man,' he noted of Erzberger, 'Typical German bourgeois.' The Kaiser's great Hochseeflotte was also to be sacrificed. The best ten battleships, six battlecruisers, eight light cruisers, fifty of the best destroyers, all of the submarines, too. As the *coup de grâce*, Weygand told them of the right of the Allies on failure of execution of any of these conditions to renounce the Armistice within forty-eight hours. By the time he had finished, Vanselow was in tears. They were told they had seventy-two hours to accept the terms. If not, the war would continue. As the proposals were essentially to demilitarise Germany, Erzberger realised it would scarcely be possible for her to renew hostilities should the Armistice break down.

The terms were not negotiable. Five weeks earlier, the Oberste Heersleitung (German Supreme Army Command or OHL) had told the Kaiser and the Chancellor that the military position on the Western Front was hopeless. On the night of 29/30 October a revolt by the sailors of the Kaiserliche Marine in Wilhelmshaven spread like the plague across the whole of Wilhelmine Germany. In the forest clearing on Sunday, 10 November Erzberger's delegates were shown newspapers brought from Paris. The Kaiser had abdicated, Prince Maximilian had been dismissed, a republic had been declared, headed by the Social Democrat Friedrich Ebert. Later that day, Erzberger was telegraphed by Ebert with instructions to accept the terms of what amounted to unconditional surrender. Winterfeldt commented to one of Foch's staff, François de Bourbon-Busset, 'We are prepared to sign one of the most shameful capitulations in history. We are obliged to because of the revolution. We don't even know there will be a Germany tomorrow.'

It was signed shortly after 0500 in the clearing, Erzberger formally protesting that the terms would lead to anarchy and famine. They were to come into effect at 1100, Paris time: the eleventh hour of the eleventh day of the eleventh month. It was a phrase like the tolling of a funeral bell. Foch himself had been seen by Erzberger only at the beginning of the meetings. Now he reappeared. '*Eh bien, messieurs, c'est fini, allez.*'

Elsewhere, it had already finished, the combatants going or gone. The Kaiser's Germany was the last and the greatest of the Central Powers to acknowledge the inevitable. Bulgaria had signed an armistice on 29 September 1918, the Austro-Hungarian Empire collapsed in the last week of October, the Ottoman Empire followed suit with the Armistice of Mudros on 30 October. On 3 November the conflict on the Italian front was ended by the Armistice of Villa Giusti. On land, peace had broken out after 1571 days of war. On the Western Front, John Buchan recorded:

Suddenly, as the watch hands found eleven, there came a second of expected silence and then a curious rippling sound which observers far behind the front likened to the noise of a light wind. It was the sound of men cheering from the Vosges to the sea ... A new era had come and the old world passed away.

The terms of the Armistice demanded the evacuation by the German army of its forces on foreign soil, notably in France and Belgium. The Allies allowed the Deutsches Heer a week's grace to begin its retreat, the embittered and exhausted battalions heading back along the roads of France and Belgium where their compatriots had marched so triumphantly in August 1914. By the end of November the tables had been entirely turned. Allied forces were now on the Fatherland's soil. Haig's columns had reached the Rhine, the great natural border that had developed in the course of the creation of the unified Teutonic state into such a powerful symbol of German nationalism. In early December the occupation of the bridgehead at Cologne on the eastern banks of the Rhine by the British was followed by that of Coblenz by the American Third Army, and by French forces in Mainz. The Union Jack, the Stars and Stripes and the Tricolour flew proudly over the great river crossings under Allied control. Soon, around a quarter of a million British Empire troops found themselves in Germany as the Armies of Occupation. Formed on 1 February 1919, they would comprise the Home Army, the Army of the Rhine, the Army of the Middle East, the Detachment of the Far North, and the Garrisons of the Crown Colonies and India. On land, the humiliation of the Central Powers was complete, a disgrace to usher in the peace negotiations that would culminate in the Treaty of Versailles in 1919.

The procedures for the surrender of Germany's sea forces, the Kaiserliche Marine, were similarly elaborate. As John Buchan reminded his readers, 'the human mind loves a dramatic finale, and asks for ostensible signs of victory.' Admiral Hugo von Meurer of the German Imperial Navy was ordered to Rosyth to take instructions dictated by the Armistice terms concerning the Imperial German Navy. At 1430 on Friday, 15 November the German light cruiser *Königsberg* steamed under Royal Navy escort into Rosyth. This was the great dockyard on the Firth of Forth, conceived in 1903 as part of the response to the need for naval bases on the North Sea, facing Germany. Like Foch in Compiègne, Admiral Sir David Beatty, the C-in-C of the Grand Fleet, was mindful of the symbolism of the scene when Meurer stepped aboard his flagship, the 33,000-ton super-dreadnought HMS *Queen Elizabeth*. Writing to his mistress, Eugénie Godfrey-Faussett, Beatty confided:

> my Dramatic Sense was highly developed at the moment. When he marched up the Gangway he was met by a blaze of light from groups of the strongest electric sunlights which lighted the Gangway and the Path he trod from there to my hatchway, outside the Path everything was inky Black and perfect stillness. Actually on the edge of the Path of Light, half in and half out, was a line of the fattest marine sentries about 2 paces apart with fixed bayonets upon which the light gleamed, wherever he looked he met a bayonet ... the wretch nearly collapsed on the Quarter Deck ... where I met him supported by my 2nd in Command O. de B [Osmond Brock] Tyrwhitt and several members of my staff.

Beatty demanded Meurer's credentials and asked him to identify his staff. Reflecting the red revolution that had swept over Germany, the admiral was attended by three delegates from the Sailors' and Soldiers' Council, three from the People's Council. Beatty read Meurer a prepared statement: the clauses of the Armistice covering naval matters and the orders necessary to carry out their terms. Beatty was unbending, Meurer aghast. Beatty continued:

Meurer, in a voice like lead, with an ashen face said, 'I do not think the Commander-in-Chief is aware of the condition of Germany' and then in dull heavy tones, began to retail the effect of the Blockades. It had brought Revolution in the North which had spread to the South, then to the East and finally to the West, that anarchy was rampant, the seed was sown, it remained for the harvest of human lives to be reaped in the interior of Germany as well as on the Frontiers. Men, women and children under six were non-existent, the latter with a wail in his voice. It had no effect. I only said to myself, thank God for the British Navy. This is your work and without it no victory on land would have been available or even possible.

Two operations were planned by Beatty and his staff. To these Meurer, of necessity, agreed. First, the surrender of the now 170-strong U-boat fleet that in 1917 had so nearly cut off the supplies of food and war materiel necessary for Great Britain to continue fighting. Second, the surrender of the High Seas Fleet of the Kaiserliche Marine, built to challenge British naval supremacy. The submarine fleet was to surrender – technically it was being interned – to Admiral Tyrwhitt's Harwich Force; the Hochseeflotte to the commander of the Grand Fleet, Beatty himself, in Rosyth. Both operations were elaborate pieces of theatre, designed to humiliate these great naval forces to the eyes of the world's press, to the newfangled newsreels and to the greatest painters of the day – hastily commissioned to record the great Allied victory for posterity. Both sides were understandably suspicious. Beatty noted, 'They prated about the honour of their Submarine Crews being possibly assailed, which nearly lifted me out of my chair.' The exchange supposedly went as follows:

Admiral Meurer: 'Will you guarantee the safety and honour of our submarine crews?'
Beatty: 'Admiral Tyrwhitt, can you guarantee the safety of the German submarine crews?'
Tyrwhitt: 'Yes, Sir'.
Beatty: 'Admiral Tyrwhitt will guarantee their safety, but their honour is entirely in their own hands.'

'When it came to signing the documents,' Beatty concluded, 'I thought he would collapse, he took two shots at it, putting his pen down twice, but we got him over it and they retired into the Fog in grim silence.'

Harwich, on the east coast of England at the confluence of the rivers Orwell and Stour, was the only safe anchorage between the Thames and the Humber. It was the base throughout the war of Tyrwhitt's Harwich Force, a squadron of light cruisers and destroyers that became a byword for naval aggression. It was in recognition of his services – at Heligoland Bight, at Dogger Bank and numerous other encounters – that Tyrwhitt had been accorded the privilege and honour of accepting the surrender of the U-boats.

On 20 November, nine days after the Armistice had been signed in the railway carriage in Compiègne, Tyrwhitt rose early. At 0430 his flagship, the 4190-ton light cruiser *Curacoa*, weighed anchor and the admiral led the force out to sea. It was still dark, there was a light frost on the destroyers, the temperature barely above freezing. How often had Tyrwhitt led his forces out of that haven, not knowing if – certainly not when – he was to return. The admiral headed northeast for his rendezvous with the U-boats, thirty-five miles off the Essex coast. At 0700, just as it was getting light, he ordered his crews to action stations. A few minutes later, through the mist and early morning sunlight, on a morning of ethereal beauty, he spotted a single line of twenty U-boats, long, grey shapes low in the water, rusty and bedraggled from their long passages at sea. Tyrwhitt steamed past, reversed course, and gradually overhauled the submarines in front of him. British prize crews were transferred to the U-boats, and the motley fleet of convicts and gaolers headed back to Harwich. Wrote a bystander in the port, 'I have just witnessed one of the most wonderful sights of the war and one that will remain in history as long as it is read – German U-boats being steamed up the harbour under the White Ensign with our lads in charge – boat after boat coming suddenly out of the mist to slip silently past to their billets'. By 1 December, 170 of the mysterious craft that had so nearly won the war for the Kaiser had been handed over to Tyrwhitt.

In Rosyth, the surrender of the Hochseeflotte was to be managed under an operation called 'ZZ'. To his mistress, Beatty had written jocularly, 'I am now in the position of commanding the High Seas Fleet as well as the Grand fleet which is a big business and am arranging some Autumn Manoeuvres with the two fleets.' On 21 November Beatty in *Queen Elizabeth* duly led the Grand Fleet out of the Firth of Forth to meet the pride of the Kaiserliche Marine. The great ships – totalling in all thirteen squadrons, 370 ships and 90,000 men – formed two columns, some six miles apart. It was the greatest fleet ever to set sail from these shores. *The Times* correspondent recorded in awestruck tones, 'The annals of naval warfare hold no parallel to the memorable event which it has been my privilege to witness today. It was the passing of a whole fleet, and it marked the final and ignoble abandonment of a vainglorious challenge to the naval supremacy of Britain.' Beatty's crews – like Tyrwhitt's – were ordered to action stations. 'Turrets and guns are to be kept in the securing positions, but free. Guns are to be empty with cages up and loaded ready for ramming home. Directors and armoured towers are to be trained on. Correct range and deflection are to be kept set continuously on the sights.' At 1000, forty miles east of Rosyth, on another bright winter's day, Beatty's fleet encountered the cream of the great German fleet: nine battleships, five battlecruisers, seven light cruisers and forty-nine destroyers, led into internment by the light cruiser *Cardiff*. Following the pattern set by Tyrwhitt the day before, the Grand Fleet reversed course, forming an escort leading the Germans into captivity. The *Glasgow Herald* called it 'The greatest naval surrender in the world's history'. It was '[a] triumph to which history knows no parallel'.

It was certainly victory; it was undoubtedly a victory of the best of all sorts: achieved without a shot being fired. As the Hochseeflotte steamed past *Queen Elizabeth*, Admiral Beatty was to be seen on her bridge, standing alone in front of his staff. A great cheer went up and Beatty raised his gold-laced cap, invariably worn at a jaunty angle, in acknowledgement. 'Thank you,' he shouted. And in an historic phrase to be flashed to the whole British fleet, 'I told you they would have to come out.' Then, as the German fleet dropped anchor at the island of Inchkeith in the outer reaches of the Firth of Forth, Beatty signalled with a peremptory note of command, 'The German flag will be hauled

down at sunset today and will not be hoisted again without permission'. It was 1537. Back at *Queen Elizabeth*'s moorings in the shadow
of the famous railway bridge, the men of the Grand Fleet cheered
Beatty again, again and again.

Well might Foch have said, 'It's over, go.' For John Buchan, the
novelist and historian, politician and government propaganda chief,
'Victory dawned upon a world too weary for jubilation, too weary even
for comprehension ... The ordinary man could not grasp the
magnitude of a war which had dwarfed earlier contests, and had
depleted the world of life to a far greater degree than a century of the
old Barbarian invasions'. Even today after a second and equally
barbarous war, the figures are staggering. The total number of civilian
and military casualties was in the order of 41 million, of which 17
million were deaths. Of the various major offensives, Tannenberg, in
what is now Poland, saw total casualties of about 180,000, Verdun
more than 700,000, with around 150,000 dead on each side. On the
first day of the Somme offensive in 1916 the British Army suffered
57,470 casualties, a third of whom were killed: the worst day in the
history of the British Army. Over the five months of the offensive, the
British suffered a total of 400,000 casualties, the French 206,000 and
the Germans around half a million. Passchendaele in 1917 saw totals
of around 500,000, according to some sources 800,000. The German
spring offensive of 1918 saw 250,000 casualties to the Germans alone.
In the course of the whole war, to the Empire's dead of more than a
million men stood the French of nearly two million, the Germans with
slightly more. Consider, in addition to the loss of human life, the
millions of women who were widowed, the children rendered
fatherless, the young women childless, the single, double and triple
amputees, the crippled, faceless and the blind, and the stupendous
financial cost of the war; consider, too, what has been well described
as 'the debasement of values and the sense of moral bankruptcy';
consider, too, the unleashing of Fascism and Communism and all that
it meant to the twentieth century, and, indeed, for the twenty-first. For
Churchill, 'victory was to be bought so dear as to be almost
indistinguishable from defeat'.

As to the Navy and the Army, the signing of the Armistice in
Compiègne and its aftermath on the Rhine, on the Firth of Forth and

at Harwich, raised questions amongst the participants as to the relative contributions made by the land and sea forces to victory. Compatriots the sailors and soldiers were; rivals too. At the height of the struggle against the U-boats in the spring of 1917 the question on everyone's lips was: 'Can the Army win the war before the Navy loses it?' Eighteen months later, on 24 November 1918 Beatty went on board his old flagship, the veteran of Heligoland Bight, Dogger Bank and Jutland, the great, battle-scarred, 26,000-ton battlecruiser *Lion* and answered that question. To the ship's company he set out the decisive role he felt they had played in victory:

England owes the Grand Fleet a great, great debt. The world owes the Grand Fleet a great, great debt. It has been said before, and will be said many times again, that the war which is now on the threshold of coming to an end, has been won by sea power ... Military successes have been great. Military victories have been achieved under circumstances which have produced difficulties, all of which have been overcome by the greatest gallantry, devotion to duty and sacrifice. But all that would have been of no value without the sea power of England.

His military counterpart, Field Marshal Sir Douglas Haig, was coupled by Churchill with Ferdinand Foch himself. 'Both these illustrious soldiers had year after year conducted with obstinacy and serene confidence offensives which we now know to have been as hopeless as they were disastrous.' Admiral Beatty was, of course, himself far from beyond reproach, not least over Jutland. Yet in his own last word on the conflict, Haig found it necessary to be as defensive as Beatty was congratulatory. His final despatch reflected on the fighting as a whole, and here the man behind the Somme and Passchendaele felt obliged to explain away the length of the war, the extent of the casualties and the persistent aggression of his tactics, the doctrine of aggression irrespective of the human cost: 'why we attacked whenever possible'. Haig argued in this apologia that the stupendous sacrifices of the first four years of the war, in particular those since his appointment as C-in-C of British forces on the Western Front in December 1915, were precisely those that made victory possible:

The rapid collapse of Germany's military powers in the latter half of 1918 was the logical outcome of the previous two years. It would not have taken place but for the period of ceaseless attrition which used up the reserves of the German armies, while the constant and growing pressure of the blockade sapped with more deadly insistence from year to year at the strength and resolution of the German people. It is in the great battles of 1916 and 1917 that we have to seek for the secret of our victory in 1918.

Subsequent assessments of Haig and his personal contribution to victory were – and remain – mixed. The commander of the American Expeditionary Force in France, General John Pershing, thought Haig was indeed 'the man who won the war'. John Buchan, who amongst many other duties was Haig's speechwriter, could say that 'The campaign – nay, the history of war – has produced no finer figure: great in patience, courtesy, unselfishness, serenity and iron courage amongst reverses and delays.' For Lloyd George, Haig was 'brilliant to the top of his boots'. For the best-known mid-twentieth-century military historian, Basil Liddell Hart, Haig:

was a man of supreme egoism and utter lack of scruple – who, to his overweening ambition, sacrificed hundreds of thousands of men. A man who betrayed even his most devoted assistants as well as the Government which he served. A man who gained his ends by trickery of a kind that was not merely immoral but criminal.

For John Bourne, 'The scale of his victories was the greatest in British military history. His countrymen have never forgiven him.'

2

By Naval Action Alone

'The differences which had prevailed about entering the war were aggravated by a strong cross-current of opinion by no means operative only in the Cabinet, that if we participated it should be by naval action alone.'

Winston Churchill

Fifty-one months earlier in August 1914, as the monstrous anger of the guns roared over Europe, Haig and his battalions had come remarkably close to completely missing the boat to France, largely at the general's own suggestion. Set in aspic, carved in the Portland stone of the Lutyens memorials as the events of the Great War now appear, Britain's involvement at all was a damned close-run thing. So too was the sending of the BEF across the Channel, the decision to harness the Army there to the huge French forces, and the crucial decision to eschew participating in the war by, in Churchill's words, 'naval action alone.'

Murder in Sarajevo. Austria–Hungary's declaration of war on Serbia on 28 July 1914 was followed by the Tsar's mobilisation of the Russian army on the 30th, Belgian mobilisation on the 31st, Germany's ultimatum to Russia – and Turkish mobilisation – on the same day. The two great European systems of alliance, the Triple Entente of Great Britain, France and Russia, the Triple Alliance of Germany, Italy and Austria–Hungary, seemed to be closing for battle with the awful inevitability of an avalanche. Yet thirty-six hours later, on 2 August 1914 Britain herself was yet to declare her hand. 'Happily, there seems no reason,' Prime Minister Herbert Asquith had written in the aftermath of Archduke Franz Ferdinand's assassination on 28 June, 'why we should be anything more than spectators.' The Treaty of London of 1839 by which Great Britain, France, Russia and Prussia

– as she then was – guaranteed Belgian neutrality remained unsullied, however many of the Kaiser's battalions were massing on the border between Belgium and Germany. Britain had committed herself to France only to the extent of assuring her that the Royal Navy would protect France's Channel ports from the attention of the Kaiser's Hochseeflotte. British public opinion, and with it the Liberal Cabinet, was divided. The peace faction of ten Cabinet ministers, led by Chancellor of the Exchequer David Lloyd George, was unbowed. It was easy for the British public to see the beckoning conflict as part of an old quarrel between France and Germany, a squabble in which the British Empire in her splendid isolation had no stake. Britain, after all, had not involved herself in the three major European conflicts that had led to German unification: Prussia's seizure of Schleswig-Holstein in 1864, the Austro-Prussian War in 1866, and the Franco-Prussian War of 1870–71. She was a world power, not merely a European one. Why involve herself now? But when, that very Sunday, the Kaiser's Germany finally declared war on Russia, the news came that Austria and Russia were already fighting, that the French had mobilised, and that the Cabinet had been told by the leader of the Conservative and Unionist opposition, Andrew Bonar Law, that his party supported intervention; Lloyd George began to waver. Two Cabinet ministers – John Morley and John Burns – resigned at the prospect of war before Sir Edward Grey's heartfelt speech to Parliament on the afternoon of 3 August finally carried the day for the war party. Even so, the Cabinet itself did not formally authorise the declaration of the war, Grey assured Parliament that no commitment had been made to send troops across the Channel, and, of course, the electorate was not consulted.

The following morning, Britain sent an ultimatum to Germany demanding her withdrawal from Belgium by 2300 in England, midnight in the Kaiser's more easterly Berlin. That evening in the Admiralty, Churchill found the minutes passing slowly.

The windows of the Admiralty were thrown wide open in the warm night air. Under the roof from which Nelson had received his orders were gathered a small group of Admirals and Captains and a cluster of clerks, pencil in hand, waiting. Along the Mall from the direction of the Palace the sound of an immense concourse singing 'God Save the King' floated in. On this deep wave there broke the chimes of Big Ben; and as the first stroke of the hour boomed out, a rustle of movement swept across the room. The war telegram, which meant 'Commence hostilities against Germany', was flashed to the ships and establishments under the White Ensign all over the world. I walked across the Horse Guards Parade to the Cabinet Room and reported to the Prime Minister and the Ministers who were assembled there that the deed was done.

Among those present was Lloyd George himself, the Welsh radical whose political gifts outshone even those of the 39-year-old Churchill. In his memoirs he recalled, 'Winston dashed into the room, radiant, his face bright, his manner keen, one word pouring out after another that he was going to send telegrams to the Mediterranean, the North Sea, and God knows where. You could see he was a really happy man.' In the cloud-capped towers, gorgeous palaces and solemn temples of pre-war Europe, of the Old World of the belle époque, of Grantchester and of Adlestrop, of Housman's idle hill of summer, nothing would ever be the same again. 'The whole prospect fills me with sadness,' wrote Asquith to Venetia Stanley, the 27-year-old socialite with whom he was besotted. 'We are on the eve of horrible things.' For John Keegan, 'the states of Europe proceeded, as if in dead march and a dialogue of the deaf, to the destruction of their continent and its civilisation.'

Yet with the Royal Navy already at war and about to fire the first shots of the conflict at the German minelayer *Königin Luise* in the North Sea, it was indeed far from a foregone conclusion that Great Britain would send troops to the Continent. Indeed, it was by no means clear what role the Army would play at all. Churchill would later write:

The differences which had prevailed about entering the war were aggravated by a strong cross-current of opinion, by no means operative only in the Cabinet, that if we participated it should be by naval action alone. Men of great power and influence, who throughout the struggle laboured tirelessly and rendered undoubted services, were found at this time resolutely opposed to landing a single soldier on the Continent.

The monumentally influential newspaper magnate Lord Northcliffe, owner of *The Times*, the *Daily Mail* and the *Daily Mirror*, declared to his underlings:

What is this I hear about a British Expeditionary Force in France? It is nonsense. We have a superb Fleet, to which we shall give all the assistance in our power, but I will not support the sending out of this country of a single British soldier. What about invasion? What about our own country? Not a single soldier will go with my consent. Say so in the paper tomorrow.

Seventeen hours after the 2300 ultimatum had expired, at 1600 on 5 August 1914 a Council of War was duly convened in Downing Street. Rather late in the day, it is often thought, it was – in Churchill's words – to decide the question, 'How should we wage the war that had just begun?'

The meeting would be chaired by Asquith in his temporary capacity as Secretary of State for War. He was supported by his deputy Lord Haldane, the Foreign Secretary Sir Edward Grey, Churchill as First Lord of the Admiralty. Its secretary was the former Royal Marine Colonel Maurice Hankey, who performed the same role for the body that was supposed to co-ordinate the efforts of the two armed services: the Committee of Imperial Defence. A phalanx of soldiers included General Sir Henry Wilson, Director of Military Operations; Field Marshal Sir John French, who would later command the British Expeditionary Force in France; Field Marshal Lord Horatio Kitchener, who had been recalled by Asquith from his post as Governor General of Egypt and was just about to step up to Secretary of State for War; and General Sir Douglas Haig himself, who would later command one of the two corps comprising the expeditionary force. There was only one admiral. The gathering was described by General Wilson in his diary as 'an historic meeting of men mostly ignorant of their subject'.

The uncharitable might argue that these comments applied equally to the military and naval chiefs, including Wilson himself. The Pax Britannica meant that neither Navy nor Army had been involved in major European conflicts since Trafalgar and Waterloo, as distant in time as we are ourselves from the Great War. Since those great battles, the breath-taking advances in naval and military technology that were children of the industrial revolution – machine guns, artillery shells, mines, submarines, torpedoes, aircraft – had challenged the abilities of the warlords to imaginatively deploy them. Of the politicians, only Churchill's brief career as a professional soldier in the 4th Hussars and Haldane's leadership of Edwardian army reforms contradicted the common claim that their innocence in such matters was complete. According to Wilson, a number of those heading for Downing Street on that August day were unaware that the city-fortress of Liège, close to where the German forces were massing, was in Belgium rather than Holland. A J P Taylor wrote simply, 'The authorities, military and civil, had no idea how to win the war.'

Still, opinions there were, and they were views steeped in the participants' understanding of the geography of these islands, their military and naval history, and above all of Great Britain's role as a sea power.

In the days before a navy, Julius Caesar's first adventure to our shores in 55 BC very nearly ended in a disaster. It arose from his unfamiliarity with the tides and storms of the Channel and the unreceptive and unwelcoming qualities of the natives, the ancestors of Boudicca. Half his fleet was wrecked and only his second expedition a year later succeeded. The Saxon and Viking raids of the Dark Ages drew bows at a venture against the storms of the North Sea. In 1066 William of Normandy was fortunate indeed to reach these shores unscathed by wind and water. In 1340 the plans of Philip of Valois for an invasion of England collapsed when Edward III destroyed the French fleet at the Battle of Sluys. Two hundred years later the pretensions of Philip II of Spain to dethrone Elizabeth I and restore the country to Catholicism foundered with the defeat of the Spanish Armada. In the first Anglo-Dutch War in the days of Cromwell's Commonwealth, the superiority of a nascent Royal Navy saw crushing victories in 1653 at Portland, the Gabbard and Scheveningen. Then came Napoleon. In 1803 the emperor established the 200,000-man *Armée d'Angleterre* to invade England. A fleet of invasion barges was constructed, detailed plans were drawn up for a tunnel under the Channel, a squadron of balloons mooted as an imaginative alternative. Yet the Channel – *La Manche* – still remained the real problem. It was England's cordon sanitaire. In 1803 Admiral of the Fleet John Jervis, 1st Earl St Vincent, commanding the Royal Navy's Channel Fleet, memorably assured the Admiralty Board, 'I do not say, my Lords, that they [the French] cannot come. I only say they cannot come by sea.' They did not. After Trafalgar in 1805, they could not. Nelson had eviscerated the fleet in which the emperor had so rashly intended to invade. These lessons in geography and history suggested that in strategic terms Britain's greatest asset was the Channel; her second best was the Royal Navy.

Yet if the service was a defence against invasion, it was also true that conquering her enemies could be accomplished by sea power. The Royal Navy was an offensive as well as defensive weapon.

Long before the Great War, the industrialised countries of Europe had lost their self-sufficiency in all the goods they needed to feed their populations, manufacture the necessities of war, and fund through taxation the making of war. In 1914 Great Britain imported 80 per cent of her wheat, 40 per cent of her meat and all of her sugar: in short, most of her food. This made her vulnerable. As Admiral Sir John ('Jacky') Fisher put it, 'If the Navy is not supreme, no army, however large, is of the slightest use. It is not *invasion* we have to fear if our Navy is beaten, it is *starvation*!' Germany, with a larger population, found herself in a not dissimilar position; indeed, in 1914 her merchant navy was second in size only to Great Britain's, the country which possessed around 50 per cent of the world's merchant tonnage. Neither nation was self-sufficient in food; neither had any indigenous supplies of vital tropical materials like rubber, rare metals like tungsten, copper, manganese and chromium, or conveniences like industrial diamonds: all materials for the making of war. Germany also had very little of one of the essential requirements of twentieth-century agriculture, fertiliser. Although, of course, not an island nation, much of what the Kaiser's Germany needed had to be imported; some from her immediate neighbours like Belgium and from across the Baltic; much that was brought across the great waters of the world by the 'Quinquireme[s] of Nineveh from distant Ophir'. Moreover, as Nicholas Lambert has pointed out:

> During the half century before the outbreak of World War I the technological revolution in communication, transportation and financial services facilitated the global spread of market capitalism ... innovations like credit financing, freight forwarding and 'just in time' orders, especially of food ... meant that industrial nations became to depend on an uninterrupted flow of maritime trade.

More than a century ago, globalisation was well under way.

The strategic implications of this dependence on overseas trade were obvious. On the outbreak of war, a belligerent with sea power at its disposal would seek to seal its enemy's ports by means of a blockade and thus bring her to her knees. As Churchill put it:

> The traditional war policy of the Admiralty grew up during the prolonged wars of antagonisms with France. It consisted in establishing immediately upon the outbreak of war a close blockade of the enemy's ports and naval bases by means of flotillas of strong small craft supported by cruisers and superior battle fleets in reserve. The experience of 200 years had led all naval strategists to agree on this fundamental principle. Our first line of defence is the enemy's ports.

In 1890 Alfred Thayer Mahan's *The Influence of Sea Power upon History 1660–1783* brilliantly articulated just such thinking; indeed, with its successor *The Influence of Sea Power upon the French Revolution and Empire, 1793–1812,* it set it in stone. In a celebrated passage on the Napoleonic campaigns, he noted:

> Amid all the pomp and circumstance of the war which for ten years had desolated the Continent, amid all the tramping to and fro over

Europe of the French armies and their auxiliary regions, there went on unceasingly that noiseless pressure on the vitals of France, that compulsion whose silence, when once noted, becomes to the observer the most striking and awful mark of the working of Sea Power.

The strategy of blockade lacked the theatrical qualities of decisive battles either on land or at sea, but – given time, given time – it was nonetheless effective. It won wars. In 1812 the British blockade had strangled American maritime trade and virtually bankrupted the United States government; the doctrine of Mahan suggested that the blockade of the French ports did as much as Waterloo to defeat Napoleon. It was true that the invention of the self-propelled torpedo in 1865 and of naval mines at much the same time made the Napoleonic policy of close blockade look hazardous for the blockading ships. This did not preclude the strategy of 'distant blockade', the practicalities of which were being explored by the British Admiralty during Churchill's early days there as First Lord in late 1911. Rather than establishing a cordon in close proximity to enemy ports, the same effect might be achieved by blocking bottlenecks. Here, geography once again played into Britain's hands. Churchill continued, 'It was rightly foreseen that by closing the exits from the North Sea into the Atlantic Ocean, German commerce would be almost completely cut off from the world.'

Such unfair advantages of geography that helped give Britain this great power, this vital maritime supremacy, did not go unchallenged. Germany, welded into a federal state by the three wars of unification, was determined to take her place as a world power. In 1897 her Foreign Secretary Bernhard von Bülow had declared, 'In one word: we wish to throw no one into the shade, but we demand our own place in the sun.' She would and did pursue a course of aggressive diplomacy, acquire an overseas empire of sorts, and build herself a navy. The consequences of this ambition were unfortunate. Since the German Naval Laws of 1898, 1900, 1906, 1908 and 1912, the naval arms race had been developing. It saw the expansion of the Kaiserliche Marine into a force intended to challenge the supremacy of the seas enjoyed since before Nelson's day by the Royal Navy. Kaiser Wilhelm II, eldest grandson of Queen Victoria, Imperial Germany's self-styled Oberster Kriegsherr, or 'supreme warlord', head of the house of Hohenzollern, was clever, cantankerous, headstrong, autocratic, anti-Semitic and wildly envious of all things British. In his memoirs, he wrote:

> I had a peculiar passion for the navy. It sprang to no small extent from my English blood. When I was a little boy ... I admired the proud British ships. There awoke in me the will to build ships of my own like these some day, and when I was grown up to possess a fine navy as the English.

These ambitions had been fiercely countered in Great Britain. She rightly saw her very existence challenged by such a policy, reliant as she was on external goods and supplies: that is, on the sea. In a meeting in 1912 with the architects of the Kaiserliche Marine, the Kaiser himself and the vaultingly ambitious Admiral Alfred von Tirpitz, Lord Haldane had explained simply, 'We (are) an island Power dependent for our food supplies on the power of protecting our commerce.' It was on this basis that Great Britain had adopted since Napoleonic times the doctrine of the 'two-power standard'. This meant that the Royal Navy should be of sufficient size to withstand the challenge of a combination of the next two largest rival naval powers. As the Kaiserliche Marine grew under the impetus of the Naval Laws, Tirpitz and the admiralty staff (the Admiralstab), so too did the Royal Navy. Fisher, from his appointment as First Sea Lord in 1904, had recognised the threat posed to the Royal Navy by its upstart rival and was ruthless in pursuing radical reform: in men, in material, in strategy and in due course in the greatest of ships, *Dreadnought*. She became the generic for all such vessels, the dreadnoughts. Typically they were some 600ft long, 90ft in beam, displacing more than 20,000 tons, drawing perhaps 25ft or more. They combined steam turbine power with all big guns in a way that revolutionised battleship design and rendered obsolete all earlier classes of battleships.

Dreadnought herself, built in Portsmouth in a year and a day and launched with great fanfare in 1906, spurred Tirpitz to commission the *Nassau* and *Helgoland* classes. In both countries, the public took this great naval race to heart. 'We want eight [dreadnoughts] and we won't wait' was the popular cry, still remembered today. Very considerable political capital on both sides of the North Sea was expended on the great fleets. Money, too. *Dreadnought* herself had cost £1,783,883. The super-dreadnoughts and battlecruisers that followed were even more costly at just over £2 million. Before his accession to the Admiralty in 1911, it was Churchill himself who contested the vast expenditure on these ships, arguing that they detracted from desperately needed social reforms like national insurance – something largely pioneered in Wilhelmine Germany. In 1908 he stood shoulder to shoulder with Lloyd George in bitterly opposing First Lord of the Admiralty Reginald McKenna's naval estimates (annual budget) of £36 million. Within three years Churchill had become an equally vehement advocate of such expenditure. The great assemblage of battleships and battlecruisers that constituted the Grand Fleet was the Sword of Albion:

> On them, as we conceived, floated the might, majesty, dominion and power of the British Empire. All our long history built up century after century, all our great affairs in every part of the globe, all the means of livelihood and safety of our faithful, industrious, active population depended upon them. Open the sea-cocks and let them sink beneath the surface ... and in a few minutes – half an hour at most – the whole outlook of the world would be changed. The British Empire would dissolve like a dream; each isolated community struggling forward by itself; the central power of union broken; mighty provinces, whole Empires in themselves, drifting hopelessly out of control, and falling prey to strangers; and Europe after one sudden convulsion passing into the iron grip and rule of the Teuton and all that the Teutonic system meant ... Guard them well, admirals and captains, hardy tars and tall marines, guard them well and guide them true.

In August 1914, largely through the efforts of Churchill and Fisher, the Royal Navy boasted twenty-two dreadnoughts, nine battlecruisers, 121 cruisers and 221 destroyers; the Kaiserliche Marine weighed in with fifteen dreadnoughts, five battlecruisers, forty cruisers and ninety destroyers. They were by then the two largest naval fleets in the world, the greatest of all national symbols of wealth, pride and fighting power. The Grand Fleet was England, England the Grand Fleet.

So, given that Great Britain could be more than adequately defended – and her enemies eventually defeated – by means of sea power, her emphasis on her land forces had been more modest. Dating from the Restoration, the Army was built on the regimental system. Each regiment was responsible for recruiting, training and running its corps of men, often from and within a single county. These organisations developed strong identities, proud traditions and a powerful *esprit de corps*. Cavalry and infantry regiments like the Coldstream Guards, the Black Watch, the Buffs, the Life Guards, the Royal Horse Guards and the Grenadiers were celebrated on stage and in song. Like the Navy, they played a significant part in the country's national identity. They fought in the Seven Years War and the Napoleonic Wars, but the focus in the nineteenth century was more on the growing Empire than the Continent. The Army could certainly be hazarded there, but to what purpose? In 1734, at a time when the Continent was wracked by war, Sir Robert Walpole could complacently observe to Queen Caroline, 'Madam, there are fifty thousand men slain this year in Europe and not one Englishman'. As well as fielding her own forces, during the Napoleonic wars Great Britain paid her European allies – Russia, Austria and the strutting Prussia – to field armies on the far side of the Channel in support of these alliances. This was dubbed the Golden Cavalry of St George. Though costly of treasure, the cavalry was not so of British blood. At Waterloo, Wellington's army was actually smaller than that of his Prussian ally, Blücher. After the establishment of the Pax Britannica, in the second half of the nineteenth century the Army's purpose became firmly established as keeping order in the Empire. For this purpose, half its strength was stationed in the colonies overseas. Most recently the Army had been despatched to South Africa to supress the nascent Boer republics, initially with indifferent success. By 1914 the army reforms of the Edwardian period had given the country a modest, well-organised, well-trained army of around 400,000 men. Of these, 247,000 were regulars, 145,000 territorials. In the words of the official history it was, 'incomparably the best trained, best organised, and best equipped British Army that ever went forth to war'.

So for Great Britain, geography dictated a large navy and small, professional army. Childers' hero Arthur H Davies in *The Riddle of the Sands* explains:

> My own idea is that we ought to ... train every able-bodied man for a couple of years as a sailor. Army? Oh, I suppose you'd have to give them the choice. Not that I know or care much about the Army, though to listen to people talk you'd think it really mattered as the Navy matters. We're a maritime nation – we've grown by the sea and live by it; if we lose command of it we starve. We're unique in that way, just as our huge empire, only linked by the sea, is unique.

By way of contrast, the other principal belligerents in the Great War, France, Germany, Russia, Austria–Hungary and, eventually, Italy were divided from their enemies not by the watery deeps of the Channel and the North Sea, but by very little. Rivers that were often fordable, mountain ranges that could be scaled, lines on a map that were no more than windswept hedgerows on arable plains admirably suited to military manoeuvres, perfect plains for ignorant armies to clash by night. The histories of these godless places bore witness to this mutability. Nice, on what is now the Franco-Italian border, was fickle in her affections and did not finally submit to France until 1860. The alpine Tyrol, pivoting on Innsbruck, was the bastard child of Austria and Italy, parents who perpetually fought for custodial rights. Poland's borders were forever being recast and redrawn by its belligerent neighbours, Russia and Prussia. The repeated *casus belli* between France and Prussia was Alsace-Lorraine, with its rich iron-fields and the arterial Rhine. The Continental powers were accordingly obliged to establish compulsory military service and – rather than professional – conscript armies of a size commensurate with the length of their porous frontiers. 'In a Continental country, with an enemy at its gates,' wrote John Buchan, 'A man was called upon to enlist in the defence of his home and his livelihood. But this was not [Great Britain's] case.' In

1911 the German army mobilised 2,200,000, France – with her smaller population – 1,700,000.

Here, then, were two very different manifestations of power. Voltaire could quip with some justice that 'Whereas some states possess an Army, Prussia is an army that possesses a State.' Its trade was war, just as that of the Habsburgs was marriage. Prussia, perforce, was a land power, in the early twentieth century the greatest in Europe. Under Prince Otto von Bismarck, courtesy of the Prussian army, the loose confederation of petty princedoms that had existed when Queen Victoria came to the throne in 1837 had become her grandson's Imperial Germany. She was a land power which – by the time of Victoria's death in 1901 – dominated Continental Europe. Britain, perforce, was a sea power: in the early twentieth century, the greatest in the world. 'Germany's a thundering great nation,' says Davies in *The Riddle of the Sands*. 'I wonder if we shall ever fight her.'

So to strategy, the means by which victory might be achieved. If Britain had no need for an army on the Continental scale, then at Asquith's meeting in August 1914 that begged an important question. Exactly what useful contribution could five or six divisions of infantry and their attendant cavalry make to the quarrels between France and Germany, Germany and Russia, Austria and Italy? It was a very good question. Given Great Britain's limited interest in Continental affairs – notwithstanding the signing of the Entente with France in 1904 – it was one which had never been satisfactorily or fully resolved.

'The Admiralty,' recorded Churchill of an earlier Committee of Imperial Defence meeting convened in August 1911 to mull over a future European conflict. 'The Admiralty thought we should confine our efforts to the sea; that if our small Army were sent to the Continent it would be swallowed up among the immense hosts conflicting there.' According to the bluff and bearded First Sea Lord, Admiral Sir Arthur Wilson, the war would be won, and won at a stroke, by fighting a second Trafalgar. If the Army was 'kept in ships or ready to embark for counter-strokes upon the German coast, it would draw off more than its own weight of numbers from the German fighting line.' The Admiralty –

and Churchill too in his time there – found the German North Sea islands of Borkum, Sylt and Heligoland particularly tempting to use as forward bases from which to launch attacks on the Kaiser's coast; also for the purposes of luring the Hochseeflotte out of its harbours for a decisive battle. It was regrettable, said Admiral Sir Arthur Wilson, that these operations would preclude any definite commitment to taking the Army anywhere early in any war. Perhaps later.

In 1911 this was a view, perhaps not surprisingly, rejected by the generals. Particularly by the Director of Military Operations, the confusingly named General Sir Henry Wilson. In the presence of Churchill, Prime Minister Asquith, Lloyd George, Haldane and other grandees, the Francophile General Wilson had set out with what proved remarkable accuracy the German plan for attacking France, her rival for power in Europe and – since the Entente Cordiale – England's friend. This was what we now rather loosely call the Schlieffen Plan, the brainchild of the late Count Alfred von Schlieffen. It was to gobble up France by outflanking her through Belgium, so sidestepping the heavily fortified Franco-German border. Churchill continued, 'It was asserted [by Wilson] that if the six British divisions were sent to take position on the extreme French left, immediately war was declared, the chances of repulsing the Germans in the first great shock of battle were favourable. Every French soldier would fight with double confidence if he knew he was not fighting alone'.

Possibly so or possibly not. For soon the pleasantry was established in Army circles that there was no military problem at all to which the solution was the token of six divisions and four mounted brigades. Sir John French said this was 'fifty divisions too few'. Kitchener wrote to Lord Esher in 1911 that it was 'puerile to suppose that the presence or absence of a ridiculously small British army at any particular time or place could affect the outcome of a Franco-Prussian war'. Asquith, too, was baffled. How was he to reconcile the opposing opinions of the Navy and the Army, between the Admiralty and the War Office, in what became known as 'the battle of the two Wilsons'? How was he to decide the way in which any Continental war might be fought and won? The prime minister, who often liked to let the passage of time resolve intractable issues – 'Wait and see' was his catchphrase – restricted himself in the aftermath of the 1911 meeting largely to moving Churchill from the Home Office to the Admiralty. This was supposedly to better prepare the Navy for war and to reconcile its plans with those of the Army. This was late in 1911 and – despite the co-ordinating role that was intended to be discharged by the prime minister himself and the Committee of Imperial Defence as well, the way by which Great Britain would wage a war involving its Continental enemies and allies was left unsettled. There was tacit acceptance that, in line with the terms of the Entente, Britain would help France, but that was all. The Anglo-French Naval agreement of 1912 put this detente on only a marginally more formal footing.

Nine years earlier, in 1903 Erskine Childers had written truculently in *The Riddle of the Sands*, 'We have no theory of national defence, and no competent authority whose business it is to give us one ... co-operation between army and navy is not studied or practised.' Little had changed since then other than the advent of the Committee of Imperial Defence itself. This might or might not be competent, might or might not reconcile the warring factions of the Army and the Navy. It had in any case no means of putting its views into practice. Although informal talks between British and French military staff on the help that France might expect in the event of a German attack continued, Lloyd George could write to Churchill in 1911, 'The thunderclouds are gathering. I am not at all satisfied that we are prepared, or are preparing.' The Army was in fact drafting a detailed operational plan with the French, but only one – not a series of options suited to different scenarios as they might arise. Neither did these talks have anything other than tepid political endorsement. The public knew nothing. As to the Navy, its efforts under Churchill to put flesh on the bare bones of Admiral Wilson's ideas, or indeed those of anyone else, were modest. According to Hew Strachan, 'In 1914, in none of the three possible areas of operations – fleet action, blockade, amphibious landing – did the Royal Navy have a viable war plan ... the obvious manifestation of pre-war rivalries ... was not accompanied by much thought as to what those navies might do with themselves in the event of war.' Childers' fears had apparently been well founded.

Still, as the politicians and warriors ambled towards Downing Street on that sunny, late summer afternoon of 5 August 1914 more than a century ago, it would have been surprising if the sort of naval solution about which Churchill himself had written had not been at the front of the grandees' minds. Geography, history, the small size of the Army, the established efficacy of blockade, Britain's longstanding status as a sea power and the king's ransom invested in the dreadnoughts of the Grand Fleet; they all pointed – surely – towards a naval strategy. It would be equally surprising if their expectations were not for a war along familiar nineteenth-century lines. A J P Taylor noted that many both within and outside the government thought that, 'The British navy would fight a great engagement with the German big seas fleet in the North Sea, while the armies of the continental Allies defeated Germany on land. All would be over in a few months, if not weeks.' Surprises, though, there would be.

Oh, to have been a fly on the wall in the Cabinet Room in Downing Street when those sixteen men, mostly in khaki uniform, chatted quietly in groups before – at a word from Maurice Hankey at 1600 – taking their seats in the Cabinet Room. The country, the great Empire that Britain then constituted, that empire of 412 million people, a quarter of the world's population, a quarter of its land surface area – was at war. How was that war to be waged? It was a difficult question. It was a question for which the War Council was really neither well qualified nor well prepared to answer; it was one for which the Continental hostilities demanded an immediate answer; and it was one which would have momentous consequences. There are various – Churchill, Grey, French, Haig, Haldane, Hankey – mildly contra-dictory accounts of its substance, but all attest Asquith's view that this was a 'somewhat motley gathering'. In a more disciplined age, perhaps someone would have set a clear agenda and managed the meeting rigorously. It might been required to debate and decide:

- Whether the war could be waged by naval power alone;
- Whether the BEF could make any worthwhile contribution, either immediately or in the future;
- If so, how large a force was needed;
- If so, under whose direction it should fight: British or French;
- If so, where it should be sent: France, Belgium – or Germany.

Or, rather, such questions should have been more fully debated and resolved by senior naval, military and political figures in the years that preceded the outbreak of the war than they, in fact, appear to have been. As it was, though, it was agreed at the outset of the meeting that the country was under a moral obligation to its old enemy, France. It might perhaps have been better argued – often was both then and subsequently – that it was not in Great Britain's interest to have the Continent dominated by Germany. Nevertheless, it was under this well-meaning impetus that Churchill – Churchill as the First Lord of the Admiralty, Churchill as the disciple of Mahan, Churchill as the man charged to advocate and to guarantee British naval supremacy – who proposed a motion not simply to despatch the Army, but to send it immediately, and to send it in some force: six divisions. This motion was carried within minutes of the opening of the Council of War.

There was then a longer discussion as to whether the BEF should be sent as planned to the Franco-Belgian frontier town of Maubeuge on the left of the French army, or whether it should be sent (as circumstances arguably now dictated) to support the Belgian army where it was fighting a fierce rearguard action in Liège. Or, as Lord Kitchener advocated, it should be held back at Amiens, a major railway junction which would have left open some options as to the force's ultimate destination. This was settled by those – mainly General Sir Henry Wilson – who pointed out that planning and logistics precluded such a change in destination at such short notice; and by Churchill, who declared that the Royal Navy could not guarantee the safe passage of forces over the voyage across the North Sea to Antwerp, the nearest port to Liège. The BEF was thus knowingly sent not to where the German armies actually were, but where they were supposed to be – according to the Allies' expectations for the Kaiser's own war, developed several years previously.

The discussion then reverted to some of the more compelling fundamentals of the despatch of the BEF. Douglas Haig was at the forefront of debate, and in some respects he was the most cogent. His views seem to reflect a letter he had written the previous day to Maurice Hankey. 'I agree that we ought not to despatch our expeditionary force in a hurry to France. Possibly had there been a chance of supporting her at the very beginning, our help might have been decisive. That moment seems to have been allowed to pass. Now we must make an Army large enough to intervene decisively – say

300,000.' Given these reservations, at the meeting he asked whether the French would be beaten if the force was not immediately despatched; whether – if they were in retreat – the force would be sufficient to turn the tide; and if the French collapsed, whether the BEF could be evacuated. Haig wanted to wait for three months to allow a build-up of forces from the Empire. This might also have allowed such an army to be used to train a larger volunteer or conscript army along the lines that eventually emerged. As it was, though, no particular conclusions were reached on the issues he raised, and the meeting broke up.

When the Cabinet met the following day – 6 August – it endorsed the Council of War's proposal to despatch the Expeditionary Force, but with a proviso about the number of divisions. An invasion scare had emerged overnight. On the occasion of Queen Victoria's Diamond Jubilee in 1897, *The Times* had talked of 'the mightiest and most beneficent Empire the world has ever seen.' The Cabinet of this great Empire declared that day that four divisions – plus one of cavalry – would suffice. This was the force that the Kaiser would reportedly and infamously dub, 'A contemptible little army'. Basil Liddell Hart would doubtless have replied that, 'It is in quality, not in quantity, that military virtue lies.'

The decision taken, the Navy then had to undertake its traditional task of transporting the Army to where it might fight. This was a perilous operation in the course of which a large part of the country's professional Army was in jeopardy. As Churchill wrote, 'All the most fateful possibilities were open. We were bound to expect a military descent upon our coast, with the intention of arresting or recalling our Army, or a naval raid into the Channel to cut down the transports, or a concentrated submarine attack upon these vessels crowded with our troops'. His dispositions against such eventualities comprised patrols by light cruiser squadrons from Harwich and the Thames, the novelty of air cover in the form of seaplanes and airships, a patrol from Dover of British and French destroyers and a British submarine flotilla, patrols by the Channel Fleet, and on 12 August 1914 – as the largest numbers of troops were being ferried across the narrow straits – the Grand Fleet steamed down from Scapa Flow. Crowed Churchill, 'Not a ship was sunk, not a man was drowned'. In ten days, 150,000 men

31

and almost as many horses had been safely transported from Newhaven, Southampton and Bristol to Le Havre, Boulogne and other French Channel ports. This was kept secret from the public until 17 August 1914, when the official announcement was made of the successful completion of the operation. Courtesy of the Royal Navy, the British Expeditionary Force was abroad. For good or ill, the die was cast. It was, says Max Hastings, 'The government's most important strategic decision of the war.'

Already, though, there were doubts, precisely the sort of concerns expressed by Haig.

Even before the force set out, Kitchener had joined the Cabinet in his official capacity of Secretary of State for War. Kitchener had won fame at the battle of Omdurman and the Second Boer War, and was seen as almost the Wellington of his day. In reality, he was a master of imperial skirmishes, knew little of Continental war, less still of war at sea and the meaning of sea power, even less of Cabinet politics and the machinations of men like Asquith, Grey, Churchill and Lloyd George. Tongue-tied amongst the canny, dissembling and articulate politicians, he was loquacious with his underlings. Rudyard Kipling dismissed him as 'A fatted pharaoh in spurs ... garrulously intoxicated with power'. Asquith had recalled him with the utmost reluctance, driven principally by political considerations of the field marshal's stellar military reputation with the public, and the widespread and entirely justifiable supposition that the Liberal Cabinet was largely bereft of any understanding of war. In desperately uncertain times, he 'was a god who breathed war'. Once installed as Secretary of State for War, Kitchener noted ironically, 'At least no one can say that my colleagues in the Cabinet are not courageous. They have no Army and declared war against the mightiest military nation in the world.' Even as the four regular divisions of the Army were entraining for the Channel ports, he was warning his Cabinet colleagues in staccato sentences to prepare for a long war; a war – he said – that could only be won by great battles on the Continent; a war that could not – he said – be won at sea; and a war to which – he said – the Empire would have to contribute armies of a size commensurate with her status as a great power. This was the genesis of the Kitchener armies, the greatest force of volunteers the world had ever seen. Soon Kitchener's image would adorn perhaps the most famous poster of all time, his finger pointing accusingly at the viewer, the headline declaring: 'Your Country Needs You'.

It was also the beginning of much else. No sooner had the four divisions set foot in France than they were joined – on Kitchener's orders – by a fifth, sent as originally planned to Maubeuge. The Expeditionary Force commanders, French in overall command, Douglas Haig and Horace Smith-Dorrien beneath him at the head of I Corps and II Corps respectively, were then ordered by Kitchener 'to support and co-operate with the French Army'. At a stroke, they thus effectively ceased to be an independent force; and a precedent was established that further forces as and when they formed would follow, as indeed they did to the tune of seventy divisions or around four million men. Lloyd George wrote, 'The general effect of the con-sultations that took place on that and the following day [5 August, 6 August] was that we should conform our strategy with that of the French.' A J P Taylor commented, 'In previous wars, Great Britain had followed an independent strategy based on sea power. In the first World war she lost this independence by accident, almost before fighting had started.'

Kitchener's nostrums in the first days of the war were received by the Cabinet, wrote Churchill, 'in silent assent'. As the First Lord of the Admiralty, as a brilliantly forceful and eloquent advocate of sea power, as a man not entirely without intellectual and dialectic confidence, and as the best qualified minister to challenge Kitchener in the Cabinet, perhaps Churchill should at this point have had something to say about the use of sea power, the wisdom of attaching a token expedi-tionary force to the coat-tails of the French, and the wisdom of creating a huge army. Lloyd George's biographer John Grigg comments, 'Lloyd George admitted that all Kitchener's Cabinet colleagues were intimidated by his presence, because of his repute and because of his enormous prestige amongst all the people outside. A word from him was decisive, and no one dared challenge it in a Cabinet meeting.' Moreover, convincingly though Churchill might have written on sea power a decade later in *The World Crisis*, in 1914 – perhaps always –

Churchill's understanding of Alfred Thayer Mahan and his doctrine was coloured by his spending his formative years in the Army, in the 4th Hussars. For his contemporary, Admiral Sir John Jellicoe, Churchill's 'fatal error was his inability to realise his own limitations as a civilian with, it is true, some early experience in military service but quite ignorant of naval warfare'. The historian Richard Ollard added, 'Churchill suffered from an inability or refusal to distinguish between the nature of land power and sea power, to recognise that there are things that ships can and should do that troops and artillery cannot, and vice versa ... [he had] ... an invincibly army approach to the use of sea power.'

In those very early days of August 1914 Great Britain had committed herself to a war she could certainly have avoided, sent the BEF to France when she could have fought – and conceivably won – the war by naval action alone, and committed what would ultimately be armies four million-strong to fight in harness with the French when she could have kept them autonomous, free to strike at will. The eventual outcome was certainly victory, but as Churchill later said, 'victory bought at a price so dear as to be almost indistinguishable from defeat.' This is hard to see as a triumph of strategy or statesmanship. It would be another ten months before a famous exchange between Asquith and General Sir Henry Wilson. On 2 June 1915 at the Army's GHQ in St Omer in the Pas de Calais, the prime minister slightly tactlessly remarked that the war had produced 'no great generals'. Wilson replied sharply, 'No, Prime Minister, nor has it produced a statesman.'

For the present, though, matters were largely in the hands of the admirals and the generals, of the Army and the Navy, of Beatty and Jellicoe, of French, Smith-Dorrien and Haig, rather than Asquith, Grey, Churchill and Lloyd George. It remained to be seen exactly what these warriors would do.

In *Testament of Youth*, Vera Brittain wrote of this time, 'To me and my contemporaries, with our cheerful confidence in the benignity of fate, War was something remote, unimaginable, its monstrous destructions and distresses safely shut up, like the Black Death and the Great Fire, between the covers of history books.' Within weeks, Brittain would go up to Somerville College, Oxford, where she was to read English. She was to have been joined at the university by her brother Edward and the man who was to become her fiancé, Roland Leighton. Both had decided against pursuing their academic studies and – inspired by the patriotic fervour that had swept the country and had already attracted 400,000 volunteers to the colours – were seeking commissions in the Army. Rupert Brooke spoke for a generation when he declared, 'Now God be thanked who has matched us with His hour.'

3

The Ides of August

'As a result, the British blockade of Germany remained in effect and increased in effectiveness throughout the war. The naval blockade of Germany is a chief reason for the defeat of the country in World War I.'

Eric Osborne

At a little before seven o'clock on 24 August 1914, Winston Churchill lay in bed in his rooms in Admiralty House. This was the mansion adjoining the main Admiralty Building that lay between Horse Guards Parade and Whitehall. It was the nerve centre of His Britannic Majesty's Royal Navy. As was his custom, Churchill was busy at work dealing with his despatch boxes. He had found that a good deal of work could be done in these early hours when few were about, when the only sounds were the clip-clop of horses in Whitehall below. There was much to be done to oversee the direction of the worldwide Royal Navy. Although the BEF had been ferried to France, it still had to be kept supplied, as did its ancillary and supporting services providing food, transport and munitions; it was the Navy's task to convoy to the European theatre of war the regular garrisons in the Empire's far-flung dependencies, and in due course the Dominion armies from Canada, from India, from South Africa, Australia and from New Zealand; the Kaiser's commerce raiders – including the cruisers *Emden, Scharnhorst* and *Gneisenau* – were still at large in the southern oceans and the Navy's forces had to be marshalled in pursuit; and the blockade of Imperial Germany – implemented within days of the war breaking out – had to be managed. The Grand Fleet itself at Scapa Flow in Orkney, Admiral Jellicoe's dreadnoughts and Admiral Beatty's battlecruisers that – in Churchill's own phrase – could lose the war in an afternoon; these great squadrons, too, could never be very far from Churchill's mind. Immersed in these labours, it was as Big Ben chimed seven that there was a rap at the First Lord of the Admiralty's bedroom door. His visitor was Lord Kitchener, the god who breathed war, the Empire's Secretary of State for War. Here was an apparition, particularly at seven o'clock in the morning. 'He had a bowler hat on his head, which he took off with a hand which also held a slip of paper. He paused in the doorway and I knew in a flash before ever he spoke that the event had gone wrong ... "Bad news", he said heavily, and laid the slip of paper on my bed.' It was indeed. During the following fortnight world history stood indecisively at a crossroads, the dropping of heels both at sea and on land determining its ultimate course. They were fourteen days which shook the world.

Kitchener's slip of paper was a telegram from Sir John French's expeditionary force on the border between France and Belgium. Here the fighting was almost at its heaviest. The field marshal announced the fall of the great Belgium fortress of Namur, the retreat of the French Fifth Army led by General Paul Lanrezac, the retreat from the mining town of Mons of the BEF itself, and the field marshal's own recommendation that the Channel port of Le Havre should be fortified to allow for the evacuation of the BEF. It was tantamount to an admission of defeat. Concluded Churchill of his bedroom encounter with the Secretary of State for War, 'I forget much of what passed between us. But the apparition of Kitchener *Agonistes* in my doorway will dwell with me as long as I live. It was like seeing old John Bull on the rack!' The truth was that in the cartoonists' terms, John Bull and his French consort Marianne were both on the Kaiser's rack.

The German war plans, forecast with considerable accuracy by General Sir Henry Wilson at the 'battle of the two Wilsons' meeting in August 1911, were in some respects simple; and like Great Britain's own altogether more lightly sketched plans, they were largely a consequence of geography. The Germany of 1914 was very roughly rectangular, with the Baltic to the north and Emperor Franz-Joseph's Austro-Hungarian Empire to the south. To the east lay Russia, to the west France, boxing in Germany. Both these countries were allied to

England in the Triple Entente: Germany's enemies, one on each side. The principal architect of the Kaiser's plans was the late Count Alfred von Schlieffen. In common with almost all European military strategists, the count recognised the considerable and obvious risks of having to fight two wars simultaneously on two fronts: one to the east with Russia, one to the west with France. Despite her large and growing population, Wilhelmine Germany simply did not have enough men to allow such a division. The solution was for the Reich to defeat one of her enemies first before turning on the other. It was true that Tsarist Russia, with a population twice that of Germany, could mobilise huge forces; it was equally true that with a scant railway network she was expected to do so only slowly. Schlieffen believed that Germany might have a period of grace of six weeks before Tsar Nicholas's bear could be on East Prussia's doorstep – or indeed in the Kaiser's front room in Berlin's Unter den Linden. Germany had fifty or fifty-five days in which to defeat France before her troops could about turn and take their tickets on the Länderbahnen east to finish the job.

This, in turn, had implications for the manner of the attack on France. The Franco-German border in 1914 ran from Basel roughly north 280 miles to the conjunction of France, Germany and Luxembourg at Schengen. Heavily fortified by both the Germans and the French, and with much of the terrain wooded, Schlieffen was little tempted to attack here. In the putative six weeks at his disposal it would be too difficult to conquer the forts, defeat the great French conscription armies, and capture Paris. Yet to the north of the border lay the wedge of the Benelux countries. Small, not particularly martial, politically neutral, for Schlieffen they were a much more attractive stepping-stone into northeastern France. Such an approach would also usefully enable him to outflank the French forces expected to mass on the Franco-German border. The plan was for a great right wheel of the German armies; as the historian David Thomson puts it, 'A hammer-swing down through Belgium into northern France, hinging on the fortress of Metz in the east.'

As a soldier careless of diplomatic nicety and indeed of international law, the political implications of the strategy, consequences which brought Britain into the war, Schlieffen discounted. His plans, subsequently modified after the count's death by his successor Field

Marshal Helmuth von Moltke, had been put into effect on 3 August 1914 by Oberste Heeresleitung, the German high command, or OHL. Five great German armies issued like slingshots from their railheads in northeastern Germany, heading at first west and then wheeling downwards to the south in the great hammer-blow towards Paris. Two – under Crown Prince Rupprecht of Bavaria and Generaloberst Josias von Herringen – were held in reserve on the Franco-German border. Despite the unexpected resistance of the Belgium army in Liège and Haelen, the burden of Sir John French's telegram to Kitchener was that the German plan was proceeding as intended. Indeed, the French armies under Generalissimo Joseph Joffre had even made a considerable contribution to their own destruction by two armies on the right – the First and Second – driving east over the Franco-German border into the arms of Prince Rupprecht and General Herringen. This was a move so patently foolhardy that Schlieffen had also discounted it. It was part of Joffre's Plan XVII, a general offensive on both sides of Metz, developed in accordance with the French doctrine of offensive known as the *offensive à outrance*. It lost the C-in-C of the French forces, the portly 62-year-old Joseph Joffre, 300,000 killed, wounded or prisoners. Joffre was an imperturbable man, whose daily rhythm of a couple of hours for lunch and eight hours' unbroken sleep was very rarely broken. Even now, the generalissimo kept to his rule.

This set the scene for the BEF on the left wing of the French. Sir John's forces were intended to support those of Lanrezac's Fifth Army. On 22 August 1914 advance elements of the BEF had reached their intended position just over the border with Belgium on the Mons–Condé canal. Here, Sir John was given aerial intelligence from the Royal Flying Corps that there were major German forces in his path. They were Generaloberst Alexander von Kluck and Generloberst Karl von Bülow's 1st and 2nd Armies: the head of the hammer descending from Belgium. Outnumbering the Allies by three to one, Lanrezac's offensive was already in difficulties with Bülow around Charleroi, twenty miles east of Mons. On 23 August, the following day, the advance guard of Kluck's 1st Army clashed with Smith-Dorrien's II Corps; at the same time Bülow's forces crossed the Meuse and threw the Fifth Army's offensive into complete disarray. For Lanrezac, instant retreat was the only way to save his army from the tsunami of field grey. For the BEF and the two corps of General Douglas Haig and General Horace Smith-Dorrien, he had little concern. Churchill concluded tartly:

> The two armies ... only escaped disaster by the timely retreat which Lanrezac and Sir John French each executed independently and on his own initiative ... Many faults of temperament and indeed loyalty to the British Army on his left are urged against General Lanrezac. Nevertheless his grasp of the situation and stern decision to retreat while time remained has earned the gratitude of France. It was a pity he forgot to tell his British allies about it.

This, then, was the situation on 24 August 1914 which had prompted French's telegram to Kitchener. It was a withdrawal soon dignified with the description, 'the Great Retreat'. Things were going badly.

Later that very same day, after Kitchener had taken his gloomy leave and Churchill had risen from his bed, the First Lord of the Admiralty received two further visitors. They were the Harwich Commodores Reginald Tyrwhitt and Roger Keyes, respectively commanding the Harwich Force of light cruisers and destroyers and the 8th Submarine Flotilla. Aged forty-four and forty-two, they were both ardent patriots, fine seamen, dashing, daring, and destined to make major marks on their profession: Tyrwhitt, tall, hook-nosed, chiselled, almost the caricature of a British naval officer; Keyes, whose mild appearance and slighter stature belied the inner fire. The pair were good friends. Now they were out for blood. With the BEF safely transported to France, the Navy was thirsting for action. In the Grand Fleet they believed they had a weapon capable – with the destruction of the Hochseeflotte – of winning the war at a stroke. They would destroy the High Seas Fleet in a decisive naval action, re-enacting Trafalgar. This would open the door for a landing on Germany's North Sea or Baltic coasts. Yet in the three weeks since the declaration of war, German naval forces in the principal theatre of the North Sea had been notable by their absence. Under the commander-in-chief of the High Seas Fleet, Admiral Friedrich von Ingenohl, no attempt had been made to disrupt the transport of the BEF and the cross-channel Army supply lines; no naval raid or large-scale invasion had manifested itself; and the

Hochseeflotte behind the bars of the Ems and Jade rivers in Wilhelmshaven and Cuxhaven had made no sortie that might have led to a decisive victory on either its own part or the Royal Navy's. 'The German staff,' wrote Churchill, 'felt that even if this [early stage of the war] was the best chance of a trial of strength, it was still a chance so hazardous and even so forlorn that it was not worth taking.' The Kaiserliche Marine did not want to lose the war in an afternoon.

Tyrwhitt, speaking for the Navy as a whole, wrote on 15 August 1914 that he was 'beginning to feel rather bored looking for nothing ... beginning to give up hope of getting at the Germans for some time'. Six days later, Keyes had written to Admiral Arthur Leveson, the operations director at the Admiralty, venting similar frustration. 'When are we going to make war and make the Germans realise that whenever they come out – destroyers, cruisers, battleships or all three – they will be fallen on and attacked? ... These are views I have heard you express – for Heaven's sake preach them!'

Based at Harwich, the fine natural harbour commanding the approaches to Great Britain from the Low Countries, the two commodores' responsibilities included patrolling the Heligoland Bight. This was the bay at the mouth of the River Elbe, centred on the Heligoland, a triangular geological oddity rising sheer out of the North Sea. It was some thirty miles from the Schleswig-Holstein coast and slightly over three hundred miles east-northeast from Harwich. The tiny fortified island guarded the High Seas Fleet anchorages at Wilhelmshaven and Cuxhaven, the German equivalents of Southampton Water or Plymouth Sound.

Churchill had long-standing designs on Heligoland. It was an island that Great Britain in 1890 had rashly exchanged with the Germans for Zanzibar. An irritated Queen Victoria had commented, 'Next we'll be giving up Gibraltar!' Like the late Queen, the First Lord recognised the strategic importance of Heligoland, planned its seizure, and dreamed of using it as a forward base for a blockade and for landing on Germany's North Sea coast. For the present, Tyrwhitt and Keyes, having observed the flotilla of destroyers and light cruisers patrolling the Bight for Royal Navy incursions, supposed the waters ideal for teaching the Kaiserliche Marine Keyes's lesson. Whenever they came out, they would be attacked. Keyes himself, having inveigled his way into Churchill's office in the Admiralty on 23 August 1914, took the 'opportunity of bursting into flame about it, which fired the First Lord'. Churchill called for a further meeting the following day to discuss the operation in more detail. Tyrwhitt, summoned at 0930, not long after Lord Kitchener's disconsolate departure from the Admiralty, was a hundred miles east of Harwich on patrol in the queasy grey waters of the North Sea. He eventually reached Whitehall at 1700. Churchill then presided over the meeting which also included the Chief of Naval Staff, Admiral Sir Doveton Sturdee, the First Sea Lord Prince Louis Battenberg, and the Second Sea Lord, Admiral Sir Frederick Hamilton.

The commodores' intelligence suggested that a German flotilla patrolled to the north of Heligoland by night, relieved at first light by a second flotilla, which patrolled by day. The plan, according to Churchill, was 'simple and daring'. Two of Tyrwhitt's own flotillas from Harwich would steam to intercept at dawn both the incoming and the outgoing German flotillas; Keyes's submarines would stand by to torpedo the heavier German ships – dreadnoughts and battlecruisers – if they ventured out of their anchorages in support. A little later, it was agreed that five battlecruisers and six light cruisers would also be made available by Admiral Sir John Jellicoe for the operation. The battlecruisers comprised a squadron of three from the Grand Fleet in Scapa Flow, to be joined by *Invincible* and *New Zealand*, stationed on the Humber. More lightly armoured and thus faster than their dreadnought battleship cousins, the experimental battlecruisers were the nautical equivalent of the cavalry. This considerable force, dubbed the 1st Battle Cruiser Squadron, would be commanded by that fine huntsman, Admiral Sir David Beatty. It was hoped that these forces would give the Kaiserliche Marine a bloody nose. Given the events in France and Belgium of which Churchill had just been told, a very timely one, too.

Just three days later, at 0500 on 27 August 1914 Commodore Tyrwhitt sortied from Harwich with sixteen destroyers of the 1st Flotilla and fifteen of the 3rd, the task force led by the light cruisers *Arethusa* and *Fearless*. Commodore Keyes, with his destroyers *Lurcher* and *Firedrake*, together with nine submarines, was already on his way.

Hostilities opened at about 0700 on 28 August 1914. Almost at once the operation went wrong. Admiral Ingenohl's HQ was immediately informed of the attack and ordered the raising of steam in the German heavy units behind the bars of the Ems and Jade rivers; the German destroyer flotillas found themselves swiftly supported by other light forces rushing to their aid, and a confused and fragmented series of actions took place in misty conditions that dramatically curtailed visibility. Tyrwhitt himself and – critically – Keyes's submarines, were not informed of the approaching Royal Navy heavy units in the Bight, very nearly sending them to the bottom; and Tyrwhitt's flagship *Arethusa,* commissioned only hours before the operation, proved a liability. Its new semi-automatic guns constantly jammed. Soon *Arethusa* was battling it out with two German light cruisers, *Frauenlob* and *Stettin*. By 0900 she had taken fifteen direct hits, lost her wireless and her torpedo tubes, and was virtually crippled. When the light cruiser SMS *Strassburg* appeared a couple of hours later, hungry to finish her off, Tyrwhitt signalled urgently to Beatty for reinforcements.

The 1st Battle Cruiser Squadron of *Lion, Princess Royal* and *Queen Mary* had rendezvoused with *Invincible* and *New Zealand* at 0500, some ninety miles northwest of Heligoland. At about 1130, Beatty on the great flying bridge of *Lion,* exposed to all weathers, was handed Tyrwhitt's signal. 'Am attacked by a large cruiser 54 degrees, 0 minutes North, 7 degrees, 12 minutes East ... respectfully request that I may be supported. Am hard pressed.' This gave Beatty, flying his flag in the 26,270-ton *Lion,* a difficult decision. As *Lion's* captain, Ernle Chatfield, remarked:

The Bight was not a pleasant spot into which to take great ships; it was unknown whether mines had been laid there, submarines were sure to be on patrol; and to move into this area so near to the great German bases at Wilhelmshaven was risky ... Beatty said to me 'What do you think I should do? I ought to go and support Tyrwhitt, but if I lose one of these valuable ships, the country will never forgive me.'

༈

Back in France, the situation went from bad to worse. The French and British armies on the left seemed bent on headlong retreat towards Paris, a withdrawal just short of a rout. In the few days immediately after Kitchener's early morning call on Churchill in the Admiralty, the British I Corps under Haig was obliged to break its retreat to fight at Landrecies and Maroilles. Smith-Dorrien's II Corps fought with considerable skill against heavy odds at Le Câteau, and was saved in the nick of time by a French cavalry corps. An ill-tempered conference that same day, 26 August 1914, at St Quentin between Lanrezac and Sir John French did nothing to ease matters. 'Lanrezac,' wrote Churchill, 'was one of those Frenchmen who have an almost physical dislike, born of centuries of tradition, for the English ... he seemed to think it a favour that their puny army should be allowed to come to the aid of France.' Field Marshal French, naturally enough, did not speak the French language, nor did the French themselves speak English. Nothing was resolved, Lanrezac gracelessly refused to lunch with Sir John, and the two armies resumed their flight. The retreat seemed unstoppable. 'Our own five divisions,' wrote Churchill, 'were for several days plainly in the very jaws of destruction ... A seemingly irresistible compulsion was pressing and forcing backwards the brave armies of France. Why should it stop? Would they ever be able to turn? If France could not save herself, nothing could save her'.

Soon the river Marne would be in sight of the great German armies plunging south. The Marne rose a hundred miles due east of Paris, and was one of the last natural barriers between Commander-in-Chief Helmuth von Moltke's forces and the French capital. Captain Walter Bloem, an officer of the 12th Brandenburg Grenadiers, wrote: 'The sun was beginning to set when suddenly, spread out at our feet, was a picture of indescribable loveliness, the valley of the Marne. The sun had sank into a misty haze of deepest gold, the whole valley steeped in the perfect stillness of a summer evening, shimmered in the golden light. Could this be war?' Indeed, to the Oberste Heeresleitung in Luxembourg so sunny did the news seem from all seven of the great German armies on the Western Front that victory, with it the vindication of Schlieffen's plans, seemed certain. So assured did it appear that a terrible temptation formed in the mind of Moltke. It was at first no bigger than a man's hand.

Contrary to the expectation of both the late Count von Schlieffen and Moltke himself, Tsarist Russia had mobilised with remarkable celerity. Not just that, but two of its armies under General Pavel Rennenkampf and General Alexander Samsonov had at once advanced west into East Prussia, the Prussian 'Home Counties'. Here, Russia's forces amounting to nine corps faced all that Moltke felt able to spare from the west. This was just one of the eight Imperial German armies, comprising four corps. At Gumbinnen on 21 August it seemed to the 8th Army's commander, General Max von Prittwitz, that he, too, was in the very jaws of destruction. East Prussia would have to be abandoned, the Germans to retreat west beyond the Vistula. This heralded catastrophe not just in the east but the west, too. John Keegan wrote, 'At OHL, Moltke was appalled by the reports of the Eighth Army's sudden predicament, which undermined the whole substance and belief in the possibility of postponing crisis in the East while victory was gained in the West. Only twenty of the vital forty days had elapsed and Schlieffen's timetable threatened to crumble before OHL's eyes'.

Moltke sacked Prittwitz and replaced him with two men later to win notoriety on the Western Front: Generalmajor Erich Ludendorff and his mentor Generaloberst Paul von Hindenburg. Within seventy-two hours these men were preparing for the great battle that would go down in history as Tannenberg. With Paris and with it victory apparently within the grasp of the seven armies in the west, it seemed entirely sensible to Moltke to send reinforcements to the east in preparation for Tannenberg. Two corps were available, having been earmarked for the siege of Namur, the Belgium fortress that – as French had telegraphed Kitchener – had already fallen. Despite Ludendorff himself disdaining such forces at the expense of those in the west; and despite the fact that the men would not complete the eight hundred-mile journey by rail to affect the outcome at Tannenberg, Moltke had his way. On the morning of 28 August 1914, just as Tyrwhitt was signalling Beatty for reinforcements in the North Sea, spies working for the Allies in German-occupied France were noting the withdrawal of the two corps from the Western Front. Soon Kitchener could wire French with some good tidings: 'Thirty-two trains of German troops were yesterday reported moving from the western field to meet the Russians'. David Thomson wrote that the success of the Schlieffen plan 'depended upon the surprise overrunning of Belgium and upon having sufficient weight in the hammer-head to sweep all before it in the descent upon Paris.' The hammer-head was now the lighter by two corps.

We left Commodore Tyrwhitt in Heligoland Bight signalling Admiral Beatty for assistance, and David Beatty turning to *Lion*'s captain for counsel. 'Beatty said to me "What do you think I should do? I ought to go and support Tyrwhitt, but if I lose one of these valuable ships, the country will never forgive me."' To this Chatfield replied, 'Surely we must go.' At 1135 Beatty signalled to Tyrwhitt. 'Am proceeding to your support.' This he did at the full speed of 27 knots of which these ocean greyhounds – perhaps bulldogs – were capable. At 1320 his five-ship squadron was spotted emerging from the mist by Tyrwhitt's hard-pressed light cruisers and destroyers in the Bight. One of his officers commented, 'There, straight ahead of us in lovely procession, like elephants walking through a pack of dogs, came our battle-cruisers. How solid they looked and how utterly earth-quaking.' For the Kaiserliche Marine forces, the Admiralstab and Admiral Ingenohl himself, Beatty's intervention was less welcome. Hitherto, light forces had fought light forces, with results far from decisive. Now at this point, Ingenohl could have released at least some of his own heavy units, which he had ordered to raise steam at 0843. For reasons that will become apparent, caution now stayed his hand – with momentous consequences. *Stettin* and *Köln*, the two light cruisers leading the German defences in the Bight, fled on Beatty's approach; neither *Köln* nor another light cruiser, *Mainz*, could escape the huge 13.5in shells of *Lion* and her sister ships. Three other German ships were badly damaged (*Frauenlob*, *Strassburg* and *Stettin* herself) and the destroyer *V187* had already been sunk. For the Kaiserliche Marine the game was up. By 1350, the British forces had cleared the Bight and were heading west towards their bases. Tyrwhitt's flagship *Arethusa* could only make 10 knots and was obliged to head, not home to Harwich, but to Chatham for repairs.

Having broken into the Bight and made hay with German forces, having lost no ships, having sustained fatalities of thirty-five to the

Kaiserliche Marine's 712, the battle of Heligoland Bight was immediately hailed as a great victory. Churchill rushed to meet Tyrwhitt's flagship, according to the commodore himself 'fairly slobbered' over him, and crowned the commodore the Royal Navy's very latest hero. Tyrwhitt was at once made a Companion of the Order of Bath; Keyes was mentioned in despatches and would soon become closely involved in the organisation of the Dardanelles campaign. Beatty, too, was hailed as a hero. Wrote Churchill, 'The news of this naval action reached the French and British armies in the dark hour before the dawn of victory and was everywhere published to the retreating troops', to be echoed by Keyes, 'We were told the news of our naval success, which was circulated to the Allied Armies, greatly heartened our hard-pressed troops.'

They needed it, for as the tidings of Heligoland Bight came in on the last two days of August 1914, the Allied armies were still retreating headlong towards Paris with a million field-grey Germans at their heels. On 30 August 1914 Sir John French telegraphed Kitchener, 'My confidence in the ability of the leaders of the French Army to carry this campaign to a successful conclusion is fast waning.' This feeling was reinforced when French's offer to fight alongside Joffre if they would turn and fight on the Marne was rejected by the French C-in-C. Once again, Sir John began to envisage the complete collapse of the French armies, and talked of the evacuation of the BEF, not from Le Havre but further west from Brittany. He was further discouraged on 2 September by the evacuation of the French government from Paris to Bordeaux, and on hearing that plans had been made to blow the Seine bridges and demolish a structure used as a military radio transmitter: the Eiffel Tower. When at last Joffre grasped the logic – indeed the opportunity – of turning to fight on the Marne, it was French's turn to prevaricate. It was the famous meeting between the two that turned the tide. To Joffre's emotional appeal to his British allies, French tried to reply in his ally's tongue. He failed. In tears, he turned to his staff officer who had some schoolboy French. 'Damn it, I can't explain. Tell him that all man can do our fellows will do.' So ended the Great Retreat.

On the morning of 5 September 1914 the British Army and the Fifth French Army turned about and advanced north together towards the Deutches Heer, themselves advancing south. All would meet on the Marne. There, indeed, would meet all seven of the German armies, five of the French and the BEF, along a front of two hundred miles. Churchill wrote:

> A collision of thirteen or fourteen armies, each containing the adult male population of a very large city, and all consuming food, material, ammunition, treasure and life at a prodigious rate per hour ... the elemental forces which there met in grapple and collision of course far exceeded anything that ever happened ... [it was] the greatest battle ever fought in the world.

From the Allies' point of view, it was also the miracle on the Marne. There the hitherto unstoppable Prussian war machine careered off the rails. By 7 September 1914 three German armies – Prince Rupprecht's, the Duke of Württemberg's and General von Hausen's – had tried to advance against the French and had failed; and a gap had opened up between Kluck's 1st Army immediately to the east of Paris and Bülow's 2nd Army, intended to be standing shoulder to shoulder with Kluck a little farther east. It was into this gap that the hitherto unhappy alliance of the BEF and the French Fifth Army were advancing. For the Germans, this spelt catastrophe. It turned the flanks of both Bülow and Kluck and made their positions untenable. If Moltke had had to hand the two corps he sent Ludendorff on the Vistula, the story might have ended very differently, but he had not. Said Churchill, 'If the immense organisms of modern armies standing in a row together find there is a gap in their ranks, and have no reserves to fill it, they cannot edge towards one another sideways like companies and battalions. They can only close the gap by advance or retreat. Which is it to be?'

As these developments were assimilated in the Oberste Heeresleitung in Luxembourg, the mood of imminent triumph turned to ashes. On 8 September 1914 Colonel Bauer, a staff officer attached to the HQ, recorded:

Desperate panics seized severely the whole army, or to be more correct the greater part of the leaders. It looked at its worst at supreme command. Moltke completely collapsed. He sat with a pallid face gazing at the map, dead to all feeling, a broken man. General von Stein [Moltke's deputy] certainly said, 'We must not lose our heads', but he did not take charge.

On 9 September 1914 the German retreat began. Following the lead of Bulow's 2nd Army, the 1st and the 3rd were obliged to follow suit; in the face of a fresh French attack on the 3rd, Moltke ordered the 4th and 5th to follow the 3rd, 2nd and 1st. Along the whole front the Kaiser's armies began their own great retreat, heading for the next river system above the Marne. This was the Aisne. 'The lines so reached,' ordered Moltke, 'will be fortified and defended.' They would, and would remain so for four years as the Western Front, the trenches. On 12 September 1914 Moltke reputedly told the Kaiser, '*Majestät, wir haben den Krieg verloren.*' 'Majesty, we have lost the war'. Within forty-eight hours he had been replaced by the 53-year-old General Erich von Falkenhayn, hitherto the Prussian minister of war.

Whether or not the remark was actually made, it was certainly true that the intertwined battles of the Marne and of Heligoland Bight were the first turning-points of the Great War. Germany's defeat on the Marne meant that she was unlikely to win the war; Heligoland Bight meant that she would probably lose it. In some respects all was decided virtually within the first month of the war; and all that remained – in Churchill's words – was 'little else ... but four years of senseless slaughter.'

At first sight it seems strange that the loss in the Bight of fewer than a thousand men, three light cruisers and a destroyer could so affect the course of the war. That it did so was a consequence of the conclusions drawn by the Admiralstab – and by the Kaiser himself – about a battle that was joined and completed in little over six hours. Despite the relatively small scale of the German losses, the fact that they had occurred virtually under the guns of the much-vaunted High Seas Fleet and in their own back yard – Churchill described the Bight seas as 'the enemy's most intimate and jealously guarded headquarters' – greatly alarmed the German Imperial Navy and the Kaiser. It pointed to vulnerability.

From the very beginning of the Kaiser's aspirations to build a great fleet to challenge British Naval supremacy, Germany faced two problems. Not only had Portsmouth a three-hundred-year head start on Wilhelmshaven, but the Empire's industrial resources were such that however quickly the shipyards of Bremerhaven, Hamburg and Wilhelmshaven built dreadnoughts, those in Portsmouth, the Clyde, the Humber and elsewhere could build them quicker. Despite the exertions of the German hare, the British tortoise would always be a few dreadnoughts and battlecruisers ahead. 'As naval competition becomes more acute,' stated Churchill in a speech in Ulster in 1912, 'we shall have not only to increase the number of ships we build, but the ratio of our naval strength will have to bear to other great naval powers'. So it proved. As we have seen, at the outbreak of war, Admiral Jellicoe boasted twenty-two dreadnoughts to Admiral Hugo von Pohl's fifteen, nine battlecruisers to Germany's five, 121 cruisers to Germany's forty, and 221 destroyers to Germany's ninety-six. As Kitchener told Churchill on the occasion of the First Lord's dismissal in the wake of the failure of the Dardanelles campaign, 'Well there is one thing at any rate they cannot take from you. The Fleet was ready'.

It was a consequence of the strength of the Grand Fleet that the Admiralstab was somewhat averse to a policy that would see the Hochseeflotte sallying out from its Wilhelmshaven bases to confront a much larger fleet with a view to a decisive naval action along the lines of Trafalgar. This would be to co-operate in its own destruction. Rather, it hoped to whittle down the British fleet in more modest encounters of its own choosing until the odds were more evenly balanced. As Eric Osborne puts it in the standard work on the battle of Heligoland Bight, 'The German High Seas Fleet would ... seek battle only under favourable circumstances in order to pursue the equalisation of strength with the British that was necessary for a cause of success – in defeating the enemy in a decisive battle'. The acid test for this strategy was the Bight, the very first significant action between the two navies. The conclusions drawn by the Kaiserliche Marine were unsettling; ultimately they were fatal. They were that, in practice, it was Pohl's Hochseeflotte rather than the Grand Fleet that was in the most danger of being cut down to size. As the official German history of the war at sea put it:

The 28th August had shown that the British would come, if at all, only with fast, heavy forces. Thus if our own battle-cruisers or a squadron of battleships were sent out to support our own scouts at sea, an action of capital ships could develop at any time. It would be difficult to break off such an engagement after damage had been done. In such an event, the participation of further squadrons was inevitable, and a battle would ensue, perhaps under conditions unfavourable to us ... Thus it came about that capital ships were held back.

Such conclusions were also drawn at the time by the Kaiser himself, who went further in attempts to minimise the threat to the fleet. 'After that outpost action,' wrote Pohl, 'His Majesty feared that the fleet might engage a superior enemy, just as the light cruisers had done'. In future, the Kaiser's express permission for any major action would be required, the operations of the High Seas Fleet would be confined to the Bight, and even within the Bight the fleet was not to seek action against forces of greater power. Admiral von Tirpitz amplified:

August 28th, a day fateful, both in its after-effects and incidental results, for the work of our navy ... The Emperor did not want losses of this sort ... Orders were issued by the Emperor ... to restrict the initiative of the Commander-in-Chief of the North Sea Fleet: the loss of ships was to be avoided, fleet sallies and any great undertakings must be approved by His Majesty in advance.

It was this curtailment of the High Seas Fleet that was to have such profound consequences. Not only did it diminish the prospects of a decisive fleet action, it also gravely impeded any attempts the Kaiserliche Marine might make to break the Royal Navy's blockade. This was enforced in the Channel and the Western Approaches, as well as in North Sea waters between Scapa Flow and Norway – far beyond the Bight. Osborne concluded: 'As a result, the British blockade of Germany remained in effect and increased in effectiveness throughout the war. The naval blockade of Germany is a chief reason for the defeat of the country in World War I.'

That the Battle of the Marne saved Paris and kept France in the war might place it – very loosely – in much the same category as Dunkirk, of a great escape. Yet it also saw the collapse of Schlieffen's plans and the consequential commitment of Germany to a war on two fronts; precisely the predicament OHL was rightly desperate to avoid. 'By frustrating the Schlieffen Plan,' wrote the historian Richard Brooks, 'Joffre had won the decisive battle of the war, and perhaps of the century'.

Yet the achievement was more that of the plump French gourmand Generalissimo Joseph Joffre than that of the BEF, bravely and skilfully though the two corps are widely recognised to have fought. 'Did the intervention of the BEF make any difference?' asked A J P Taylor. 'Not much. The Germans would have fallen back in any case when they saw the gap between their 1st and 2nd armies.' Much more recently, the military historian Allan Mallinson commented, 'Having the BEF in the line may well have boosted French morale ... but it is unreasonable to suggest that the French would not have been able to manage on their own. Indeed, there would have been considerably more cohesion.' Even though Churchill, being Churchill, calls French's efforts 'decisive', Haig surely had had a point in counselling caution concerning the BEF, caution about when it should be sent, about its size, about where it should be sent, ultimately – by implication – whether it should have been sent at all. Hadn't someone mentioned the idea that, 'If we participated, it should be by naval action alone'? They had, though perhaps not in Kitchener's hearing. So what would really have happened if the BEF had not been despatched? On balance, Niall Ferguson's conclusion seems about right. 'If the proponents of a neutral or a naval strategy had prevailed ... and Britain had not sent the BEF, the German chances of victory over France would without question have been enhanced.'

4

Lord Kitchener Intervenes

'If the Fleet gets through, Constantinople will fall of its own accord, and you will have won not the battle but the war.'

Lord Kitchener

It was a scene a novelist, a novelist at least of the realistic school – a Joseph Conrad, Henry James, Kingsley Amis or a Julian Barnes – might hesitate to conjure up, so contrary did it seem to laws of probability, plausibility and common sense. The occasion was the ninth meeting of Asquith's War Council, held at 1130 on 28 January 1915. The setting, the Cabinet Room in Downing Street; centre stage the Secretary of State for War Lord Horatio Kitchener and the First Sea Lord 'Jacky' Fisher, with the Prime Minister Henry Asquith, the First Lord of the Admiralty Winston Churchill, the Foreign Secretary Sir Edward Grey, the former prime minister Arthur Balfour (1st Earl of Balfour) and Maurice Hankey in attendance; the atmosphere: sulphurous; the topic: the Dardanelles. Churchill opened the session by flying a kite. He asked if the council 'attached importance' to the proposal to force the narrow straits that led from the Aegean into the Sea of Marmara and beyond to the citadel of Constantinople. These were the straits that opened up the heart of the Ottoman Empire, the gateway to the Black Sea and to Tsar Nicholas's Russia, to England's ally. Fisher, the First Sea Lord, with a face as thunderous as a broadside from one of his great dreadnoughts, responded to his political superior's question by saying tersely that he had understood the subject was not to be raised at the meeting. The prime minister, he added, turning to face Asquith across the Cabinet Room table, was familiar with his views on the adventure. To this, Asquith replied that given the importance of the Dardanelles operation and the planning that had already been undertaken, its discussion could not be set aside. It was at this point that Fisher rose abruptly, left the Cabinet Room table, and stalked over to one of the great windows that overlooked the Downing Street garden. So contrary was this to the custom and etiquette of such meetings that Kitchener also got to his feet. Briskly, with a military tread, he followed the First Sea Lord to the window. There, according to Fisher, in an account verified by Kitchener himself, Fisher told the Secretary of State for War that he would not return to the council table; that he was resigning as First Sea Lord forthwith, that his earthly powers he there abjured. In his memoirs, Fisher suggested that the tableau might furnish material for the greatest historical picture of the war. It would be Sir John Lavery's masterpiece, a secular interpretation of the Passion.

The recall of 'Jacky' Fisher as First Sea Lord had followed the discreditable episode of his predecessor's resignation. Few supposed that Prince Louis of Battenberg possessed the force of personality to withstand the young Churchill in full flight. Indeed, he was sufficiently supine in the face of the First Lord's energy, force of argument and willpower to have acquired the nickname 'Quite concur'. This was the note he appended to the spate of proposals, ideas, suggestions, instructions, diktats and orders that spewed from Churchill's pen and which made him, in the words even of Roy Jenkins, a sympathetic biographer, 'the most operationally interfering First Lord in the history of the Admiralty'. Few, equally, certainly today, feel that the prince should have been hounded from office by the force of press and public opinion on account of his German birth and – entirely imagined – leanings towards the Kaiser. In 1914 xenophobia in England was rife. Churchill's replacement of Prince Louis by the 73-year-old Fisher was a courageous move that culminated catastrophically for both Fisher and Churchill – not to mention hundreds of thousands from the Kitchener and Dominion armies. 'My bringing Fisher back to the Admiralty in 1914 was one of the most hazardous steps I have ever had to take in my official duty,' wrote Churchill. 'Certainly, so far as I was personally concerned, it was the most disastrous.' Yet it also led to one of the most important attempts to win the war through sea power.

Born in Ceylon in 1841, Fisher joined what was still the Royal Navy of sail at the age of thirteen; it was virtually Nelson's Navy: the heroic, chivalric force of C S Forester's Horatio Hornblower and Patrick O'Brian's Jack Aubrey. Fisher saw action in the China wars and in the conflict with Egypt in 1882, where he commanded HMS *Inflexible*. She was an intriguing token of the evolution of warships, sporting as she did both sails and torpedo tubes – an arrangement as incongruous as a horse trough on a motorway. Ten years later he was appointed one of the Lords of the Admiralty, from 1897–99 commanded the North American and West India Station, and in 1904 began his first term as First Sea Lord, the professional head of the Royal Navy. It was in this role that, in circumstances of great controversy, he led the modernisation of Britain's greatest armed service. He scrapped obsolete ships, revived naval gunnery, selected officers on the basis of intelligence rather than influence; he introduced destroyers, torpedoes, submarines, turbine propulsion, oil firing and much else besides. He was very far from unopposed. It is as father of the dreadnought battleships for which Fisher is best remembered, but his broader impact was incalculable. As Robert Massie remarked, 'Fisher looked beyond, imagined new men, new rules, new ships, new worlds that broke tradition so violently that they constituted revolution.' A man of great personal charisma, a brilliant lecturer, a terrible factionalist, to Churchill 'a veritable volcano of knowledge and inspiration' and 'the most distinguished British Naval officer since Nelson'. He was a very great man.

And yet, and yet. David Beatty, then a lowly rear admiral, had sought out Churchill in Whitehall shortly after his appointment as First Lord of the Admiralty in late 1911. 'You look young for an Admiral,' the 37-year-old Churchill is reputed to have said to a man of a very similar age. To which Beatty responded with all the confidence of his talent, background and natural insouciance, 'And you seem young for a First Lord!' Certainly, Churchill was much taken by the man who was in fact the youngest flag officer in the fleet, indeed the youngest admiral since Nelson.

Of Anglo-Irish patrician stock, Beatty was born in 1871. His schooling was largely restricted to equestrianism. He joined the Navy in 1884, distinguishing himself as a riverboat commander in the Sudan, subsequently seeing action at the battle of Omdurman. Here he encountered both Kitchener and Churchill, the latter in his guise as a cavalry officer in the 4th Hussars. Beatty made commander in 1891 ahead of 400 other candidates, again distinguished himself in the Boxer Rebellion, and was given his first command in 1902. By 1910 he was a rear admiral and married to the American department store heiress Ethel Tree. His swashbuckling character appealed to Churchill and – after their encounter in the Admiralty – Beatty found himself appointed naval secretary to the First Lord. Wrote Churchill, 'Working thus side by side in rooms which communicated, we perpetually discussed during the next fifteen months the problems of a naval war with Germany'. Beatty knew Churchill, Churchill knew Beatty . . . and Beatty also knew Fisher; was, in fact, his protégé. 'Any mortal thing you want, animate or inanimate, you shall have if you send me a telegram,' cooed Fisher to Beatty. In December 1914, in the wake of Fisher's late October recall to the Admiralty, Beatty wrote to his wife Ethel with foreboding and with the sort of perspicacity with which he is not always credited. 'Two very strong and clever men, one old, wily and of vast experience, one young, self-assertive with great self-satisfaction but unstable. They cannot work together, they cannot both run the show'. Such was Beatty's verdict, Beatty whose audacity had saved Tyrwhitt's light cruiser *Arethusa* in Heligoland Bight, Beatty whose courage that day in command of the battlecruiser squadron had effectively stopped Tirpitz, the Kaiser and the Hochseeflotte in its tracks; Beatty, whose failure on 31 May 1916 to keep Jellicoe informed of both his own movements and those of the Hochseeflotte would lead to one of the many lost opportunities of the Great War, that of the battle of Jutland.

In practice, with Fisher and Churchill for two months all went well. At Fisher's instigation, the loss at Coronel of Admiral Cradock's squadron to Admiral von Spee's *Scharnhorst* and *Gneisenau* was swiftly avenged by the battlecruisers *Inflexible* and *Invincible*. This was at the Falklands in the South Atlantic on 8 December 1914. It was the episode which brought to an end the threat to British merchant shipping from the Kaiserliche Marine's surface fleet in all the world. As Churchill states, 'Its consequences were far-reaching, and affected simultaneously our position in every part of the world ... All our enterprises, whether of war or commerce, proceeded in every theatre without the slightest hindrance [it had] immense importance to the whole naval situation.' For Beatty, 'The victory belongs to old Fisher and nobody else.' At Fisher's insistence, work on the submarine defences at Scapa Flow and on the creation of a more southerly base for the battlecruisers at Rosyth on the Firth of Forth was redoubled. On Fisher's orders, a great ship construction programme was initiated – submarines, destroyers, anti-submarine vessels, monitors, motor launches, light cruisers, battlecruisers and landing craft – indeed, what amounted to virtually a new navy, a navy to which the success of the blockade and the defeat of the U-boats may be partly attributed. 'Its creation on such a scale,' wrote Churchill, 'is one of the greatest services which the nation has owed to the genius and energy of Lord Fisher'. Finally, under Fisher's auspices a cryptanalysis section was set up in Room 40 in the Admiralty. It based its work on a captured German naval codebook, *Signalbuch der Kaiserlichen Marine*, and on maps with coded squares passed on to the Admiralty by the Russians. The office provided intelligence of a very high order on German naval movements throughout the war, and it was a forerunner of Bletchley Park in the Second World War. Then came the Dardanelles.

By Christmas of 1914, Lord Kitchener's August prophecy of a long war had proved all too accurate.

Mercifully, Schlieffen's plans had failed; but after the Anglo-French victory at the Battle of the Marne in September 1914 the Kaiser's armies had fallen back to the high ground overlooking the Aisne river system. A tributary of the Oise, the Aisne rose in the forest of Argonne, then flowed north and west before joining the Oise near Compiègne where, four years later, the Armistice would be signed. This valley of death General von Falkenhayn's men proceeded to entrench. Attempts by both great armies to turn each other's flank, a series of operations rather misleadingly called the 'race to the sea', had ended with impasse. That Christmas of 1914 the trenches ran from the North Sea to the neutral territory of the Swiss Alps. It was a line congealed in blood. There, virtually without variation or movement, it would stay until the great German offensives of Ludendorff and Hindenburg in March 1918. The only thing that changed was the ever-lengthening list of casualties on both sides. The MP Valentine Fleming wrote:

> Imagine a broad belt, ten miles or so in width, stretching from the Channel to the German frontier near Basle, which is positively littered with the bodies of men and scarified by their rude graves; in which farms, villages and cottages are shapeless heaps of blackened masonry; in which fields, roads and trees are pitted and torn and twisted by shells and disfigured by dead horses, cattle sheep and goats, scattered in every attitude of repulsive distortion and dismemberment ... [made] hideous by the incessant crash and whistle and roar of every sort of projectile, by sinister columns of smoke and flame, by the cries of wounded men, by the piteous calls of animals of all sorts, abandoned, starved, perhaps wounded.

Sir John French's first battle of Ypres in west Flanders, fought in late October 1914 at the western end of the great line, had demonstrated to some but by no means all Allied strategists that a more imaginative means was required to wage the war. Up until that time total casualties – killed, made prisoner or wounded – amounted to 854,000 for the French, 677,000 for the Germans, and 85,000 for the much smaller British contingent. This, though, did mean that the BEF had been virtually destroyed. For Basil Liddell Hart, 'No praise can be too high for the indomitable spirit which inspired their collective endurance ... Ypres saw the supreme vindication and the final sacrifice of the old Regular Army. After the battle was over, little survived, save its memory in spirit.' In the context of nineteenth-century warfare, indeed the whole history of European warfare, sacrifices at this level were stupendous. Total losses at Austerlitz in 1805 amounted to 45,000; at Waterloo in 1815 to 65,000; at Solferino in 1859 to 40,000. In 1914 the result of these terrible sacrifices on both sides was not victory but deadlock. At its simplest, at that time well-constructed trenches defended by machine guns – one of the great fruits of civilisation – and barbed wire could not be overwhelmed by frontal attack of infantry, even when supported by heavy artillery. Of Hiram Maxim and his machine gun, Liddell Hart declared that 'his name is more deeply engraved on the real history of the World War than that of any other man.' This situation would not change until improvements in artillery, more imaginative tactics and the advent of tanks later in the war. In the meantime, in January 1915 Kitchener rightly concluded in a letter to Sir John French that:

> I suppose we must now recognise that the French army cannot make a sufficient break through the German lines of defence to bring about the retreat of German forces from Northern France. If that is so, then the German lines in France may be looked upon as a fortress that cannot be taken by assault and also cannot be completely invested, with the result that the lines may be held by an investing force while operations proceed elsewhere.

A J P Taylor commented, 'No other military leader saw things so clearly.' The Secretary of State for War had, however, no concrete alternative ('operations elsewhere') to frontal attack on the Western Front to propose. Surely there had to be a better way to win the war into which Great Britain had entered somewhat thoughtlessly?

Maurice Hankey – sometime Royal Marine – Lloyd George and Churchill himself rushed impetuously to fill the vacuum. The lucky prime minister received three missives from these stripling strategists in the quiet days between Christmas of 1914 and the New Year. Churchill's summarised most graphically the problem facing the Allies.

> I think it is quite possible that neither side will have the strength to penetrate the other's line in the Western theatre ... My impression is that the position of both armies is not likely to undergo any decisive change – although no doubt several hundred thousand men will be spent to satisfy the military mind on the point ... On the assumption that these views are correct, how ought we to approach our growing military power? Are there no other alternatives than sending our armies to chew barbed wire in Flanders?

Whatever mistakes had been made by Asquith's Council of War in August 1914 in first sending the BEF to the Continent and then in attaching it irrevocably to the French flank, this was a very good question. Hankey and Lloyd George asked much the same, based on very similar analyses. Of the impasse on the Western Front until the Kitchener armies could be trained, perhaps even then; of the difficulty in forcing a decisive battle on the Eastern Front in the wake of Tannenberg; of the conundrum of luring out the Hochseeflotte from its bases for a conclusive encounter in the North Sea – despite its hit and run raid of the east coast on 16 December 1914 that would lead to that awkward question, 'Where was the Navy?' As things stood, they all argued, there was no prospect of victory. Neither for the Entente nor what were now being called the Central Powers. Neither on land nor at sea. All three in essence also proposed the same solution. The historical precedent, wrote Hankey, was that 'an attack has been delivered elsewhere, which has compelled the enemy so to weaken his forces that an advance becomes possible'. Adds Liddell Hart:

> The strategical solution was to go round the trench barrier. Its advocates – who became known as the 'Eastern' in contrast to the 'Western' school – argued that the enemy alliance should be viewed as a whole, and that modern developments had so changed conceptions of distance and powers of mobility, that a blow in some other theatre of war would correspond to the historic attack on an enemy's strategic flank.

Asquith, in his leisurely manner, might have contemplated these papers at his convenience over the port, stilton, charades and Christmas cake at his country house in Berkshire's Sutton Courtenay had it not been for Russia. For from there, on 2 January 1915 came an urgent call from Grand Duke Nicholas, commander-in-chief of Russian forces. The Ottoman Empire had joined the Triple Alliance in October 1914. Italy still remaining neutral, this added a third enemy to the Tsar's struggle with Emperor Franz-Joseph's Austria–Hungary and the Kaiser's Imperial Germany. The Turks were now attacking Russia in the Caucasus, the mountain range between the Black Sea and the Caspian Sea that divided Turkey from Russia. This appeal soon reached Churchill's desk – or bedroom – in the Admiralty, the telegram passed on to him by Kitchener. Grand Duke Nicholas, read Churchill over his morning tea:

> asked if it would be possible for Lord Kitchener to arrange for a demonstration of some kind against Turks elsewhere, either naval or military, and to spread reports which would cause the Turks, who he says are very liable to go off at a tangent, to withdraw some of the forces now acting against Russia in the Caucasus, and, thus ease the position of Russians.

It was a call from an ally difficult to ignore; and it was a plea that added impetus to the appeal for alternatives to the BEF chewing barbed wire in Flanders. Like Helmuth von Moltke sending a couple of corps to help out Hindenburg and Ludendorff at Tannenberg, like the Marne and like the battle of Heligoland Bight, it was a request which also created one of the war's sliding doors.

Adhering to the principle so often adumbrated by Fisher that the Army was a projectile to be fired by the Navy, Hankey, Churchill and Lloyd George all advocated operations that would turn Germany's flank. Hankey proposed an attack on Turkey; Lloyd George, offensives in Salonika, Syria or the Dalmation coast in the Balkans; Churchill advanced the old Admiralty chestnut of the attack on the coast of Schleswig-Holstein; or alternatively, he suggested, the forcing of the Dardanelles. All these ideas had a certain logic. As things stood, the Kaiser's armies in Flanders and beyond lay between the Allies and the Fatherland. They could be circumvented – in military parlance outflanked – either to the northwest or southeast, albeit at a very considerable distance from the Western Front. Given Great Britain's command of the seas, forces could be landed on either of Germany's two coasts: in the North Sea and the Baltic – the latter potentially seeing Russian armies setting foot on German soil only ninety miles north of Berlin. In the south, the narrow straits of the Dardanelles in the Aegean Sea led to Constantinople, itself the gateway to the Black Sea. Most of Russia's trade with the world passed through the Bosporus, so the seizure of the Ottoman capital would constitute just the sort of 'demonstration' for which the Grand Duke appealed.

Moreover, it was supposed that the fall of Constantinople would bring the hitherto neutral Balkan states of Greece, Bulgaria and Romania into the welcoming fold of the Entente. It would also open up the arterial Danube, the waterway that led to Budapest and Vienna, the two great cities of the Habsburgs' Dual Monarchy. Landings in Salonika in neutral Greece would also support Russia's struggles in the Balkans against Austria–Hungary. All were good examples of the opportunities open to what Churchill in 1916 would christen 'the great amphibian', a nation with the ability to fight both on land and at sea – at places of its own choosing. For Liddell Hart, such operations 'would be in accordance with the traditional amphibious strategy of Britain, and would enable it to exploit the advantage of sea power which had hitherto been neglected.' There were, however, snags.

A tactical distraction was a plan to blockade Zeebrugge, the Belgian North Sea port that had fallen into German hands in October 1914. It was proving a hornet's nest for U-boats, not to mention the light surface vessels – destroyers and torpedo boats – which threatened the Royal Navy's vital endless chain of supplies to the BEF in France, the Army's umbilical cord. Then it was Kitchener who himself later observed, 'We have to make war as we must, and not as we should like.' Wise words, and relevant in the context of the ingénue strategists' grander designs. These tended to overlook elementary logistical issues. If the Army was to be used for these adventures, precisely which one? The BEF had been decimated at Ypres and Kitchener's great volunteer armies were still being trained; Sir John French would hardly countenance the salami-slicing of his much depleted forces on the Western Front, and indeed was desperate for reinforcements. The Russians had yet to recover from the extravagant blood-letting at Tannenberg. So there was no Army – though there could have been if the BEF had not been sent the previous August so hastily to France. If the Navy, the landing craft that Fisher had certainly envisaged for use against the German coasts were still in the shipyards, the Grand Fleet was otherwise occupied shadowing the Hochseeflotte. A J P Taylor summarises, 'All these schemes were debated without staff advice or consideration of detailed maps. There was no inquiry whether shipping was available, nor whether there were troops to spare – Kitchener ineffectively observing there were none. The War Council cheerfully assumed that great armadas could waft non-existent armies to the end of the earth in the twinkling of an eye.'

There was also the First Sea Lord, Jacky Fisher himself. His support was essential, for of course the Army would be going nowhere without the Navy. As Churchill put it somewhat defensively, perhaps regretfully, 'Only the First Sea Lord can order ships to steam and the guns to fire'. In a letter to Churchill written on 3 January 1915 in his most characteristic and delightful prose, Fisher commented:

> I've been informed by Hankey that War Council assembles next Thursday, and I suppose it will be like a game of ninepins! Everyone will have a plan and one ninepin in falling over will knock over its neighbour! I CONSIDER THE ATTACK ON TURKEY HOLDS THE FIELD! – BUT ONLY IF IT'S IMMEDIATE! However, it won't be! Our Aulic [like a prince's court] Council will adjourn till the following Thursday fortnight!

Churchill reasonably regarded this as a vote of confidence for the Dardanelles scheme – certainly as far as it went. Accordingly, and given Kitchener's insistence that no troops would be available for the venture, he wrote that same day to the commander of Royal Navy forces in the eastern Mediterranean. This was Vice Admiral Sackville Carden. 'Do you consider the forcing of the Dardanelles by ships alone a practicable operation?' This query, by Churchill's own admission, was 'purely exploratory. I was still thinking a great deal of the Northern theatre, of Borkum and of the Baltic.' As indeed was Fisher, who, 'was deeply convinced that the command of the Baltic, and the consequent letting loose of the Russian armies upon the whole of the unprotected Northern seaboard of Germany, would be a mortal blow.'

Carden's reply to Churchill was read out by the First Lord at the War Council meeting on 5 January 1915. From Churchill's point of view, it was encouraging. 'With reference to your telegram of 3rd instant, I do not consider the Dardanelles can be rushed. They might be forced by extended operations with large number of ships.' Churchill commented:

> Everyone seemed alive to all its advantages, and Admiral Carden's telegram ... was heard with extreme interest. Its significance lay in

63

the fact that it offered a prospect of influencing the Eastern situation in a decisive manner without opening a new military commitment on a large scale; and further it afforded an effective means of helping the Grand Duke without wasting the Dardanelles possibilities upon nothing more than a demonstration.

It would use the Navy, not the Army.

The Dardanelles plan, in so far as it had been formulated, was to assemble a squadron of obsolete British and French battleships and supporting vessels at the mouth of the Straits. The defending Turkish batteries would be reduced one by one by naval gunfire as this superannuated fleet worked its way up the forty-five miles of narrow straits and into the Sea of Marmara – at the eastern end of which stood Constantinople. It was believed that the Ottoman capital would then fall of its accord, without the use of what another age would call ground forces: without the Army. Not least because there wasn't one to spare. Thereafter, in the second week of January, the scheme gained momentum through the apparent support of all concerned, including Fisher. According to Hankey, as Churchill promulgated the plan, 'The whole atmosphere changed. Fatigue was forgotten. The War Council turned eagerly from the dreary vistas of a "slogging match" on the Western Front to brighter prospects as they seemed, in the Mediterranean.' For the present, Hankey's own ideas and those of Lloyd George were shelved, like Fisher's fallen ninepins.

Then on 11 and 12 January 1915 a further factor was introduced which, as Churchill said, 'greatly affected the issue.' It was the commissioning of the super-dreadnought *Queen Elizabeth*, and the prospect of the support of her enormous 15in guns in forcing the Dardanelles. For Churchill, the battleship capped the argument for breaking into the Straits by what might be termed 'naval action alone'. Paradoxically, for Fisher, she eventually became the stratagem for making no such attempt at all. This 33,000-ton, 644ft battleship was the apotheosis of Fisher's conception and of the dreadnought design. Launched in 1913, seven years after her famous predecessor, she built on the experience of *Dreadnought* by being faster, better armoured, and above all better armed. *Dreadnought* herself boasted ten great guns, each firing 850lb shells, 12in in diameter. Through the vision, enthusiasm and drive of both Churchill himself and Fisher, her successor carried 15in guns. Those three inches allowed the weight of the shell to be increased from 850lbs to a monstrous 1920lbs. Imagine something the weight of a small car, a car packed with high explosive, hurtling towards you at around 2000mph. This was what *Queen Elizabeth* could do. It was a broadside which could be blasted around 35,000yds or twenty miles, say from Westminster to Windsor; it was 40 per cent heavier than anything the Kaiserliche Marine could fire; it would be decisive at sea; surely, on land, too, thought Churchill. It seemed an excellent idea.

Queen Elizabeth, the lead ship of a class of vessels, was commissioned on 22 December 1914. According to Churchill's biographer Roy Jenkins, she was 'the finest ship under the Admiralty, and maybe in the whole world'. She was earmarked as the Grand Fleet's flagship and was the apple of Fisher's eye. At a pinch the ships already earmarked for the Straits were expendable: mostly too old, too slow, too poorly armed and armoured to be part of the Grand Fleet. They were one thing. *Queen Elizabeth* was quite another. The plan had been for her to test and calibrate her armament in the Mediterranean. Here she would be free from the prying eyes of the Hochseeflotte, and the weather was better. Churchill's naval staff now proposed to send her further east into the Aegean. The Dardanelles were defended by a series of forts. None of the batteries had a range anything like 35,000yds, so making *Queen Elizabeth* untouchable, at least by the forts. They would, argued the staff, provide admirable target practice for the splendid new battleship, the pride of the Navy, the toast of the Empire, the delight of King George V – not only the monarch but, of course, an Admiral of the Fleet too. At first, Fisher acquiesced in, perhaps even made, this proposal. Then, as the month of January wore on, his doubts began to surface – with the prompting of the commander-in-chief of the Grand Fleet.

Admiral Sir John Jellicoe was a slightly surprising figure to have ended up in command of Great Britain's principal instrument of war. Born in 1859 into a naval family, he served with Fisher in the Egyptian war of 1882, and survived the notorious collision between HM Ships *Victoria* and *Camperdown* in 1893, the sword of honour from Norman Dixon's *On the Psychology of Military Incompetence*. Jellicoe worked with Fisher to modernise the Navy as an advocate of the dreadnoughts, torpedoes and the development of the submarine. He had a good deal of his superior's native intelligence, passion for the Navy, capacity for hard work, and determination to create a service fit to fight the Kaiserliche Marine. Yet he had little of the First Sea Lord's exuberance and charm; little of Beatty's swashbuckling dash and flair or film-star looks. On naval historical matters, Beatty's biographer Stephen Roskill judged him 'almost illiterate'. A master of detail, organisation and planning, Jellicoe was a kindly, decent man beloved by the lower deck. He was also Fisher's creature through and through. According to Robert Massie, 'Jellicoe was in command because, over the years, Fisher had guided his career and insisted that no one else would do.' For Churchill, he 'was in experience and administrative capacity unquestionably superior to any British Admiral ... knew every aspect and detail of his profession ... [and had] won equal confidence from those he served and those he led.'

Yet as Europe's armies mobilised in the first days of August 1914, it was Jellicoe who deplored Churchill's decision to replace Sir George Callaghan as commander of the Grand Fleet with Jellicoe himself. At 2230 on 2 August 1914 he wired Churchill:

Personal: detained Wick by fog. Am firmly convinced after consideration that the step you mentioned to me is fraught with the gravest danger at this juncture and might easily be disastrous owing to extreme difficulty of getting in touch with everything at short notice. The transfer even if carried out cannot safely be accomplished for some time. I beg most earnestly that you will give matter further consideration with First Sea Lord before you take this step. Jellicoe.

It is difficult to imagine Nelson, Wellington or – in Churchill's parlance – any of the great captains of the past responding to their promotion to the pinnacle of their careers in anything like this way. It was also Jellicoe whose decisions at Jutland, though undoubtedly defensible, did enable Admiral Scheer's Hochseeflotte to snatch survival from the jaws of defeat, destruction, death and perhaps the end of the war.

At the precise time of the ruminations on the Dardanelles, Jellicoe was – and was expressing himself as – extremely concerned about the balance of power between the British and German navies. Several of the Grand Fleet's dreadnoughts were undergoing routine maintenance, two were being repaired after a minor collision, and Jellicoe had come to believe that von Tirpitz's Kaiserliche Marine had followed the example of *Queen Elizabeth* in fitting much heavier guns to their dreadnoughts. 'His letters to the First Sea Lord,' wrote Churchill, 'were filled with disquieting computations on the relative strengths of the British and German navies in the event of a great battle'. This worried Fisher. It also sufficiently concerned Asquith for him to write to Churchill on 21 January 1915. The prime minister was summoning a War Council at which Jellicoe should be present, to be held on 28 January 1915. Churchill wrote circumspectly:

I did not think that it was right to bring Sir John Jellicoe away from his fleet to London in order to attend a War Council during a period admittedly one of stringency in our own strength, and during which from every indication enemy activity might well be expected. I therefore resisted the summoning of Sir John Jellicoe to London.

On 28 January, then, Jellicoe would not be present. Churchill's caution was in fact justified within hours by the emergence from Wilhelmshaven of a squadron of Kaiserliche Marine battlecruisers. Caught by Beatty and Tyrwhitt on the Dogger Bank on 24 January 1915, the battlecruiser *Blücher* was sunk with the loss of more than nine hundred men. Due to a series of mistakes and mischances, the remainder of the German squadron and its destroyers escaped. Yet as Churchill stated, the action meant that 'The German Emperor was confirmed in the gloomy impressions he had sustained after the action of August 28, 1914 [at Heligoland Bight]. All enterprise in the German Admiralty was again effectually quelled'.

In the meantime, on 25 January Fisher had sent Churchill a paper – perhaps a bombshell would be more apt – which opened, 'First Lord, I have no desire to continue a useless resistance in the War Council to plans I cannot concur in, but I would ask that the enclosed may be printed and circulated to its members before the next meeting.' The First Sea Lord was digging in his heels. The key to Fisher's suspiciously subdued and thoughtful paper was that 'We play into Germany's hands if we risk fighting ships in any subsidiary operations such as coastal bombardments or the attack of fortified places without military co-operation, for we thereby increase the possibility that the Germans may be able to engage our fleet with some approach to equality of strength'. With regard to the Dardanelles themselves, the operative phrase here is 'without military co-operation'. That is, without the Army. It was a point underscored towards the end of the paper with a gusto more characteristic of Fisher:

> It has been said that the first function of the British Army is to assist the fleet in obtaining command of the sea. This might be accomplished by military co-operation with the Navy in such operations as the attack on Zeebrugge or the forcing of the Dardanelles, which might bring out the German and Turkish fleets respectively. Apparently, however, this is not to be. The English Army is apparently to continue to provide a small sector of the allied front in France, where it no more helps the Navy than if it were at Timbuctoo.

For Fisher and many, but by no means all, of his underlings in the Admiralty, the Dardanelles could not be forced 'by naval power alone'. The batteries on shore needed to be tackled by substantial ground forces, not by the small naval raiding parties that were to hand. To attempt to do so was to unduly imperil the Royal Navy's precious ships, not to mention their crews. Of both there was a limited number, and for Fisher the North Sea was the priority. 'A failure or check in the Dardanelles would be nothing,' he wrote later. 'A failure in the North Sea would be RUIN!' Churchill himself later wrote that such caution was 'absolutely counter to all my convictions'. He also dismissed Fisher's urgings in a carefully argued memorandum, dated 27 January 1915. He assured Fisher of the relative strength of the Grand Fleet against the Hochseeflotte, and declared that those ships to be used in the Dardanelles would not compromise the strength of the fleet. This was not good enough. By way of response, Fisher expressed his intention of boycotting the War Council meeting set for 28 January, the very next day. Churchill, having successfully resisted the attendance of Jellicoe, now insisted on the presence of Fisher. As an olive branch, he proposed that the two of them should hold a private meeting with Asquith for twenty minutes before the War Council met at 1130 on 28 January. To this Fisher agreed. The trio would meet at precisely 1110.

Not all that much can be accomplished in twenty minutes. You might stroll from Buckingham Palace to Admiralty Arch, take a couple of turns round the deck of a dreadnought or – if you were Churchill – smoke a small cigar. You could neither thread a camel through the eye of a needle nor persuade Fisher that the forcing of Dardanelles by naval forces was practicable.

Fisher took the opportunity to express his reservations about both the Zeebrugge and Dardanelles proposals. His preference was for the Army – which one he did not specify – to advance along the Belgium coast with the Navy in close support; or, better still, deploy his long-cherished operation in the Baltic that would jeopardise Berlin. Churchill argued for both the Zeebrugge and Dardanelles schemes; but in deference to Fisher, conceded that of the two, Zeebrugge might be abandoned. According to Churchill, Asquith, in the tradition of 'Quite concur' Battenberg, 'expressed his concurrence with my views, and decided that Zeebrugge should be dropped and that the Dardanelles should go forward'. At this the brief meeting broke up, Churchill claiming that 'Lord Fisher seemed on the whole content'. The trio then went downstairs from Asquith's office to the ground-floor Cabinet Room to join the main War Council meeting of 28 January 1915. Very soon Fisher, with Kitchener in his wake, had abandoned the conference and the pair were at loggerheads in the window. Here was a great confrontation of Navy and Army, of the great field marshal and the professional head of the Royal Navy quarrelling offstage while Rome burned; here was the small, stout 73-year-old Admiral, overshadowed by the magisterial presence of the moustached 6ft 2in Secretary of State for War, resplendent in his field marshal's uniform; there, from those great windows, stretching from floor to ceiling, Fisher looked north towards where lay the Admiralty, Trafalgar Square and Nelson's Column – raised by public subscription, the

69

design chosen by the 1st Duke of Wellington, erected in 1843. What would the heroes of yesteryear have counselled? Fisher was in no doubt. To the Secretary of State for War, Fisher explained that he was resigning forthwith.

Kitchener was persuasive. He pointed out that the prime minister had already decided that the campaign should go ahead; he claimed that Fisher himself was the 'only dissentient'; he argued that at this time of national emergency, it was his duty to continue in the role of First Sea Lord. He said – he certainly said later – that if the fleet got through, Constantinople would fall of its own accord and what would be won was 'not a battle but the war'. Eventually, he induced the unhappy and volatile First Sea Lord to return to the table and to the meeting. Said Fisher, 'I reluctantly gave in to Lord Kitchener and resumed my seat.' There Fisher heard Kitchener himself proclaim that he considered the attack 'vitally important'. He listened to Balfour assuring the council that it would put, 'Constantinople under our control and ... open a passage to the Danube'. He watched as Grey declared that it would 'finally settle the attitude of Bulgaria and the whole of the Balkans'. Fisher's face darkened as the council moved inexorably towards charging the Admiralty – his Admiralty – to proceed with the storming of the Dardanelles by the Navy. As Asquith noted to his inamorata Venetia Stanley, the great man himself maintained 'an obstinate and ominous silence'. For the naval historian Richard Hough:

> The scene matches that in any Greek tragedy: the ageing, bewildered and momentarily indecisive old warrior whose past industry and patriotism had created the war machine he now saw being abused by misguided and opportunistic politicians holding him to his post for fear of their own reputations. It is a sad and unlovely picture.

Above all, Fisher feared that the campaign might compromise the Grand Fleet – with all that meant. What was it that Churchill would write in *The World Crisis* of the great ships of the Grand Fleet? 'Guard them well, admirals and captains, hardy tars and tall marines, guard them well and guide them true.' Guard them well and guide them true?

With this sort of line, Churchill's hazarding of the newest and greatest addition to the fleet, *Queen Elizabeth*, in an Aegean adventure, in a sea infested with mines and U-boats, rang very far from true. For Fisher, risking the great new ship in the Dardanelles when she should have been at the head of the Grand Fleet in Scapa Flow or sweeping the North Sea for the Hochseeflotte was apostasy to the very idea of sea power. 'A failure or check in the Dardanelles would be nothing. A failure in the North Sea would be RUIN!' Basil Liddell Hart glosses:

> From the outbreak of war British naval strategy was governed, rightly, by the appreciation of the fact that maintaining sea supremacy was even more vital than defeat of the German fleet. Instantaneously, that sea supremacy had come into force and upon was based the whole war effort of Britain, and her Allies, because upon it depended the very existence of Britain. Churchill has epitomised the issue in a graphic phrase – 'Jellicoe was the only man on either side who could lose the war in an afternoon.'

With the decision taken on the principle of the Dardanelles operation, Fisher's own Admiralty was now required to put this into effect. The first naval bombardment would take place barely three weeks later on 18 February 1915. 'And one of the First World War's human catastrophes resulted,' concluded Roy Jenkins. Within little more than twelve weeks, Fisher, Churchill and with them the country's very last Liberal government would fall; and with them the chance to save hundreds and thousands of British lives. Without Kitchener's intervention, it is reasonable to speculate, if not to assume, that Fisher would have resigned on 28 January 1915. He might have taken with him the whole idea of forcing the Dardanelles by naval forces alone, perhaps of the Gallipoli operation as a whole. What would surely not have been abandoned were the alternative operations still waiting in the wings, operations that could have avoided sending Kitchener's armies to chew barbed wire in Flanders, initiatives that provided a way out of the deadlock on the Western Front. Because of the failure of the Dardanelles against an enemy at least imagined to be second rate, no amphibious operations against Germany were even attempted. For the British and French, this left the Western Front.

With the war in such a state, Vera Brittain was considering leaving her studies in Oxford to train to be a nurse. Her brother Edward and her lover Roland Leighton had now succeeded in enlisting. The latter was lieutenant in the Worcesters, and had the expectation of being sent to France. 'At the beginning of 1915,' wrote Brittain, 'I was more deeply and ardently in love than I have ever been or am ever likely to be.' With the prospect of Leighton's posting to the trenches, she tackled him on the issue of his survival:

> 'If you return,' I emphasised, determined to face up to things for both of us, and when he [Roland] insisted: '"When," not "if"'; I said that I didn't imagine he was going to France without fully realising all it might involve. He answered gravely that he had thought many times of the issue, but had a settled conviction that he was coming back, though perhaps not quite whole.
> 'Would you like me any less if I was, say, minus an arm?'
> My reply need not be recorded. It brought tears so near the surface again that I picked up the coat which I had thrown off, and abruptly said I would take it upstairs – which I did the more promptly when I suddenly realised that he was nearly crying too.

On 31 March 1915 Leighton was sent to the front. To his mother he had remarked, '*Je suis fiancé; c'est la guerre.*'

King George V inspects troops en route to France.

'What is this I hear about a British Expeditionary Force in France? It is nonsense. We have a superb Fleet, to which we shall give all the assistance in our power, but I will not support the sending out of this country of a single British soldier . . . Not a single soldier will go with my consent. Say so in the paper tomorrow.' Despite the protestations of the newspaper magnate Lord Northcliffe, in August 1914 Great Britain sent five infantry divisions of her army to fight alongside sixty-seven French, the Allies still being outnumbered by the Kaiser's seventy-eight western divisions. Northcliffe was amongst many who believed that the war should have been left to the greatest naval force of the day, and fought 'by naval action alone.'

HMS *Dreadnought*, the battleship that revolutionised naval warfare.

The battle of the Marne was the first turning-point of the war. It ensured that the Germans could not win, and heralded the creation of the Western Front. The French, though buttressed by the small British Expeditionary Force commanded by Sir John French, were the real victors. Here French troops await a German assault.

Expectations that the war would be brought swiftly to a close by a great British naval victory proved misplaced. The German High Seas Fleet was reluctant to engage the numerically superior British Grand Fleet, and the autumn of 1914 saw more modest actions culminating in the battle of Heligoland Bight. In this artist's impression a German torpedo passes beneath the stern of a British vessel.

With deadlock established on the Western Front, by Christmas 1914 Winston Churchill was far from alone in asking whether there were no alternatives to 'sending our armies to chew barbed wire in Flanders?' The failure to force the Dardanelles in the spring of 1915 cost 300,000 Allied casualties, very nearly ended the First Lord of the Admiralty's political career, and stilled all serious attempts to win the war away from the cauldron of Flanders and France. Here, above, HMS *Irresistible* gainsays her name while the Kaiser turned to a novel weapon, below, the U-boat.

HMS Cardiff leading the German Fleet.
Charles Dixon. 1919.

On 21 November 1918 the light cruiser HMS *Cardiff* led the pride of the German Navy, the High Seas Fleet, into internment in Rosyth. For the *Glasgow Herald*, this was 'The greatest naval surrender in the world's history . . . a triumph to which history knows no parallel.'
(© National Maritime Museum, Greenwich, London)

HMS CARDIFF

SMS *Nassau* and HMS *Spitfire* at Jutland.

Hailed by the Kaiserliche Marine as a great victory, the battle of Jutland actually precipitated the return of the Imperial German Navy to 'unrestricted' U-boat warfare – a decision that cost the Kaiser the war, his country, and his throne. The Somme, opening a month after Jutland in July 1916, was also a contributory factor to this verdict, albeit at a far greater human cost.

Wounded soldiers on the Somme battlefield near Ginchy.

The intervention of the United States in the war in April 1917 was its turning-point, not only because of her forces on land but those at sea. Here the British marine artist B F Gribble depicts the arrival eight months later of the Battleship Division Nine of the US Navy at Scapa Flow, cheered by the sailors of Beatty's flagship HMS *Queen Elizabeth*. (Courtesy of the U.S. Navy Art Collection, Washington, DC)

Meanwhile, the pursuit of victory on the Western Front reached its nadir that autumn during the Third battle of Ypres, at Passchendaele. When Reginald Blomfield's great memorial to the fallen of Ypres at the Menin Gate was unveiled in 1924, Siegfried Sassoon wrote that the dead of the Ypres salient would 'deride this sepulchre of crime.' (Trabantos/Shutterstock)

Said Lloyd George, 'Germany has been broken almost as much by the blockade as by military methods.' In defeating the U-boats and successfully prosecuting its own blockade of the Central Powers, the Royal Navy did much more than is sometimes assumed to win the war. The German authorities attributed just under three-quarters of a million civilian deaths to the Royal Navy's 'starvation blockade.' Here, the beaten German army retreats in September 1918.

For John Buchan, the Royal Navy was, 'the weapon on which all others depended.' For Lloyd George, 'The sea front turned out to be the decisive flank in the gigantic battlefield'. For Basil Liddell Hart, the 'Navy was to win no Trafalgar, but it was to do more than any other factor towards winning the war for the Allies.' These were lessons learned rather late by the statesmen responsible for what Churchill called the 'victory bought so dear as to be almost indistinguishable from defeat.' Here, Lloyd George (centre) lords it over – amongst others – Foch, far left, and Clemenceau. (All uncredited illustrations Everett Historical/Shutterstock)

5

Culture and Anarchy

'In his diagnosis of the German character Lord Fisher was right and the Admiralty wrong.'

Winston Churchill

Among the more mature officers of one of the world's oldest navies, and in 1915 undoubtedly the greatest, there was a deep-rooted suspicion of submarines. A straight fight between battleships, some conspicuous acts of personal bravery and even of self-sacrifice, the striking of a ship's colours, and the treatment of enemy officers and crew with civility, dignity and respect. Such was the code – indeed the law – of naval warfare. It was one in which there remained distinct elements of chivalry. The submarine was a thief in the night, able to damage or destroy without even disclosing its presence. Such vessels contravened all notions of the fair and honourable waging of war. Admiral Sir Arthur Wilson – he who had put the Navy's general case for the prosecution of the naval war to the Committee of Imperial Defence meeting in August 1911 – had this to say ten years earlier about the newfangled submarines. They were 'underwater, unfair and dammed un-English. We cannot stop invention in this direction, but we can avoid doing anything to encourage it'. It might have been a line out of *HMS Pinafore*.

Yet his views were shared neither by the maverick Fisher nor his protégé Roger Keyes.

In his initial spell as First Sea Lord between 1904 and 1910, Fisher had been the man behind the establishment of the Royal Navy submarine flotilla. These vessels had become viable only at the turn of the century. It was then that the problems of underwater propulsion in the absence of the oxygen necessary for petrol or diesel engines to function, of safely diving and of surfacing, had been tentatively solved.

The early vessels were tiny, less than a couple of hundred tons; they had crews of barely a dozen or so; and for the purposes of war they were seen as little more than scouts, sentries or coastal defence vessels. Fisher's many critics called them his toys. The visionary admiral saw their potential. As early as 1904, he had written, 'It's astounding to me ... how the very best among us absolutely fail to realise the vast impending revolution in naval warfare and naval strategy that the submarine will accomplish.' At the end of 1913 he circulated a famous paper which anticipated that not only would the Germans use such craft against merchant shipping, that they would – without warning – sink such cargo vessels as they were unable to bring into port. This was the requirement of international maritime law to protect both vessel and crew. Churchill and the then First Sea Lord Prince Louis Battenberg bridled at this suggestion, abhorrent as it was 'to the immemorial law and practice of the sea'. For Fisher, though, understated as ever, 'The essence of war is violence. Moderation in war is imbecility!'

Keyes, born in 1872, son of General Sir Charles Keyes of the Indian Army, joined the Royal Navy at thirteen, having assured his parents from an early age, 'I am going to be an Admiral.' Like his friend Reginald Tyrwhitt he was schooled in destroyers, taking his first command of HMS *Opossum* in 1898. During the Boxer Rebellion he had led cutting-out expeditions ashore reminiscent of the young Horatio Hornblower. He made captain in 1905, excelled himself in diplomatic and intelligence work, and then focused on the nascent submarine flotilla. He was promoted Inspecting Officer of Submarines in 1910, commodore of the service as a whole in 1912. He shared Fisher's views on the likely German use of the Admiralstab's small fleet of German submarines: *Unterseeboote*, or U-boats as they were called. Following his successful proposal – with Tyrwhitt – of what became known as the battle of Heligoland Bight, preferment beckoned. At the end of 1914 he became embroiled in Churchill's plans for the Dardanelles; in February 1915 he became chief of staff to Vice Admiral Sir Sackville Hamilton Carden. It was Carden who had advised Churchill that the Dardanelles might be forced by naval action. For Keyes, this meant that submarines would have to play their part in the Dardanelles, as indeed they already had. In the meantime, though, it was the U-boats that first showed the submarines' mettle. Wrote Churchill, 'Neither the British nor the German Admiralty understood at the outbreak of hostilities all that submarines could do'.

Pathfinder, a small British cruiser, was torpedoed on 5 September 1914 in the Firth of Forth. She was a victim of *U-21*, some 650 tons with a crew of twenty-nine. The presence of the submarine in British coastal waters set alarm bells ringing both at the Admiralty in London and at the base of the Grand Fleet in Scapa Flow. Later that month, much worse was to follow. Three old British cruisers, *Aboukir*, *Cressy* and *Hogue*, had been detailed to patrol an area of deep water close to the Dutch coast known as the Broad Fourteens. They were intended to guard against purported plans by the Admiralstab to block the Schelde estuary. So vulnerable were they considered to be, they were known in the Navy as the 'live-bait squadron'. At daybreak on 22 September 1914 they were spotted by Kapitänleutnant Otto Weddigen of *U-9*. Weddigen torpedoed *Aboukir* at close range at 0620. She sank within half an hour, leaving her crew floundering in the bitter waters of the North Sea. *Cressy* and *Hogue* at once came to the rescue, and were themselves sunk by the lurking Weddigen. The crews of these three vessels, mainly cadets and married reservists, amounted to 2200, of whom 1469 were drowned. It was characteristic of the ever-vigilant Tyrwhitt that he found himself picking up the survivors. Churchill, even in 1915 the inheritor of a more civilised tradition, custom and usage of war – he had famously fought at the Battle of Omdurman under Kitchener himself, commented that 'the destruction with his [Weddigen's] own fingers of fourteen hundred persons was an episode of peculiar character in human history'.

The crews, though, were servicemen; the vessels were battleships on war patrol. The case of Kapitänleutnant Walther Schwieger of *U-20* was rather different.

The U-boat had left its base on Borkum – the Frisian island that so attracted Churchill's interest and attention – on 30 April 1915. She headed northwest across the North Sea, rounded Scotland and Ireland, and broke into the Irish Sea from the south. On 5 May 1915 she stopped a small trading schooner, *Earl of Lathom*, forced her crew to take to the boats, and destroyed the vessel with grenades. Two days later at 1320, off a prominent headland in County Cork called the Old

Head of Kinsale, a lookout on the surfaced U-boat made out
something the identity of which he was unsure. Amidst clouds of
smoke he could see several masts and funnels; he called the captain to
the conning tower. Schwieger was at first similarly puzzled; then, as
the vessel slowly neared, he gradually made out a large steamer. With
her plunging vertical stem, white superstructure, and four great
smokestacks picked out in her owners' black and scarlet livery, she was
reminiscent of another great liner, RMS *Titanic*. The White Star
flagship had sunk on 15 April 1912 on her maiden voyage with the loss
of more than 1500 lives. Schwieger's sighting was another British
passenger liner, the 44,000-ton Cunarder RMS *Lusitania*. She was
inward bound to Liverpool from New York under the command of
Captain William Turner. Her passengers and crew numbered 1959.

Here was a far more substantial target than a schooner. Schwieger
ordered *U-20* to dive.

On 4 February 1915, a week after Lord Kitchener's momentous
intervention with Lord Fisher, the Admiralstab had declared that, 'All
the waters surrounding Great Britain and Ireland, including the
whole of the English Channel, are hereby declared to be a war zone.
From February 18 onwards every enemy merchant vessel found
within this zone would be destroyed, without it being always possible
to avoid danger to the crews and passengers.' This strategy had been
adopted by the Kaiserliche Marine in response to the destruction of
its surface fleet of commerce raiders, notably Spee's squadron in the
Falklands six weeks previously. It meant the institution of a
submarine blockade against Great Britain, and one which would put
innocent lives in jeopardy.

For Churchill – at the time still embroiled with Fisher and the
Dardanelles – the declaration was strictly in defiance of the
'immemorial law and practice of the sea'. More specifically, it was in
contravention of the custom firmly established since well before the
Napoleonic wars and enshrined in prize law, or the 'cruiser rules'. This
required belligerents to force their victims to stop by raising a pennant
or by means of a shot across their bows; it permitted the inspection of
the ship's manifest; and allowed for her seizure or destruction if
carrying contraband. Critically, though, the law dictated the rescue of
crews. These practices were upheld by the Royal Navy in prosecution

of its own blockade against Germany; and they were rules which Schwieger had himself followed with the schooner *Earl of Lathom*. He chose to ignore them in the case of *Lusitania*.

It was the practice which Fisher had foreseen, which Churchill 'did not believe a civilised nation would ever resort to', and which demonstrated that 'in his diagnosis of the German character Lord Fisher was right and the Admiralty were wrong'. Ultimately, the Germans were now contravening such dispositions as the Lieber Code of 1863. Drafted during the US Civil War, part of this put a clear case for morality in warfare:

> Men who take up arms against one another in public war do not cease on this account to be moral beings, responsible to one another and to God ... Military necessity does not admit of cruelty – that is, the infliction of suffering for the sake of suffering or for revenge, nor of maiming or wounding except in fight, nor of torture to extort confessions. It does not admit of the use of poison in any way, nor of the wanton devastation of a district. It admits of deception, but disclaims acts of perfidy; and, in general, military necessity does not include any act of hostility which makes the return to peace unnecessarily difficult.

This formed one of the bases for the laws of the conduct of warfare laid down in the Hague Conventions of 1899 and 1907, subsequently by the London Declaration concerning the Laws of Naval War in 1909. At the first of these conferences Fisher himself had been one of the British delegates, inscribing in a journalist's autograph book, 'The supremacy of the British Navy is the best security for the peace of the world.'

Schwieger, with *U-20* now underwater at periscope depth and invisible to Captain Turner on *Lusitania*, set a course to intercept what he now realised was a large passenger liner. At 1400 the steamer and the U-boat had closed to barely half a mile. Ten minutes later, Schwieger ordered a single torpedo to be fired. In the log of *U-20* he recorded:

Torpedo hits starboard side right behind bridge. An unusually heavy detonation takes place with very strong explosive cloud. The explosion of the torpedo must have been followed by a second of (boiler or coal powder?) The ship stops immediately and heels over to starboard very quickly, immersing simultaneously at the bow ... the name *Lusitania* appears visible in golden letters.

Lusitania began to list to starboard almost immediately, and then to go down by the head. *Titanic* had sunk two hours and forty minutes after her collision with the iceberg; for *Lusitania* it was a mere eighteen minutes. This was barely time to lower the ships' lifeboats. When she sank, eleven miles from the Irish coast, she took with her 1195 passengers and crew. Chrissie Aitken was a 17-year-old survivor.

The women were very calm and the crew were just splendid. One of the crew noticed that I had not a belt and he took off his own and fastened it round me. The ship was dipping over to one side terribly, and after we got into the boat, and it was lowered, a remark made by one of the stewards made me think our boat was to be swamped like the one before it, and I jumped overboard. I don't remember anything then for a long time, but the lifeboat seems to have got away all right, for afterwards I saw some ladies who were in it, and they hadn't even got wet. But a lot had happened before I regained consciousness. When next I remember anything I was floating amongst the wreckage, and the ship had gone. Everything seemed calm then, but I was a bit dazed and don't remember clearly. A little bit away there was an upturned boat and three men on it. I struggled to it and the men pulled me up. We stayed there for a time – I don't know how long, and then a collapsible boat took us off, and later a minesweeper took us into Queenstown.

Those rescued alive from the sea were brought ashore at Queenstown. So, too were the bodies. One witness wrote of 'piles of corpses like cordwood began to appear among the paint-kegs and coils of rope of the shadowy old wharves'. Day after day they were buried in the graveyards of the Old Church Cemetery in Queenstown and the Church of St Multose in Kinsale.

The sinking of RMS *Lusitania* was the herald of what came to be known as 'unrestricted' U-boat warfare, unconstrained by custom and law. In 1915 the Kaiserliche Marine had too small a fleet of U-boats to prosecute such warfare on a large scale. This would change, the thirty-three vessels of the U-boat fleet commissioned by the Imperial German Navy in 1914 eventually rising to more than three hundred. The Admiralstab estimated that monthly losses of 600,000 tons of merchant shipping would force Britain to the negotiating table in five months. The result of this spree of U-boat construction and of the Kaiserliche Marine's calculations will become apparent a little later.

The sinking of the liner and the loss of so many civilian lives was a double-edged sword. It was scarcely surprising that the death of so many non-combatants would be castigated by Churchill as the 'crowning outrage of the U-boat war [which] resounded throughout the world'. It made Rudyard Kipling see the war as a crusade for civilisation against barbarism, between culture and anarchy. Of the 139 US citizens on board the *Lusitania*, all but eleven lost their lives. Since those innocent days we have become all too familiar with the loss during war of civilian lives: indeed, it has become commonplace. Coventry, Dresden and Hiroshima were all steps on a downward path that began with German atrocities in Belgium in the autumn of 1914 – notably at Louvain – continued with *Lusitania*, and led more recently to 9/11. At that time though – and at a time, too, of a great deal of US ambivalence about the British blockade of the Central Powers – this was a diplomatic catastrophe. The Munich medallist Karl Goetz tactlessly struck a medal to celebrate the sinking of the *Lusitania*, albeit with the wrong date; the German Admiralty heaped on Schwieger the laurels of a national hero; and in a clever stroke of propaganda the British put it about that schoolchildren in Germany had been granted a day's holiday to celebrate the sinking. The *Los Angeles Times* wrote that Germany had placed itself 'outside the pale of civilisation'. For the *New York Nation*, 'the torpedo that sank the *Lusitania* also sank Germany in the opinion of mankind.'

In response to the public outrage among the Allies, and the Americans, the Germans argued that *Lusitania* was carrying munitions, as indeed she was; and was therefore a legitimate military target. This was so neither in the court of international law, that of public opinion, nor the code of ethics of the age. If an inspection had confirmed the existence of a cargo of munitions, passenger and crew should have been allowed to take to the lifeboats, as in the case of the *Earl of Lathom,* following the cruiser rules. Among other things, these stated 'Everyone on board must be placed in safety with their goods and chattels if possible.' The Admiralstab's counterblasts were to no avail. President Woodrow Wilson of the United States issued three Notes to the German government in the months after the sinking. He called on the Germans to abandon submarine warfare, rejected their arguments that the British blockade was illegal and – finally – declared on 21 July 1915 that the United States would regard further sinkings as 'deliberately unfriendly'. This was a code easy to decipher. The sinking by *U-24* of ss *Arabic,* outward bound for the United States on 19 August, fuelled the fire. The Kaiser was obliged to temporarily suspend such warfare.

For Germany, the destruction of *Lusitania* was the end of the beginning, an atrocity that would eventually bring the United States into the war. She has been nicely described as the ship which failed to bring 200 American citizens to Liverpool in 1915, but in 1917 and 1918 brought two million US soldiers to France. Just as Helmuth von Moltke told the Kaiser, '*Majestät, wir haben den Krieg verloren,*' they had indeed lost the war; though not yet; and the means of that loss was not an action on land, but at sea.

6

Lord Fisher's Modest Proposal

'If the British fleet had attacked in the first week of the war, we should have been beaten. Under cover of the British navy, the Russian armies, then available in great numbers, could have landed on the coast of Pomerania and could have easily marched to Berlin.'

Admiral Reinhard Scheer

While the consequences of the sinking of the *Lusitania* were beginning to become apparent in *Große Hauptquartier* in Berlin in the early summer of 1915, in Whitehall the necessity of finding alternatives to chewing barbed wire in Flanders was becoming daily more pressing. On both the Eastern and the Western Fronts, the exigencies of winter meant that December to March was largely a closed season for battle – the more so after the catastrophic consequences of the Ottoman attack on the Tsar's armies in the Caucasus filtered through. At the battle of Sarikamish there survived perhaps 18,000 men from a Turkish force of around 95,000. Of the 77,000 losses, about 30,000 men froze to death. It was an outcome that might have been anticipated in a mountain range that rises to 18,000ft, loftier than Switzerland's Matterhorn. This was Enver Pasha's ill-conceived campaign that had led to Grand Duke Nicholas's *cri de coeur* to Lord Kitchener in early January 1915, the plea for a 'demonstration' on the Eastern Front that had inspired the Dardanelles operation. Given that the outcome of the campaign was the Ottomans' worst defeat of the war, there was no longer an absolute necessity for a show of strength. The Dardanelles had gone ahead nonetheless because finding an alternative to barbed wire was paramount. The British, French – and German – burying parties on the Western Front now all worked overtime.

For the fresh new season of hostilities in the spring of 1915, Generalissimo Joseph Joffre, still eating well, had planned a campaign that he at least professed would lead to total victory. The Kaiser's forces, he argued, were particularly vulnerable in the salient or bulge on the front line between Flanders and the great French fortress of Verdun, some two hundred miles east of Paris in the Meuse *département*. The supply lines to Crown Prince Rupprecht's 6th Army comprised two railway systems. Cut these arteries by attacking each side of the Noyon salient, and the 6th would be obliged to fall back to avoid bleeding to death. The prince might even become encircled. Then that would be that. Finis! In the north the attack would be against the Aubers and Vimy ridges. These protected the steel ribbons in the Douai plain, the line between Lille and Metz. In the south the Champagne ridge protected the metals from Meziers to Hinson. Decisive victory beckoned, said Joffre.

There were preliminaries in early March 1915 with a British attack under Sir John French at Neuve-Chapelle. Here a thousand yards were gained at a cost of around 12,000 casualties. The main assault was set for early May, just as *Lusitania* was sailing from New York. The BEF 'old contemptibles' who had been decimated at 'First Ypres' in November 1914 had been reinforced by territorial forces and by the first of Kitchener's volunteers. A number of these came from Scotland, with the Cameron Highlanders boasting a territorial unit of whom twenty-eight came from Portree on the Isle of Skye. Elements of both these groups formed the 1st Army under Sir Douglas Haig, increasingly uncomfortable under the yoke of Sir John French. On 9 May 1915, while the victims from the *Lusitania* were still being buried, Haig's forces attacked the Aubers Ridge. The French under General Henri Pétain followed against the Vimy Ridge a few days later. Haig's numerically superior army, wrote John Keegan, 'was simply stopped in its tracks'. Churchill was a witness, writing later of the 'hideous spectacle' of the wounded. 'More than a thousand suffering from every form of horrible injury, seared, torn, pierced, choking, dying were being sorted according to their miseries ... from the back door corpses were being carried out at brief intervals to burying parties constantly at work.' Pétain's XXXIII Corps reached Vimy Ridge in time to see the railway lines glinting below in the spring sun; also just in time to be decisively counter-attacked. When Haig renewed the 1st Army's efforts to the south of the Aubers Ridge in Festubert on 15 May, the results

were equally catastrophic. No strategic or tactical advantage whatsoever was gained. The losses merely ensured that in the rich earth a
richer dust lay concealed. Haig's casualties in the two battles numbered
around 27,000. Of these ten came from Portree, all killed on the night
of 17 May 1915. The impact on the community of the island, where
everyone knew everyone else, may be imagined. Prince Rupprecht's
6th Army lost between a quarter and a third that number, probably
fewer than 9000. If, that is, 9000 is few. 'These so-called battles,' states
A J P Taylor dismissively, 'have no meaning except as names on a war
memorial.' Inspired by the death that month of a fellow Canadian
artillery officer at Ypres, Major John McCrae wrote one of the most
famous poems of the war:

> In Flanders fields the poppies blow
> Between the crosses, row on row,
> That mark our place; and in the sky
> The larks, still bravely singing, fly
> Scarce heard amid the guns below.
>
> We are the Dead. Short days ago
> We lived, felt dawn, saw sunset glow,
> Loved and were loved, and now we lie
> In Flanders fields.
>
> Take up our quarrel with the foe:
> To you from failing hands we throw
> The torch; be yours to hold it high.
> If ye break faith with us who die
> We shall not sleep, though poppies grow
> In Flanders fields.

The British failure was variously attributed to the intrinsic
vulnerability of the offensive infantry to the defenders' entrenched line,
barbed wire and machine guns, the multi-layered German defence,
and to a shortage of shells. Indeed a telegram from the famous war
correspondent Charles à Court Repington now led to the breaking of
the 'shells scandal'. *The Times* journalist had witnessed the debacle of

Aubers Ridge, was horrified by the losses sustained by his old regiment the Rifle Brigade, and – encouraged by Sir John French – attributed the disaster to the shortage of high-explosive shells. This was, in fact, a problem for the whole of the front held by the British. It rapidly became a major political scandal, fuelled by *The Times*'s proprietor, Lord Northcliffe, who had Lord Kitchener in his sights. Amongst much else, too much else, the Secretary of State for War was responsible for the manufacture and supply of munitions.

This all suggested incompetence on the part of both Kitchener himself, and Asquith's Liberal administration more generally, in the waging of the war. It was an impression reinforced by the news from the Gallipoli peninsula, the rugged slip of land that forms the northern side of the Dardanelles Straits in the Aegean.

Admiral Sir Sackville Carden, who had planned the naval operation in the Dardanelles, proved unable to cope with the stress and strain involved. He had been replaced by Vice Admiral John de Robeck, who Churchill dismissed as a stand-in. 'One could not feel that his training and experience had led him to think deeply on the larger aspects of strategy and tactics.' On 18 March 1915 de Robeck had called off the naval attack in the Dardanelles after the loss to mines of five old British and French battleships. Kitchener believed that British prestige in the Middle East would be fatally damaged by failure. He so decided that the Army, after all, should play a part; in this he was vehemently supported by Fisher. For Churchill, this decision 'withdrew the Fleet from the struggle, and laid the responsibilities of the Navy on the Army.' At Kitchener's disposal were the Australian Imperial Force and the New Zealand Expeditionary Force, both training in Egypt for posting to the Western Front. Consolidated into the Australia and New Zealand Army Corps (ANZAC), the Mediterranean Expeditionary Force men would be led by the 62-year-old General Sir Ian Hamilton. According to Taylor, Kitchener provided him with 'one inaccurate map, no information about the Turkish army and little about the fortifications of the Dardanelles, no firm guidance as to the forces which he could expect.' For de Robeck's chief of staff Roger Keyes, this initiative was a gross misjudgement. He believed that with a more concerted effort the fleet could still have got through:

I wish to place on record that I had no doubt then, and have none now – and nothing will ever shake my opinion – that from the 4th April onwards, the Fleet could have forced the Straits, and with losses trifling in comparison with those the Army suffered ... and would have led immediately to a victory decisive upon the whole course of the war.

Unlike Fisher and Kitchener, Keyes was actually on station in the Dardanelles; and it emerged after the war that when de Robeck called off the attack the Turkish forts had been badly damaged and – according to some, but by no means all, accounts – were virtually out of ammunition.

Landings by five divisions on the Gallipoli peninsula had taken place a month later in April 1915. The interval had given ample time for the Turks – led by Enver Pasha working under the German direction of General Otto Liman von Sanders – to reinforce defences. Admiral Henry Francis Oliver, Churchill's naval secretary, commented neatly, 'On 18 March, the Fleet was single. Now it has a wife ashore'. Unfortunately, the marriage proved tempestuous. Hamilton's initial landings cost 20,000 men. By early May – just as the *Lusitania* was being torpedoed – the remaining forces of French, British and Empire troops, including the Anzacs, found themselves entirely pinned down by six Turkish divisions. The campaign intended to circumvent the stalemate on the Western Front was itself deadlocked. On 9 May de Robeck despatched a telegram to the Admiralty. He noted that, 'A condition of affairs approximating to that in Northern France is threatened.'

In England, the combination of this news from Gallipoli and Haig's disasters at Aubers Ridge and Festubert put the blackest possible complexion on the prosecution of the war. On 11 May 1915 Churchill felt obliged to write to the secretary and members of the Admiralty Board as follows. 'Please inform all heads of Department in the Admiralty, that for the present it is to be assumed that the war will not end before December 31 1916.' This missive accompanied a political crisis precipitated by the shells scandal, and on 15 May 1915 the resignation of Lord Fisher as First Sea Lord.

Having been frogmarched by Kitchener back to the table of the Council of War on 28 January 1915, Fisher had endured over the next three months the fulfilment of most of his gloomiest prophecies about the Dardanelles operation. It was only by dint of threatening resignation – not by any means for the first time – that he had induced Churchill to agree to the withdrawal of the great battleship that at least so far had survived, the new super-dreadnought *Queen Elizabeth*. Now enough was enough. This time he really meant to go – or at least that either he or Churchill himself should depart – preferably the latter. Having delivered his letter of resignation to the prime minister in Downing Street, Fisher went into hiding in the Charing Cross station hotel, leaving the other more junior Sea Lords to fend for themselves as best they might. At this moment Lloyd George, the master of political chicanery, saw his opportunity. He argued that the crisis in confidence could only be overcome by the formation of a national coalition government with the Conservatives. On 17 May 1915 he told Asquith that he, too, would resign unless such an administration was formed. The prime minister had little choice. When Churchill saw him that day to recommend Admiral Sir Arthur Wilson as Fisher's replacement, Asquith broke the news:

'No, this will not do. I have decided to form a national Government by a coalition with the Unionists, and a very much larger reconstruction will be required.' He told me that Lord Kitchener was to leave the War Office, and then added ... 'What are we to do for you?' I saw at once that it was decided I should leave the Admiralty.

To season this dismissal, Churchill, on returning to the Admiralty to clear his desk was told that intelligence from Room 40 indicated that the Hochseeflotte was again at sea: indeed, the whole German fleet. To Jellicoe, Churchill at once telegraphed, 'It is not impossible that tomorrow may be The Day. All good fortune attend you.'

Churchill had been made the scapegoat for a campaign that he had certainly done a great deal to originate and to inspire, but which had been pursued without much competence, conviction and, perhaps above all, sense of urgency and purpose either by the Navy in the form of Admirals Sackville Carden and de Robeck nor – latterly – the Army in the guise of General Sir Ian Hamilton. In an analysis with which relatively few historians disagree, the Turkish leader Enver Pasha took Roger Keyes's part. 'If the English had only had the courage to rush more ships through they could have got to Constantinople.' The evacuation of the forces from the Gallipoli Peninsula would not take place for another seven months, but its failure was becoming increasingly clear. Roger Keyes was, in fact, just about the only senior officer in either of the armed services to display much zest for engaging the enemy more closely; his former charge, the Royal Navy Submarine Flotilla, the only military or naval unit to achieve any measure of success. Several submarines successfully ran the gauntlet of the Straits; Martin Dunbar-Nasmith made HMS/M *E11* the first enemy ship to reach Constantinople in five hundred years, sinking eighty small ships. By the summer, sea communications – supplies – to the Turkish forces on the Gallipoli peninsula had been entirely cut. With much justice, Churchill summarised, 'Not to persevere, that was the crime.'

On the Western Front, the failures of the French at Vimy Ridge and the BEF at Neuve-Chapelle, Aubers Ridge and Festubert seemed to have vindicated Kitchener. It was he who had written to Sir John French on 2 January 1915, 'I suppose we must now recognise that the French army cannot make a sufficient break through the German lines of defence to bring about the retreat of the German forces for northern France'. He had ignored his own judgement and its implications about the wisdom of offensives on the Western Front.

If this all meant that it was time for Plan B – or perhaps C – this was something that Jacky Fisher, at least, had up his heavily braided sleeve. On 19 May 1915, just as Asquith was busying himself with forming the Coalition government with the leader of the Conservatives, Andrew Bonar Law, he received a modest proposal from the First Sea Lord. These were the terms on which Fisher was prepared to remain in office. More importantly, they were also about how to win the war.

His buoyant ultimatum to Asquith read as follows:

If the following six conditions are agreed to, I can guarantee the successful termination of the war, and the total abolition of the submarine menace.

I also wish to add that since Lord Ripon wished, in 1885, to make me a Lord of the Admiralty, but by my request made me Director of Naval Ordnance and Torpedoes instead, I have served under nine First Lords and seventeen years at the Admiralty, so I ought to know something about it.

(1) That Mr Winston Churchill is not in the Cabinet to be always circumventing me. Nor will I serve under Mr Balfour.

(2) That Sir A. K. Wilson leaves the Admiralty, and the Committee of Imperial Defence, and the War Council, as my time will be occupied in resisting the bombardment of Heligoland, and other such wild projects. Also his policy is totally opposed to mine, and he accepted the position of First Sea Lord in succession to me, thereby adopting a policy diametrically opposed to my views.

(3) That there shall be an entire new Board of Admiralty as regards the Sea Lords and the Financial Secretary (who is utterly useless). New measures demand New Men.

(4) That I should have complete professional charge of the war at sea, together with the sole disposition of the Fleet and the appointment of all officers of all ranks whatsoever.

(5) That the First Lord of the Admiralty should be absolutely restricted to Policy and Parliamentary Procedure, and should occupy the same position toward me as Mr Tennant, M.P., does to Lord Kitchener (and very well he does it).

(6) That I should have the sole absolute authority for all new construction and all dockyard work of whatever sort whatsoever, and complete control over the whole of the Civil Establishments of the Navy.

[Initialled] F.

19.5.15

PS – The 60 per cent of my time and energy which I have exhausted on nine First Lords in the past I wish in future to devote to the successful prosecution of the war. That is the sole reason for these six conditions. These six conditions must be published verbatim, so that the Fleet may know my position.

88

Churchill wrote that, 'this amazing document was answered only by the curt acceptance of Fisher's resignation.' For dereliction of duty when the Hochseeflotte sallied out – impotently, as it so transpired – on 17 May 1915, Asquith thought the First Sea Lord should have been shot. 'There is a political crisis just now,' Vera Brittain commented in her diary on 20 May 1915. 'A national non-Party Government is to be formed for the duration of the war.' Four days later she noted that Italy – hitherto allied to the Central Powers but in practice neutral – had declared war on the side of the Entente.

It is difficult to feel that Fisher had not become a little unhinged by the rough and tumble of working with the human dynamo of Churchill, of the slow-motion car crash of the Dardanelles, of his night-thoughts of *Queen Elizabeth* and of the North Sea theatre, and of the conundrum that the whole war had become. He was also seventy-four.

Still, perhaps this was not such a wild proposal after all. As Michael Hickey remarked in *Gallipoli*, Asquith's acceptance of Fisher's terms would have seen the creation of a 'warlord with even greater powers than Kitchener.' Or as Richard Hough puts it more theatrically, 'Lord High Admiral! Supreme Dictator of the Royal Navy!' Yet it would at least have put the war at sea in the hands of a man who really did understand the nature – and the limitations – of sea power. With Kitchener's huge volunteer armies still a work in progress – and in any case to be squandered at Loos, on the Somme and at Passchendaele – perhaps Fisher had a better chance of turning the country's greatest asset to account. One of his sayings was 'Mad things come off'; and had not Churchill assured him shortly before the First Lord's enthusiasm for the Dardanelles caught fire that it was the Baltic that was 'the only theatre in which naval action can appreciably shorten the war ... the Russians [must] be let loose on Berlin'? Not only had he done so but detailed plans were in development that – according to Fisher – would have seen a major series of amphibious operations in northern waters on 23 July 1915. These, in his words, 'would have finished the war'. He also wrote to Churchill in October 1918 reminding him of a conversation that had clearly been going on for some time: 'The shortest way to Berlin is by sea. The quickest route to end the war is by the sea.'

Of course, this great amphibious design was easier said than done. The obvious difficulties were two. Navigating the Grand Fleet into the Baltic through the Danish Straits and combating the threat posed to an invading force by the Deutsches Heer. As a serious alternative to the Dardanelles, it has generally been dismissed. Still, Admiral Sir Reginald Bacon, Fisher's biographer, commented:

> It is impossible to say, now, whether the scheme would have survived the detailed and critical examination essential before such an operation could be justifiably undertaken; but it is unjust to dismiss the project offhand as impracticable and with a shrug of the shoulders to say that it was madness on Lord Fisher's part to have proposed it. Scientific and thorough preparation would certainly have caused many of the objections which have been hastily advanced to fall into insignificance. The German Battle Fleet would have been placed in a difficult situation, for they would have been forced by public opinion to take some action, and this would have had to have been carried out in the Baltic, in the face of a large fleet of submarines and an extensive and unknown minefield.

Admiral Reinhard Scheer, who was soon to replace Hugo von Pohl as C-in-C of the Hochseeflotte, commented in his memoirs, 'If the British fleet had attacked in the first week of the war, we should have been beaten. Under cover of the British navy, the Russian armies, then available in great numbers, could have landed on the coast of Pomerania and could have easily marched to Berlin.' Scheer, of course, had his own axe to grind, but in terms of elementary logistics two points might be made. In the first week of the war most of the German army was indeed tied up a long way away from Berlin, either executing Schlieffen's plans or trying to hold back the Russians in Prussia; and the Hochseeflotte – though it could steam from the North Sea to the Baltic through the Kiel Canal built for just such a purpose – was in the former not the latter. In the autumn of 1915 and the spring of 1916, in these two respects not much had changed. The naval historian Andrew

Lambert concluded that after Fisher's resignation, 'Without his direction the Baltic concept faded, but the logic endured.'

As things turned out, 27 May 1915, the first day of the new coalition, saw in post Lloyd George in the new and very necessary role of Minister of Munitions. There was also a new First Lord of the Admiralty in the shape of the former Conservative PM Arthur Balfour; and as First Sea Lord Admiral Sir Henry Jackson. Tyrwhitt regretted the passing of Fisher, cut as they were of much the same martial cloth. By Balfour he was charmed. 'He is a delightful person to talk to. He could not have been nicer and I left prepared to die for him!' For Keyes, though, this was a calamitous turn of events, of war's labour lost:

> Thus ended a remarkable association with wonderful possibilities. The Navy lost in the course of a few days the services of an Admiral who was one of the outstanding figures of the last hundred years ... and of an Administrator to whom it owed, in great measure, its readiness for war in August 1914. Moreover, one who was responsible for placing a few old battleships on a stage on which they might have won imperishable glory for the Navy, in a feat of arms which ... would have shortened the war by two years and spared millions of lives.

7

The Squadron Which Could
Win Us the War

'The conviction came into my mind with absolute assurance that the simple soldiers and their regimental officers, armed with their cause, would by their virtues in the end retrieve the mistakes and ignorances of Staffs and Cabinets, of Admirals, Generals and politicians – including, no doubt, many of my own. But, alas, at what needless cost! To how many slaughters, through what endless months of fortitude and privation would these men, themselves already the survivors of many a bloody day, be made to plod before victory was won!'

Winston Churchill

In any case, Fisher and Asquith, Keyes and Churchill should all have taken comfort from the fact that at least one strand of the maritime strategy actually was operating largely as intended. Far from the limelight of Gallipoli, Aubers Ridge and Jellicoe's dreadnoughts in Scapa Flow, far from David Beatty's dashing battlecruiser squadrons – now based in Rosyth on the Firth of Forth – and far from Tyrwhitt's pugnacious Harwich Force, this was the very largely unsung operation of the blockade. While Fisher fulminated in Whitehall, while Kitchener, French and Haig pondered the next slaughterhouse in the Artois, it was the largely unknown and now forgotten Admiral Sir Dudley Rawson de Chair who was slowly grinding down Wilhelmine Germany. In the seas lying to the northeast of the British Isles, hour after hour, day after day, week after week, month after month, the tenacious 10th Cruiser Squadron was on guard. Wrote de Chair in his memoirs:

When one considered that we had to watch a line 610 miles long ... where the blockade-runner could choose his time and place to get through, it required constant and unremitting watch, both night and day, summer and winter ... [a] vigil [which] had to be kept in latitudes where winter gales were incessant ... where enemy submarines were constantly searching for the ships maintaining the blockade ... it was remarkable that the work proved so successful.

Yet so it was, eventually.

De Chair was born 1864 and joined the Navy at fourteen. His idiosyncratic name derived from his Huguenot extraction and must have been a source of much innocent amusement on the lower decks. He was in the same term at Dartmouth as the future King George V and his brother, though by no means as persistent as Douglas Haig in turning such friendships to account. He distinguished himself in 1882 during the bombardment of Alexandria. Ordered to carry despatches ashore, he was captured by the Egyptians rebelling against British rule, brought before their leader Arabi Pasha and then escaped – but not before Queen Victoria had herself asked for prayers to be said for his safety. This attracted the attention of Fisher and, in due course, of Jellicoe. De Chair made commander in 1897, captain in 1902, and was then sent as naval attaché to the United States. In 1913 he replaced David Beatty as Churchill's naval secretary, the beaten path – one anyway – to high command. De Chair worked with the First Lord until Churchill appointed him to command the Navy's training squadron in May 1914. This was redesignated the 10th Cruiser Squadron on 1 August 1914. De Chair was disappointed not to be given a more warlike appointment and was ambivalent about his political master. He was very far from the only man in dark blue uniform to admire Churchill's intelligence, imagination and astonishing energy, while at the same time noting his tendency to over-reach himself. 'We thought he considered himself more like Napoleon and Marlborough than any living man.' This was not a compliment.

Following a plan originally set out in the Admiralty War Orders of 1912, the Navy had deployed its blockading force less than a week after hostilities opened in August 1914. Denied the opportunity by enemy submarines, mines, torpedo boats and destroyers to conduct a close blockade of Germany's North Sea ports, the operation guillotined her western supply lines by closing the two routes by which vessels could break out into the Atlantic, or could reach the Fatherland from the great waters. The narrow Channel straits between Kent and the Pas de Calais were guarded by a cordon of destroyers forming the Dover Patrol; on the Atlantic trade routes and the Western Approaches a force of cruisers stood sentinel. This left the area between the northeast tip of Orkney and the Norwegian coast. As de Chair implies, this was the most tempting route for blockade-runners; indeed, really, the most realistic one, given how narrow were the Dover Straits. Here, from those balmy August days of 1914 to the bitter winter of First Ypres, patrolled the 10th Cruiser Squadron – or the Northern Patrol as it was generally called – under de Chair's command.

De Chair reported to Jellicoe in Scapa Flow. The orders of the C-in-C were in some respects simple. The Northern Patrol was first to intercept German warships and merchantman, and to capture or sink them. Secondly, it was to stop and search all neutral vessels suspected of heading for the German ports and to identify their cargo. Under the terms of the Declaration of London of 1909, this was regarded as falling into three categories. Absolute contraband was material that could only be used for military purposes, such as guns and munitions. Conditional contraband comprised materials which were capable of being turned to the purposes of war, such as fuel and clothes. The 'free list', falling entirely outside the category of banned goods, included items like raw cotton – a raw material of national importance to the economy of the United States. The patrols were ordered to furnish ships thought, suspected or discovered to be carrying contraband with prize crews, and to take them into British harbours for examination; in the case of the Northern Patrol, into Kirkwall in Orkney or Lerwick in Shetland. As German commercial shipping outside the protected waters of the Baltic had entirely ceased at the outbreak of war – a token of British naval supremacy – the vast majority of ships concerned would be flagged as neutrals. Many of them would be from Scandinavia, Holland or – mostly – the United States.

Naturally enough, the legality of this blockade was much contested both in Berlin and by those neutral countries whose trade with

Germany had collapsed. 'The arguments on both sides,' wrote Churchill, 'were technical and interminable, and whole libraries could be filled with them.' It is sufficient to say here that whereas the 1909 Declaration of London was a legitimate and reasonably even-handed attempt to codify the rules of war at sea, it required ratification by its signatories: Great Britain, Austria–Hungary, France, Germany, Italy, Japan, the Netherlands, Russia, Spain and the United States. Once Whitehall ratified, the lesser sea powers would follow. Despite the support of the Admiralty and the Foreign Office, the House of Lords refused endorsement, presciently arguing that the declaration provided an insufficient security of the country's food supply in times of war. Although the Foreign Secretary Sir Edward Grey had intended to override the Lords, the war intervened. The declaration never came into effect and its legal status was uncertain. This had implications that will become apparent for both Britain and Germany's blockades.

Irrespective of its legality, from the beginning of what turned out to be the longest continuous operation undertaken by the Royal Navy in the whole of the war, prosecuting the blockade proved far from a sinecure.

The core of the original Northern Patrol comprised eight *Edgar*-class cruisers of around 7700 tons: *Grafton, Gibraltar, Hawke, Royal Arthur, Theseus, Endymion, Crescent* and *Edgar* herself. These were all the Admiralty could spare at a time when the focus was on the Grand Fleet and a decisive – and supposedly imminent – action with the Hochseeflotte which would end the war. In the autumn of 1914 de Chair discovered that he had not enough vessels to patrol his designated area. This meant that some blockade-runners were slipping through, especially at night. Neither were his cruisers themselves fit for purpose. *Edgar* herself was twenty-one years old, her sisters little younger. In an age of headlong maritime technological development they were septuagenarians, perhaps old maids. Armed with varying combinations of modest 9in and 6in guns, they were virtually defenceless against the Admiralstab's surface and underwater forces; thus they were dubbed 'the cheese in the mousetrap'. On 15 October 1914 *Hawke* was torpedoed by *U-9*, the submarine that had already accounted for the cruisers *Aboukir, Cressy* and *Hogue*. Of a complement of almost 600, only seventy of the cruiser's crew survived.

The *Edgar*s, with their low freeboard and rackety old engines, were also unseaworthy. The stretch of water over which the Northern Patrol stood sentinel was one of the least hospitable seaways in the world. Summer's lease of 1914 proved as brief as usual, and the remaining seasons were characterised by icebergs drifting down from the Arctic, mountainous seas, fog and a continuous succession of icy gales. In the depths of winter there were no more than four, or at the most five, hours of daylight. Less than a month after the loss of *Hawke*, de Chair was pursuing two German minelayers close to Shetland when the weather suddenly worsened. The admiral, sheltering in his duffel coat on the open bridge of his flagship, *Crescent*, recounted:

As we approached the Fair Island Channel, the sky began to darken, the glass fell with extraordinary rapidity, and I knew we were in for a really bad time. There was nothing for it but to go on to try and catch those German minelayers, who could do so much damage if left to their own devices. As we came through the Channel we felt the full blast of the westerly gale, which blew with astonishing violence, and increased in force every hour. The noise of the wind was like one continuous peal of thunder – one could not hear what anyone said, however hard he shouted. Enormous waves roared at us, their crests shorn off by the gale, and the icy-cold water was flung all over the ship, even to the mastheads. Just before our wireless aerial was blown away a signal from Admiral Jellicoe, who with the rest of the Grand Fleet had sought refuge in Scapa Flow, was received, telling us to seek shelter, but it was impossible to turn the ship without danger of capsizing. Boats were washed away from their davits, hawser reels of large size were torn out of the deck and flung to leeward, the upper deck and ship sides began to give, and the seams of the deck to open, letting the water down to the boiler-rooms. The fires in the foremost boiler-rooms were put out, as the water rose above the furnaces, but fortunately the after boiler-rooms held, and we were able to steam sufficiently fast to keep the ship head to wind ... At the height of the gale the bridge was smashed by sea and became untenable, so we had to steer from the conning-tower ... Men were blown about the deck like feathers, and some were seriously hurt; my sea-cabin was swept overboard ... the ship was plunging heavily into the sea, descending rapidly into the vast troughs, and rising as if exhausted to the summits of the big waves ... This was quite the most appalling gale I ever experienced in all my years at sea, and we really did not think the old ship would weather it.

As even the great 25,000-ton dreadnoughts of the Grand Fleet had been forced to shelter from this early winter storm, in December 1914 Jellicoe called time on the remaining seven *Edgars*.

They were replaced by passenger liners taken up from the merchant marine, designated armed merchant cruisers (AMCs). Equipped with small-calibre armament to waylay the blockade-runners, RMS *Lusitania* had been earmarked for this role. Reflecting the Admiralty's view of the increasing importance of the blockade – and the fact that the seven *Edgars* were insufficient to provide a solid sea wall – the patrol was allotted twenty-four of these vessels. Most, but by no means all, were larger and more modern than the *Edgars*, and could stay at sea for longer. De Chair's new flagship was the 18,000-ton Atlantic liner SMS *Alsatian*, commissioned in 1914, and a good deal more seaworthy than his old cruiser. Yet even the AMCs soon ran into trouble. Between Christmas and New Year of 1914, the time at which Asquith was pondering the ideas advanced by Churchill, Hankey and Lloyd George for sidestepping the Western Front, the 5000-ton *Clan MacNaughton* was despatched to the Hebrides. She soon found herself rolling 45 degrees each way in the teeth of a southwesterly gale. Nicolas Monsarrat painted an exceptionally vivid picture of this sort of experience in a Second World War corvette:

Apart from the noise it produces, rolling has a maddening rhythm that is one of the minor tortures of rough weather. It never stops or misses a beat, it cannot be escaped anywhere. If you go through a doorway, it hits you hard: if you sit down, you fall over; you get hurt, knocked about continuously, and it makes for extreme and childish anger. When you drink, the liquid rises towards you and slops over: at meals, the food spills off your plate, the cutlery will not stay in place. Things roll about, and bang, and slide away crazily: and then come back and *hurt* you again. The wind doesn't howl, it *screams* at you, and tears at your clothes, and throws you against things and drives your breath down your throat again. And off watch, below, there is no peace: only noise, furniture adrift, clothes and boots sculling about on the deck, a wet and dirty chaos.

Despite this sort of experience, over Christmas 1914 de Chair's Hebridean sentinel stayed on guard. In a storm later that winter, *Clan MacNaughton* disappeared. Only some telltale wreckage hinted of her fate. A victim of a mine, torpedo or simply another storm, her crew of 241 were all lost. In his diary, Commander F H Grenfell of HMS *Cedric* commented sharply:

> The *Clan MacNaughton*'s officers were firmly convinced that nothing could save the ship from capsizing if she met really bad weather and their fears were unfortunately all too well founded. The Constructor's Department at the Admiralty ought to render up some victims for hanging after the war; it is they who have passed the ships and allowed them to go to sea with empty holds and guns on deck and nobody with the least idea how these novel conditions would affect their stability.

At worst, operating in these waters could indeed mean the loss of a vessel to weather, but on a day-to-day basis the sea state also meant that inspecting the goods of a merchantman was in itself frequently hazardous. This required boarding parties from the Northern Patrol to transfer from their patrol vessel to the merchantman. This was a procedure normally undertaken in a 27ft whaler, essentially a lifeboat and not a craft noted for its sea-handling qualities. Although the patrol's cruiser would station itself upwind of the merchantman to provide a degree of shelter, lowering the boat in the first place, boarding her, rowing – sometimes sailing – a few hundred yards across to the cargo vessel and boarding her in any sort of a seaway called for absolutely first-class seamanship. As Terence Lilley remarks:

> The book cover artist for Chatterton's work *The Big Blockade* has caught all the apprehensions and tensions at the moment of boarding. The sea boat is about to pitch to the next wave, whilst the

coxswain squares his shoulders to keep firm control of the tiller in readiness for the pitch. Two seamen with boathooks struggle to fend the boat off, in the hope of preventing it from smashing against the ship's side. One sailor watches anxiously at the progress of the visiting officer on the ladder. The two remaining sailors perhaps contemplate the perilous row back to their parent ship and the task of the boat being hoisted aboard.

Once in the lee of the blockade-runner, a warm welcome was hardly to be expected. A boarding party of a lieutenant or midshipman and a half a dozen armed ratings would scramble aboard the merchantman with the minimum of help and assistance, struggling up an accommodation ladder as the ship pitched and rolled in the heavy seas. Led grudgingly up to the bridge, the officer presented his credentials to the vessel's master and demanded to see the ship's papers. These would include logbook, proof of nationality, registration and the ship's cargo manifest and port of discharge. While these were being sought, the ratings checked the vessel for hidden armament. Soon a search of the ship would begin for contraband. Inspecting a ship's cargo at sea in these waters was very rarely easy or safe, especially as it would normally involve raising hatch covers. Blockade-runners established the practice of hiding contraband under innocuous goods at the bottom of the ship's hold, behind false bulkheads, decks or even in hollow masts. Some managed to disguise rubber as onions. If nothing was discovered the ship was allowed to continue its voyage; if a cargo of contraband was discovered or suspected, a prize crew was left on board and the ship directed to Lerwick or Kirkwall. The boarding party then had to regain the relative comfort of their own ship across half a mile of the leonine North Sea. Yet having safely despatched the blockade-runners for inspection, a significant number of suspect vessels were released. The Foreign Office was fearful of offending neutral states and was susceptible to pressure from the embassies – much to the annoyance of the men of the Royal Navy.

It was no wonder that the squadron was also called 'the Terrible Tenth'. The patrol was the early twentieth-century equivalent of Mahan's 'far-distant, storm-beaten ships, upon which the Grand Army never looked, [but which] stood between it and the dominion of the world.' Before the *Edgars* left station in December 1914, they had stopped and despatched for inspection more than 300 vessels.

On 11 March 1915, as the naval assault on the Dardanelles got under way, the noose of the Royal Navy's blockade was tightened further. Partly in response to the German declaration of British waters as a war zone – the announcement that would see the sinking of the *Lusitania* – the Admiralty issued a directive that no vessels whatsoever would be permitted through the blockade to the German North Sea ports; that vessels leaving these ports would have to be given clearance. As the Dardanelles campaign faltered and Haig's 1st Army was torn apart in the Artois, the Northern Patrol continued its work. With the larger force of AMCs, four lines of patrol were possible; fewer and fewer blockade-runners got through. The Admiralstab then redoubled its own efforts to retaliate. Of de Chair's force, *Bayano* and *India* were both sunk by submarine, respectively on 11 March 1915 and 8 August 1915. *Arlanza* was mined, and *Viknor* lost with all hands. The total toll was 863.

Still, by the end of 1915, more than 3098 merchant vessels had been intercepted by the Northern Patrol. Of these, 743 were discovered to be carrying contraband. HMS *Alsatian* herself had been at sea for 262 of the year's 365 days, and had steamed 71,500 miles. For this work, de Chair was accorded the KCB. Admiral Sir David Beatty wrote from his flagship, *Lion*, 'Hearty congratulations, my dear de Chair, on the recognition of your great services. Nobody in the Navy deserves it better or has done better service.' This was perhaps more than halfway between platitude and statement of fact. Within a couple of months de Chair had been appointed naval adviser to the Ministry of Blockade. Established on 23 February 1916, this body was intended to co-ordinate the efforts by which economic pressure was brought to bear on Germany and her allies. Through the remainder of the war, the ministry held together the Cabinet, the Foreign Office, and all sorts of other bodies in creating a mesh of agreements, embargos and prohibitions which – every day – made things more difficult for the Central Powers. For John Buchan, this all meant that 'the British Navy was winning without striking a blow.'

The consequence was that by 1916 German imports had fallen since 1914 by 55 per cent, exports by 53 per cent.

These are monumental figures. Some of the cargoes lost were raw materials vital for the purposes of war, including rare metals, rubber and industrial diamonds. Others included bulk fertiliser, equally essential to the German agricultural economy. By the end of 1915 this had already begun to have a serious impact on the harvest of such staples as potatoes and wheat; these in turn affected the production of meat and dairy products. A few months earlier, the new First Lord of the Admiralty, Arthur Balfour, had remarked that it was 'unlikely that we shall starve Germany into submission; and I am not sure I would do it if I could.' Now, both of these ideas – of practicality and of morality – looked questionable and were being questioned. For Wilhelmine Germany, what became known as the *Steckrübenwinter* (Turnip Winter) loomed, the winter when the population would be reduced to eating animal fodder, largely turnips. Wrote Churchill a few years later, 'It was rightly foreseen that by closing the exits from the North Sea into the Atlantic Ocean, German commerce would be almost completely cut off from the world. It was expected that the economic and financial pressure resulting from such a blockade would fatally injure the German power to carry on the war.' Recent scholarship has called into question the efficacy of the blockade in the first two years of the war, and it was certainly the case that the ministry was created to better co-ordinate work which was hydra-headed and clearly susceptible to circumvention. Nevertheless, there was certainly justice in Beatty's postscript to de Chair that, 'The squadron which enforced the blockade ... formed the one unit which could win us the war.'

By much the same time British casualties on the Western Front had grown to 415,000; 1915 alone saw a toll of 285,000. Of these, a staggering proportion had been amassed from the resumption of hostilities in the autumn in the Artois, scene of the failures at Aubers Ridge and Festubert in the late spring. At the battle of Loos, fought from 25 September to 8 October 1919, 59,200 of French's men had been expended at a cost to Crown Prince Rupprecht's 6th Army of around 26,000. Kitchener, along with many others, did not think much of this use of the forces which he himself had supplied in the form of the volunteer armies. He wrote to the Chief of the General Imperial Staff, Sir William Robertson, 'Joffre and Sir John [French] told me in November that they were going to push the Germans back over the frontier; they gave me the same assurances in December, March and May. What have they done? The attacks are costly and end in nothing.'

To Stalin is attributed the remark that although one death is a tragedy, a million is a statistic. All the casualties, though – British, French, and German alike – were somebody's son or friend, somebody's brother, uncle, cousin, husband or father. Rudyard Kipling's only son John – then eighteen – was one of those of who died at Loos and had no known grave. To mark the gravestones of all unidentified servicemen, his father coined the phrase 'A soldier of the Great War known unto God'. Another victim of Loos was the poet Charles Sorley. In his kit recovered after his death was found his last poem, with perhaps some of his most famous lines:

> When you see millions of the mouthless dead
> Across your dreams in pale battalions go,
> Say not soft things as other men have said,
> That you'll remember. For you need not so.
> Give them not praise. For, deaf, how should they know
> It is not curses heaped on each gashed head?
> Nor tears. Their blind eyes see not your tears flow.
> Nor honour. It is easy to be dead ...

Churchill was by now himself serving in the trenches with the 2nd Battalion of the Grenadier Guards. It was a posting for which none of the other leading politicians of the Great War volunteered. Leading a platoon up to the front line near Laventie, some twenty miles west of Loos, he, too was mindful of the scale of the losses:

> The conviction came into my mind with absolute assurance that the
> simple soldiers and their regimental officers, armed with their cause,

would by their virtues in the end retrieve the mistakes and ignorances of Staffs and Cabinets, of Admirals, Generals and politicians – including, no doubt, many of my own. But, alas, at what needless cost! To how many slaughters, through what endless months of fortitude and privation would these men, themselves already the survivors of many a bloody day, be made to plod before victory was won!

The battle of Loos proved the death knell of Sir John French, as well as so many of his foot soldiers. His conduct of the war on the Western Front had long been questionable and long questioned, not least by his second in command Sir Douglas Haig. The catastrophe at Loos – the first large-scale offensive on the Western Front by the British Army – was debated at length in the British press, with Haig and French publicly disagreeing over the disposition of reserves. These were forces that might have turned failure into a tactical success. Haig's wife Dorothy was a lady-in-waiting to Queen Mary, and Haig had long enjoyed privileged access to her husband, King George V. In the last week of October the King had visited the front at Ypres to boost morale and to find out for himself what had happened at Loos: notably, who was to blame. He asked Haig.

Haig, born in 1861, was the son of the head of the famous whisky distillers, Haig & Haig. As a boy not regarded as particularly bright, he found his way to Oxford University at a time when the academic barriers to entry were low. When John Buchan became a member of Haig's college – Brasenose – in 1895, his biographer described it as 'a small college of about a hundred undergraduates, with a reputation for sport, hard drinking, and disorder'. Haig was accepted by the Royal Military College at Sandhurst in 1884, and made lieutenant a year later in a cavalry regiment, the 7th (Queen's Own) Hussars. This was an affiliation which would long colour his conduct of war. He served in India, the Sudan and the Boer War, and in 1902 was appointed ADC to King Edward VII. In 1904 he came the youngest major general in the Army. On his return from India he married Dorothy Vivian, one of Queen Alexandra's maids of honour, a connection that cemented his position as part of the royal entourage. He worked with Richard Haldane on the army reforms that stemmed from the Boer War, and in 1910 became Chief of Staff, India. The following year he returned to England to take command at Aldershot. In this role he was instrumental in training the corps that in 1914 became the BEF. Aged fifty-three at the outbreak of the war, he was efficient, perhaps more professional, but arguably no more talented than many of his contemporaries and colleagues. Innately conservative and with a perhaps misplaced confidence that his plans enjoyed divine guidance, he was at best a thoroughly professional soldier of his time. He was not much of a match for the man who would soon become his opposite number, General Erich von Ludendorff.

On 24 October 1915 Haig recorded:

After dinner, the King asked me to come to his room, and asked me about Sir John French's leadership. I told him I thought the time to have removed French was after the Retreat [of early September 1914], because he had so mismanaged matters ... and showed great ignorance of the essential principles of war ... French's handling of the reserves in the last battle, his obstinacy and conceit, showed his incapacity, and it seemed impossible for anyone to prevent him doing the same things again. I therefore thought strongly that for the sake of the Empire, French ought to be removed. I personally was ready to do my duty in any capacity.

The King, a more thoughtful and competent figure than some of his predecessors and successors, took this vague hint. On his return to London – unfortunately on a stretcher, having been badly thrown by one of Haig's own horses – there followed consultations with Asquith and Kitchener. The latter had just survived the attempt to unseat him as Secretary of State for War. Haig duly succeeded Sir John on 16 December 1915.

Vera Brittain's fiancé Roland Leighton expected to be home for Christmas 1915. He had telegraphed from France, 'Shall be home on leave from 24th Dec.–31st. Land Christmas Day. R.' On Boxing Day Brittain was called to the phone in the hospital in which she was working:

Believing that I was at last to hear the voice for which I had waited for twenty-four hours, I dashed joyously into the corridor. But the message was not from Roland ...; it was not to say that he had arrived home that morning, but to tell me he had died of wounds at a Casualty Clearing Station on December 23rd.

The Western Front now stood largely where it had been entrenched twelve months before in December 1914. In some places it was a few hundred yards closer to Germany, in some a few yards further away, in all places better fortified. In Gallipoli the evacuation of the peninsula was completed on 7 January 1916. The attempt to outflank the Western Front had failed. Casualties to British Empire and French forces totalled 302,000. Falkenhayn had focused on the Eastern Front in 1915, mounting a major offensive at Gorlice in the late spring. This saw the Russians losing Galicia, Poland and three-quarters of a million men as prisoners of war. The Tsar's line reformed 300 miles to the east. Summarised Martin Gilbert:

> At the end of 1915 the Central Powers were in the ascendant. Serbia was entirely under Austrian and Bulgarian occupation. Russian Poland and Belgium were under German control. At sea, the sinking of Entente shipping had been continuous and destructive. The German plans for 1916 for victory included [the resumption of] unlimited submarine warfare, and an attack on the French forces surrounding Verdun and its ring of forts.

The aim was to knock out Britain's western ally and then make a separate peace with England.

For the Entente land forces, to Haig now fell the opportunity to demonstrate what he could do to turn the tide and to win the war on the Western Front. He now had at his disposal the Kitchener armies on a scale beginning to match their Continental counterparts: 38 divisions to 95 of the French, 117 German. At this point his men had all the enthusiasm of the volunteers that they were, though their training was inevitably limited and their experience of battle modest

– particularly by comparison with their French allies and German enemies. Arguably, though, the newly promoted field marshal could do no worse than Sir John French, Sir Ian Hamilton in Gallipoli or his French opposite number Generalissmo Joseph Joffre. At a meeting at the French headquarters in Chantilly in early December 1915 representatives of the French themselves, the British, the Russians – and now the Italians who had joined the Entente – met to co-ordinate their efforts. A tentative step towards combined operations, the Allies agreed to synchronise their offensives in such a way as to discourage Falkenhayn from transferring his forces from one sector or front to another to defend against an Entente offensive. There would be simultaneous attacks on what had become the three main fronts of the war: the Western, Eastern and Italian. To ring in the New Year, on 29 December 1915 Haig agreed with Joffre that he would mount an offensive on the Somme, so enabling French forces to operate further south of the river. Neither Falkenhayn, though, nor Emperor Franz Joseph of Austria–Hungary entered into such agreement, the Oberste Heeresleitung having plans of its own for Verdun.

Admiral Sir David Beatty, whose year – whose career – would culminate at Jutland on 31 May 1916, found himself in a similar position to Haig in so far as he could do no worse than Admiral de Robeck, Hamilton's opposite number in the Dardanelles. Unless, that is, he conspired with his chief, Admiral Sir John Jellicoe, to 'lose the war in an afternoon'. To borrow another phrase of Churchill's, this one from the Second World War, it seemed to both Beatty and Haig that 1916 would prove 'the hinge of fate'.

8

Independence Day

'The powers that be are beginning to get a little uneasy in regard to the situation. The casualties are mounting up and they are wondering if we are likely to get a proper return for them.'

General Sir William Robertson, 29 July 1916

Bliss it was in that dawn to be alive, but to be young was very heaven. Independence Day, 4 July 1776, the day that rings down the centuries, when the thirteen American colonies declared their independence from British Rule. In the years that followed, a tradition was established of celebrating the day as a national holiday with parades, bonfires, fireworks, gun salutes and performances of patriotic songs like 'The Star-Spangled Banner' and 'God Bless America'. Yet 140 years later in 1916, for many Americans there was little cause for joy; for Theodore Roosevelt, president from 1901 to 1909, none at all. On that day in 1916, almost a year before the United States entered the war, he was moved to write a eulogy for a young American who had spurned the politics of his mother country and volunteered to fight beside the Entente in France. Victor Chapman was a corporal in the American Flying Squadron in France who had died on 17 June over the trenches near Douaumont, close to Verdun. Roosevelt, a Republican, found President Woodrow Wilson's policies abhorrent. The Democrat had declared that America was 'too proud to fight'. Now he was campaigning for a second term on a platform of the country remaining neutral. His slogans were 'America First' – now hijacked by Donald Trump – and 'He kept us out of the war'. This is less plausible as a Trump property. For Roosevelt, who had been appalled by the German atrocities – 'the rape of Belgium' – in August and September 1914, and by the sinking of the *Lusitania* in May 1915, this was anathema. He wrote:

The American nation has had scant cause for pride during the past two years, and much cause for bitter shame and humiliation. We are therefore indebted to these young men [who showed] they were not too 'proud to fight' but were proudly willing to die for their convictions ... they have partially redeemed us as a nation from the twin curses of gross materialism and silly sentimentalism.

Churchill, himself half American, likewise deplored US neutrality, seeing the intervention of his mother's country as one of the best chances of the Entente winning the war. He had finally returned to civilian life in May 1916, escaping from the trenches without injury but bringing with him a wealth of experience which made him unique among the politicians of his day. His six months on the Western Front had convinced him of the futility of attempting to break the deadlock in Flanders, indeed the whole of the front in the west. As the man determined as early as December 1914 to find alternatives to sending soldiers to chew barbed wire in Flanders, he needed little further persuasion.

Although the presidential election of November 1916 would see Wilson returned to office, the tides of history and the turn of events in Europe were inexorably drawing the United States into the war. In July 1916, around halfway through the conflict, two virtually con-current battles, one at sea and one on land, cast the die for the United States. The battle of Jutland and the battle of the Somme. These were also the operations in which Admiral Sir David Beatty and Field Marshal Sir Douglas Haig would play such prominent and contro-versial parts, both at the time and ever since.

When the news came through on 3 June 1916 from the Danish peninsula of Jutland of the great losses suffered by the Royal Navy, of men and of ships, Lord Fisher cried, 'They've failed me, they've failed me! I have spent thirty years of my life preparing for this day, and they've failed me!' With the Kaiserliche Marine sinking almost 113,300 tons of the Royal Navy's warships against its own losses of 62,300 tons; killed or wounded 3058 to 6768, the Kaiser could crow, 'The spell of Trafalgar is broken.' Within forty-eight hours, on 5 June 1916 came the news that Lord Horatio Kitchener, the constable of England and Secretary of State for War, had been lost when the cruiser *Hampshire* struck a mine off Orkney. Reduced to no more than a great poster in the eyes of Margot Asquith and her husband's Cabinet colleagues, for the public he had remained the symbol of the nation's fighting spirit. Vera Brittain saw the news on the streets:

The words 'KITCHENER DROWNED' seemed more startling, more dreadful, than the tidings of Jutland; their incredibility may still be measured by the rumours ... that he was not dead, that he had escaped in another ship to Russia, that he was organising a great campaign in France, that the wreck of the *Hampshire* was only a 'blind' to conceal his real intentions, that he would return in his own good time to deliver the final blow of the War.

Three weeks later on the first day of the Somme, 1 July 1916, the British army suffered 57,470 casualties, of whom 19,240 died. This was the worst day in the history of the British army, the heaviest loss it had – or has – ever sustained, and the worst day's toll of any army in the Great War. It left a scar on the national psyche that, a century on, has barely healed.

For the British people in those summer days of July 1916, it seemed that neither the Navy nor the Army could save them from disaster and defeat. The Somme blundered, crawled then crept on all fours through the mud into the autumn and the early winter. On 15 November, just as Haig was finally abandoning his efforts in Picardy, David Lloyd George remarked to Maurice Hankey, 'We are going to lose this war.' He might well have been right. Yet Jutland was not as it first seemed and – at least for Haig and his apologists – neither was the Somme. One and perhaps both were pivotal to the war.

The battle of Jutland has been described too many times to justify any but the briefest of descriptions.

The caution displayed by the commander of the Hochseeflotte, Admiral Hugo von Pohl, in the aftermath of the battle of Heligoland Bight and Dogger Bank five months later was somewhat qualified by the appointment early in 1916 of Reinhard von Scheer. Born in 1863,

Scheer joined the Kaiserliche Marine in his sixteenth year, only the seventh of the Imperial German Navy. He progressed rapidly through the ranks, made his name as a torpedo specialist, and in the early 1890s became a protégé of Admiral von Tirpitz, stepfather of the navy. Of severe appearance and a strict disciplinarian, he was nicknamed 'the man with the iron mask'. Scheer reached flag rank by the age of forty-seven. At the outbreak of war he was in command of the 2nd Battle Squadron of the High Seas Fleet. Like his predecessor Pohl, he hoped to whittle, pare and scrape down the superiority of the Grand Fleet until such time as some sort of parity (*Krafteausgleich*) existed. Then he would fight a battle on his own terms. Like Churchill on the far side of the North Sea, he believed that the destruction of the Grand Fleet would knock Great Britain out of the war. If it could be accomplished in an afternoon, all the better. No such celerity was imaginable on either the Eastern or the Western Fronts.

With this in mind, in the late winter and spring of 1916 the Vizeadmiral undertook a series of sorties in the North Sea intended to destroy some of the units of the Grand Fleet. One of these on 10 February cost Commodore Tyrwhitt his flagship *Arethusa* when she hit a mine outside Harwich. Another on 25 April saw a Hochseeflotte raid on Lowestoft and Yarmouth, again at some cost to Tyrwhitt – this time to his new flagship *Conquest*. Eventually, Scheer set a successful trap in which the lightly armoured battlecruisers of Beatty were lured under the guns of the heavier battleships of the High Seas main fleet. The bait comprised Beatty's opposite numbers, the battlecruiser squadron of Rear Admiral Franz von Hipper. This great day – the Admiralstab called it *Der Tag* – came on 31 May 1916. Off the Danish peninsula of Jutland, battle was joined between the twenty-eight battleships and nine battlecruisers of the Grand Fleet, and the sixteen dreadnoughts and five battlecruisers of the Hochseeflotte. With the accompanying light cruisers and destroyers, 250 vessels were present, a sight and sound which few of those 100,000 men present ever forgot. Correlli Barnett wrote:

Perhaps no sight more impressive has been seen at sea – not even Nelson's two divisions standing in to destroy Villeneuve – than

Jellicoe's 24 [four had been detached] blue-grey battleships in six columns abeam, the left-centre column led by *Iron Duke* wearing Jellicoe's flag – a red St George's cross on a white ground – their bow waves curling higher and higher, and the thick, soft smoke streaming away from their funnels into the still, sunlit afternoon.

The British, having broken the signal code of the Admiralstab, were forewarned by Room 40 of the Hochseeflotte's sortie, therefore forearmed. At 1645 Beatty's battlecruisers (reinforced by the four battleships) duly acted as the lure in Jellicoe's own trap, allowing themselves to be engaged by Hipper's battlecruisers before drawing away, apparently in flight. In so doing Beatty lost a third of his batlecruiser squadron – *Indefatigable* and *Queen Mary* – and very nearly had his flagship *Lion* blown up from under him. Churchill captures the moment, casting Beatty as the hero of the hour:

Meanwhile the Vice-Admiral, pacing the bridge among the shell fragments rebounding from the water, and like Nelson of old in the brunt of the enemy's fire, had learned that the *Indefatigable* and *Queen Mary* have been destroyed, and that his own magazines are menaced by fire ... the enemy, whom he could not defeat with six ships to five, are now five ships to four. Far away all five German battle-cruisers – grey smudges changing momentarily into 'rippling sheets of flame' – are still intact and seemingly invulnerable ... The movement of these blind, inanimate castles of steel was governed at this moment entirely by the spirit of a single man. Had he faltered, had he taken less than a conqueror's view of the British fighting chances all these great engines of sea power and war power would have wobbled off in meaningless disarray. This is a moment on which British naval historians will be glad to dwell ... The *Indefatigable* had disappeared beneath the waves. The *Queen Mary* had towered up to heaven in a pillar of fire. The *Lion* was in flames. A tremendous salvo struck upon or about her following ship, the *Princess Royal*, which vanished in a cloud of spray and smoke. A signalman sprung on to the *Lion*'s bridge with the words '*Princess Royal* blown up, sir.' On this the Vice-Admiral said to his Flag-Captain, 'Chatfield, there seems to be something wrong with our bloody ships today. Turn two points to port.' i.e. two points nearer the enemy. Thus the crisis of the battle was surmounted.

Only when Scheer's pursuing fleet were confronted at 1815 with Jellicoe's superior force did the Vizeadmiral realise that the hunter had become the hunted. Despite the loss of another British battlecruiser, *Invincible*, the heavier weight of fire, speed and number of Jellicoe's battleship fleet soon began to tell. Jellicoe himself executed a superb manoeuvre which 'crossed the T' of Scheer. This allowed almost all the Grand Fleet's guns to bear on the Hochseeflotte while the latter could only bring its forward turrets to bear. At 1835 Scheer turned tail, and ran away west – towards England – in an attempt to disengage, perhaps trailing his coat towards an unseen and underwater enemy. Committing what was regarded by some as a sin of omission for which he has never been forgiven, Jellicoe failed to pursue Scheer's bedraggled fleet. He exercised a tactic long agreed with the Admiralty that, threatened by the prospect of German mines and submarines, he would abstain from such a course should the temptation arise. Engage the enemy more closely, not he.

Then, for reasons that have been forever debated, the Hochseeflotte reappeared, blundered into the middle of the British line, again came under very heavy fire, and then once again turned tail towards the west. As the light faded, Scheer still had Jellicoe and his Grand Fleet between the Hochseeflotte, Wilhelmshaven and safety. With contact lost and night falling, Jellicoe was obliged to guess which of four routes back to sanctuary Scheer and Hipper might hope to take. Jellicoe wrote later:

> I was loth to forgo the advantage of position, which would have resulted from an easterly or westerly course, and I therefore decided to steer to the southward, where I should be in a position to renew the engagement at daylight, and should also be favourably placed to intercept the enemy should he make for his base by steering for Heligoland or forward to Ems and thence along the north German coast.

Jellicoe miscalculated as Scheer headed home by the Horns Reef, and the Hochseeflotte escaped its day of reckoning. The battle of Jutland was over, the only major encounter between the two fleets in the whole of the war.

Besides the men killed on both sides, the Grand Fleet had lost the three battlecruisers, three cruisers and eight destroyers; Scheer lost one battleship, *Pommern*; one battlecruiser, *Lützow*; four light cruisers and five destroyers. The Hochseeflotte reached its rather closer bases before the Grand Fleet and at once declared a great naval victory. An exhausted Beatty, realising that the chance to immortalise his own memory had just slipped through his fingers, threw himself down on the settee in *Lion*'s chart room and remarked wearily, 'There is something wrong with our ships. And something wrong with our system'. Yet as Scheer was to write both in his initial and final report to the Kaiser – the latter submitted on 4 July 1916 – there was also something wrong with the Hochseeflotte and its strategy.

Six thousand men is a lot to lose in one day; 20,000 is profligate. It was like an asteroid strike on – say – Luton, Bradford, Bath or Slough. The Somme bloodbath touched not just those who died or the further 40,000 who were injured on that day, but their families, friends and the whole nation beyond. During the Crimean War, John Bright had written that 'the angel of death has been abroad throughout the land; you may almost hear the beating of his wings.' It had come again. For John Keegan, the Somme 'was and would remain their [the British] greatest military tragedy of the twentieth century, indeed of their national military history.'

Like Jutland, the battle of the Somme has been described too often to be rehearsed once again. For a battle of such a scale and of such a human – let alone material – cost, it was curiously ill-conceived. To be fair to Haig, now master and commander of the battle on the British side, it was not his conception. He agreed only reluctantly to the operation in a spirit of co-operation with Generalissimo Joseph Joffre, shortly after the dismissal of Sir John French in December 1915. Originally, the battle was to be a joint operation between the British and the French, forty French divisions supporting twenty-five British at a point where the Allies met on the Somme, the river that rises above

St Quentin and drains into the Channel. Then came the inconvenience of the OHL and the supreme commander Falkenhayn – the enemy – having his own plans by way of the February attack on Verdun, the stroke which aimed to knock the French out of the war. This reduced the French contribution on the Somme first to match that of the British, then to just five divisions; indeed, from now on the British did most of the fighting on the Western Front. It was in any case never very clear what strategic aim would be achieved by success, and the terrain of the upper reaches of the Somme basin was characterised by the Germans holding the higher ground towards which the British were obliged to climb. The chalk proved admirably suited for the construction of defences, and the Germans had worked hard to make the most of natural advantage. Haig himself wrote, 'During nearly two years' preparation he [the enemy] had spared no pains to render these defences impregnable'; indeed, Haig's forces were knowingly attacking where the defences were at their strongest. The British, for all the enthusiasm of the new Kitchener armies, were poorly trained and minimally experienced – in some respects no better than raw recruits. The artillery barrage intended to cut the wire defending the German defences largely failed to do so. Despite the herculean efforts of Lloyd George's Ministry of Munitions to provide more than 1.5 million shells for the initial offensive, in some parts of the line shortage still prevailed, many were duds, more still misdirected.

At 0730 on 1 July 1916, just a month after Jutland, the huge artillery barrage lifted and some nineteen British divisions set off into no man's land. No sooner had they done so than the Germans emerged from their bunkers, set up their machine-gun posts:

'Get ready!' was passed along our front from crater to crater, and heads appeared over the crater edges as final positions were taken up for the best views and machine-guns mounted firmly in place. A few minutes later, when the leading British line was within 100 yards, the rattle of machine-gun and rifle fire broke out from along the whole line of craters ... whole sections seemed to fall, and the rear formations moving in closer order, quickly scattered. The advance rapidly crumbled under this hail of shells and bullets. All along the line men could be seen throwing their arms in the air and collapsing never to move again. Badly wounded rolled about in their agony, and others less severely injured crawled to the nearest shell-hole for shelter ... again and again, the extended lines of British infantry broke against the German defence like waves against a cliff, only to be beaten back ... It was an amazing spectacle of unexampled gallantry, courage and bull-dog determination on both sides.

As early as 4 July the pattern and likely outcome of the battle had been established. On that day the British captured Bernafay Wood to the east of Montauban; the French captured Estrées, Belloy-en-Santerre and Sormont Farm. Haig reported, 'To sum up the fighting of those five days on a front of over six miles ... the troops had swept over the whole of the enemy's first and strongest system of defence ... they had driven him back over a distance of more than a mile, and carried four elaborately fortified villages'. However, as Churchill later pointed out, 'These gains had been purchased at the loss of nearly a hundred thousand of our best troops'. The only independence these men marked on 4 July was shuffling off their mortal coil. Vera Brittain was now working as a nurse in Camberwell, dealing with the tens of thousands of seriously wounded ferried back by hospital ships from France.

On that morning, July 4th, began the immense convoys which came without cessation for about a fortnight, and continued at short intervals for the whole of that sultry month of August. Throughout those 'busy and strenuous days' the wards sweltered beneath their roofs of corrugated iron; the prevailing odour of wounds and stinking street lingered perpetually in our nostrils, the red-hot hardness of paths and pavements burnt its way through the soles of our feet. Day after day I had to fight the queer, frightening sensation – to which, throughout my years of nursing, I never became accustomed – of seeing the covered stretchers come in, one after another, without knowing, until I ran with pounding heart to look, what fearful sight or sound or stench, what problem of agony or imminent death, each brown blanket concealed.

By the end of July, Allied casualties had already reached the 200,000 mark, German around 160,000. The front line had moved three miles. After the abandonment of the campaign on 18 November 1916, the advances made by the Allied armies were barely discernible on a map, merely later on gravestones, in the cemeteries, and in the great memorials commemorating those with no known grave, of those soldiers 'of the Great War, known unto God'. The French ultimately suffered 200,000 casualties, the British more than twice that number, around 620,000 in all. 'The Somme,' wrote John Keegan, 'marked the end of an age of vital optimism in British life which has never been recovered.' Wilfred Owen wrote in 'Anthem for Doomed Youth':

> What passing-bells for these who die as cattle?
> Only the monstrous anger of the guns.
> Only the stuttering rifles' rapid rattle
> Can patter out their hasty orisons.
> No mockeries now for them; no prayers nor bells,
> Nor any voice of mourning save the choirs, –
> The shrill, demented choirs of wailing shells;
> And bugles calling for them from sad shires.
>
> What candles may be held to speed them all?
> Not in the hands of boys, but in their eyes
> Shall shine the holy glimmers of goodbyes.
> The pallor of girls' brows shall be their pall;
> Their flowers the tenderness of patient minds,
> And each slow dusk a drawing down of blinds.

It was also in the early days of July, just as the full extent of the casualties on the Somme was beginning to become apparent, that Vizedamiral Admiral Scheer completed and despatched his report of what the Germans had come to call the battle of Skagerrak (*Skagerrak-schlacht*) to the Kaiser. Despite the fulsome, indeed vehement, declarations of victory that had appeared in the German press on 2 June 1916, despite the national holidays and the nationwide rejoicing, despite the Iron Crosses that the Kaiser, the supreme warlord, had showered on the crews of the Hochseeflotte, this joy was far from being shared by Scheer. On the contrary, the Vizeadmiral's analysis was virtually an admission of defeat of the whole project to build the

Imperial German Navy. This ambition had been pursued at enormous cost in the face of three factors that not just the benefit of hindsight made such immovable objects. First, the relative geography of Britain and northern Germany that placed the British Isles – in Mahan's terms – as a vast breakwater between Germany and the freedom of the great waters beyond. Secondly, the lead in the construction of all big-gun ships that had been established on 10 February 1906, the day King Edward VII launched Fisher's *Dreadnought*. Thirdly, the virtually ungovernable demands of human, financial and material resources that in Imperial Germany were devoted to its great army, the Deutsches Heer. As the respected German military journal *Marine-Rundschau* had put it very simply before the war, 'Boxed in between France and Russia, Germany has to maintain the greatest army in the world. It is obviously beyond the capacity of the German economy to support at the same time a fleet that could outgrow the British.'

Omitting the last point perhaps as something that went without saying, in the sober aftermath of *Skagerrakschlacht*, on 4 July 1916 Scheer wrote to the Kaiser:

There can be no doubt that even the most successful result from a high sea battle will not compel England to make peace. The disadvantages of our geographical situation as compared to that of the Island Empire and the enemy's vast material superiority cannot be coped with to such a degree as to make us masters of the blockade forced on us.

It was for these reasons that although Scheer did not despair of the Kaiserliche Marine as a means of breaking the stranglehold of the blockade and of winning the war, he certainly did so of the Hochseeflotte. It was a name that – penned in as the fleet was into the North Sea – was beginning to look ironic. For Scheer and many of the other staff at the Admiralstab, the strategy of unrestricted U-boat warfare was beginning to seem the only possible approach to breaking the stalemate that the war on land had become. Moreover, by early July 1916 it had also become apparent to Falkenhayn that his attempt to win the war by breaking the French army at Verdun had failed. General Henri Pétain, who was to turn fame into infamy – in modern parlance from hero to zero – in 1940 by volunteering to collaborate with the Nazis, had promised, 'They shall not pass'. The Germans had not. Indeed, they had suffered total losses in the order of 337,000. On the French side the cost was the spirit of the fighting army, and a monstrous casualty list of perhaps 380,000 men. To the Kaiser's increasing discomfort, to the German losses were added the consequences of General Aleksei Brusilov's June offensive in Poland. This performed the comparable task of destroying the will to fight of the Austro-Hungarian army, the Kaiser's allies on the Eastern Front; and, as we will see, it held important lessons for the Western Front.

It was no wonder that Scheer turned to other ways and means of winning the war at sea. His 4 July letter to the Kaiser continued, 'A victorious end to the war at a not too distant date can only be looked for by crushing the economic life through U-boat action against British commerce'.

It was, of course, not only at the Admiralstab that men had been reflecting on the battle of Jutland. In Whitehall and Downing Street, in the villages, market towns and cities of England, the talk that summer was of little other than what was generally seen as – at best – a strangely inconclusive battle, at worst a crushing betrayal of trust by the shield of Albion, the Royal Navy. For Vera Brittain, still in mourning for her fiancé Roland Leighton, the question at the time was: 'Were we celebrating a glorious naval victory or lamenting an ignominious defeat? We hardly knew; each fresh edition of the newspapers obscured rather than illuminated this quite important distinction.' As Churchill wrote in 1923, 'The disappointment of all ranks was deep; and immediately there arose reproaches and recriminations, continued to this day.'

There was certainly something to justify reproach. The losses of the three battlecruisers *Indefatigable*, *Invincible* and *Queen Mary* (*Princess Royal*, in fact, survived) was almost at once attributed to a casual handling of cordite propellant charges for the great guns which had allowed flash fires to ignite the ships' magazines. This could be – and was – immediately rectified, but the tragedies also posed questions about the whole idea of placing the lightly armoured battlecruisers in the line of battleship fire. Fisher, the creator of the battlecruisers, had always argued that their speed was their principal means of defence. Jutland gainsaid him. The loss of the Royal Navy's last battlecruiser, HMS *Hood*, to *Bismarck* on 24 May 1941 capped the argument – at the loss of another 1415 men. By comparison, the Hochseeflotte had rectified its own propellant handling laxities after nearly losing *Seydlitz* at the battle of Dogger Bank in January 1915. The Royal Navy had failed to learn from a comparable incident on Beatty's own *Lion* in the same battle, or, rather, had neglected to ensure its lessons were passed on to her sister ships. Scheer's fleet also proved superior in range-finding, gunnery, its shells, certain aspects of ship-handling, and in signalling. Throughout the battle – a battle spread over an area the size of Yorkshire – the British captains fell down in their duty of keeping their superiors abreast of the location and heading of the Kaiserliche Marine's ships. Few were worse than Beatty himself. As Jellicoe's scout, his main job was to let the Grand Fleet battleships know where the enemy was. In this Beatty was culpably negligent. There is something rather pathetic about Jellicoe's signals to Beatty in the afternoon of 31 May inquiring plaintively of the whereabouts of the Hocheseeflotte. Richard Hough wrote:

We see John Jellicoe ... standing on *Iron Duke*'s compass platform. He is dressed in a much worn blue raincoat, white muffler round his neck, old cap with tarnished brass on his head – an unpretentious, rather plain figure, below average height, and standing erect. At 6.01 Jellicoe sights the *Lion* at a distance of about five miles to the south-west. She is moving fast, on an easterly heading, and bearing evidence of the fierce battle that she has been fighting since 4 o'clock. The *Iron Duke*'s captain recalled this moment. 'Beatty in the *Lion* appeared out of the mist on our starboard bow, leading his splendid battlecruisers, which were engaged with an enemy invisible to us. I noticed smoke pouring from a shell-hole on the port side of *Lion*'s forecastle and grey, ghost-like columns of water thrown up by heavy enemy shells pitching among those great ships.' Jellicoe at once ordered the signal, by searchlight, 'Where is the enemy battle-fleet?' The answer was not satisfactory and the C-in-C was not pleased: 'Enemy battle-cruisers bearing SE.'

Beatty also failed to concentrate his force by allowing the 5th Battle Squadron of four battleships to keep in close touch with him, made a series of tactical errors, and had poorly trained his squadron in gunnery. Only 3 per cent of the fleet's salvoes hit their targets, the battlecruisers faring worse. A dashing and flamboyant leader, a gallant man, he was not fit for the heroic role in which Churchill had generously cast him. Jellicoe himself cannot be fairly criticised for his failure to pursue Scheer. This was merely in accordance with a policy carefully debated and agreed in October 1914 in the early months of the war. Indeed, as Allan Mallinson points out, 'Jutland was one of the few battles of the First World War which was fought to a cogent strategy as previously agreed.' Neither can Churchill's part be taken, who blamed Jellicoe for failing to act upon intelligence on Scheer's intentions from a source that had already twice proved misleading, intelligence from Room 40 which would have enabled the Grand Fleet to ambush Scheer at Horns Reef on his way home on 1 June 1916. For John Buchan, 'In a fog of uncertainty, Jellicoe handled the affair ably and, if he was cautious, such was not only the man but the essence of his policy. He could not have destroyed Scheer without taking risks which could have destroyed himself and with him would have gone down the Allied cause.' Jellicoe can be more fairly indicted for his failure to possess the quality that Napoleon prized most highly in his captains: good fortune. The Admiralty alone must bear responsibility for keeping Tyrwhitt's Harwich Force out of the battle, fearing a lunge south by Scheer which the Harwich Force would have had to beat off. Tyrwhitt, who in his home port had followed the signals traffic from Jutland, was so frustrated that he set to sea without orders from the Admiralty, only to be sharply recalled. Commented Tyrwhitt, 'I might as well have gone on mowing the lawn!' Wrote a young lieutenant on one of the flotilla destroyers at the battle, 'The destroyer business in the night at Jutland was an awful mess-up. If only they allowed Com. T [Tyrwhitt] to be there ... things might have been very different.' Jacky Fisher said much the same thing.

On 3 June 1916 Tyrwhitt's good friend Roger Keyes, still chief of staff to the Eastern Mediterranean Squadron, wrote to his wife, 'In the evening we got a bit of German wireless [about Jutland] which was too depressing tho' one knew it was an exaggeration, or at any rate their losses had been minimised'. Like the general public, he thought that the country had been robbed of another Trafalgar, of a decisive victory at sea. The irony was that Scheer, and in due course the Kaiser, correctly concluded that this was exactly what Jellicoe – almost unknowingly – had achieved. On 5 June 1916 the British admiral, barely twenty-four hours after his return to port, was able to tell the Admiralty that the Grand Fleet, in the form of twenty-six of its dreadnoughts and six of the remaining battlecruisers, was once again ready for sea. Scheer, with all his battlecruisers badly damaged and one sunk, was able to make no such announcement to the Kaiser about the Hochseeflotte until August, repairs being delayed by materials denied to the German fleet by the British blockade. A J P Taylor summarises, 'The real danger to Britain did not come from any German belief that they had won the Battle of Jutland. It came from an appreciation that they had lost it, or at any rate that they could not gain from fighting another battle of this kind.'

After Scheer's memorandum of 4 July and into the summer and autumn of 1916, debate continued in Berlin. On the one hand were those who cautioned the Kaiser about the diplomatic consequences of unrestricted submarine warfare; on the other, those of Scheer and Tirpitz's party who increasingly saw this as the best and perhaps only hope of victory. Amongst the latter was Vizeadmiral Hoffman, who noted astutely a few days after the battle, 'The result incidentally strengthens my conviction that the days of the super-dreadnoughts are numbered. It is senseless to build 30,000 ton ships which cannot defend themselves against a torpedo shot.' This was a legitimate criticism of both Germany's and Great Britain's splendid surface fleets, their commanders increasingly believing that they were too valuable and too vulnerable to be risked in battle. Accordingly, Imperial Germany duly committed herself to undersea warfare with a building programme that saw the doubling of the size of the U-boat fleet. By the time the fighting on the Somme had been abandoned in the face of the November rains, the Admiralstab had almost a hundred vessels at its disposal, around half of which might be at sea at any one time. More were on the stocks in the yards of Wilhelmshaven, Bremerhaven, Hamburg and Kiel.

This was the real fruit of Jutland, and for the Germans it was to prove poisoned. When the Kaiser finally sanctioned unrestricted submarine warfare in January 1917, he signed his own instrument of abdication. And although it is inaccurate to say that the Hochseeflotte never ventured out again after Jutland, it did so that year only twice and then ineffectually – on 19 August and 19 October 1916. These were both operations in which the indomitable Tyrwhitt was again entangled. The final aborted sortie of the Hochseeflotte planned by Scheer for 30 October 1918 was the trumpet call for the revolution, itself ultimately the consequence of the admiral's 4 July memorandum. 'The Navy!' wrote Lieutenant Commander Ernst von Weizsäcker on 5 November 1918, 'It sprung forth from the hubris of world power, and for twenty years it has been ruining our foreign relations. It never kept its promises in wartime. Now it sparks revolution!'

If Jutland was a victory that looked like a defeat, of the Somme even its apologists have had to bend over backwards to make it look like much other than an unmitigated disaster.

Our national history is written in the red letters that spell the victories at Crécy, Poitiers and Agincourt over the French, over the Spanish Armada, over the French and the Spanish at Trafalgar, over the French (again) at Waterloo, and over the Germans at both the Battle of Britain and El Alamein. The rather shorter roll call of military catastrophe is headed by the Somme, with the Charge of the Light Brigade, the siege of Kut, Gallipoli, Singapore and, of course, Passchendaele as also-rans. 'Strategically,' claimed A J P Taylor, 'the Battle of the Somme was an unredeemed defeat'. It has become a byword for the futility of trench warfare, a synonym for military incompetence, the tragic embodiment of the idea of lions led by donkeys, the watershed in the national consciousness and confidence. It was also the most brutal possible baptism of fire for the remarkable creation of the late Lord Kitchener. As to Haig himself, he certainly might have learned from General Aleksei Brusilov and his Polish campaign on the Eastern Front, the battle that preceded the Somme offensive by three weeks. Brusilov employed no preliminary bombardment that forewarned the defenders, eschewed attacking at the strongest point, avoided concentrating his troops, and simply attacked the Austro-Hungarian front line south of the Prippet Marshes where it seemed most vulnerable. The front duly collapsed. Brusilov advanced forty miles, and within three weeks the Russians had taken 250,000 prisoners. For Keegan it was, 'the greatest victory seen on any front since the trench lines had been dug on the Aisne two years before.' By contrast, in the face of persistent failure – with the exception of a night attack and a half-hearted use of the new tanks – Haig merely persisted. Of the Dardanelles, Churchill concluded, 'Not to persevere, that was the crime.' Of the Somme it might be said, 'To persevere, that was the crime.'

Despite this, the Somme cannot and should not be dismissed. It has been said that war should be pursued using the minimum of resources to achieve decisive victory by means of the stratagems of manoeuvre, concentration of force and surprise. The Dardanelles was an attempt to employ just such means as an alternative to chewing barbed wire in Flanders. Its failure had momentous consequences, nothing so bold being attempted again, not least the amphibious attack against the German coastline planned for July 1915.

Kitchener had then pointed out the necessity of waging war not as we would wish to, but as we must. In 1916 Haig was accordingly far from alone in believing that in the absence of any possibility of manoeuvre and – apparently – little of surprise, attacking head-on and grinding the Germans down was the only way to break the stalemate. Joffre argued likewise, though both of them had a tendency to promise breakthroughs and – when they failed to materialise – argue that their intention had been attrition. Like Verdun, the Somme at least became an attempt to wear down the enemy by means of continuous losses in personnel and war materiel – as a war of attrition is defined. There is clearly logic in this approach if your resources are superior to your enemy's, and it was, of course, true that Germany had three enemies – France, Britain and Russia – to fight on two fronts. Britain, in practical terms, had on land only one. Haig's own defence of the Somme was essentially this. Indeed, as he claimed in his final despatch:

> The rapid collapse of Germany's military powers in the latter half of 1918 was the logical outcome of the previous two years ... It would not have taken place but for the period of ceaseless attrition which used up the reserves of the German armies, while the constant and growing pressure of the blockade sapped with more deadly insistence from year to year at the strength and resolution of the German people. It is in the great battles of 1916 and 1917 that we have to seek for the secret of our victory in 1918.

This is supported by the decision taken by Hindenburg in Cambrai on 5 September 1916 to build a new front some way behind the Somme fortifications. This is taken by some to be an admission of defeat. Likewise, the Great War historian Gary Sheffield argues that, on balance, the Somme did more damage to the Germans than the Allies, that the British learned from the experience, emerging a much improved fighting force, that Haig 'had a critical role in transforming the inexperienced, poorly trained army of July 1916 into the war-winning force of 1918.' Thus for John Buchan, 'The Somme had shown [Germany] that her military machine was being strained to breaking-point.' Allan Mallinson adds that, 'The Somme had, indirectly, ensured that the Germans could not now win ... for it reinforced the post-Jutland conviction that the U-boat must be allowed to do its worst, and when the Kaiser finally conceded this in February 1917, his decision brought the United States into the war within months.' In this sense, Jutland and the Somme, both seen as disasters of very varying degree, both in reality contributed to a greater and lesser extent to the Allied victory.

It was at the end of July 1916 that the Chief of Imperial General Staff, General Sir William Robertson, wrote a note of concern to his superior, Sir Douglas Haig. 'The powers that be are beginning to get a little uneasy in regard to the situation. The casualties are mounting up and they are wondering if we are likely to get a proper return for them.' If conflict has to be regarded in such reductive terms – and, of course, to an extent it must – it is worth considering the relative contributions made respectively by Jutland and the Somme to the winning of the war; and to consider, too, their cost in so doing. In Bertrand Russell's clinical phrase, the objective of a war economy was the 'maximum slaughter at the minimum expense'; or in Keegan's more emollient phrase, consideration must be given to the 'return on sacrifice'.

It has been said that Jellicoe was no Nelson, nor Jutland another Trafalgar. Still, the fact remains that despite the much higher British losses in men and ships, Imperial Germany did indeed conclude in the aftermath of Jutland that little was to be gained by seeking another such encounter. Another means had to be found to win the war. This was the U-boat warfare, which indeed actually lost her the conflict. This result was achieved by the loss of the three battlecruisers, three cruisers, eight destroyers and casualties of 6768 men. Haig himself made no such claims of the Somme and its 620,000 Entente casualties. He did suggest that the battle was a step on the path towards victory; the other major factor he cites in the passage quoted above being the naval blockade. It is also arguable that without the British participation in the Somme, the French would have been knocked out of the war.

Still, we are left with the fact that for every naval casualty at Jutland, around a hundred were sustained in the trenches on the Somme. This heartless actuarial argument is simply that of Robertson's 'proper return' on resources, Keegan's 'return on sacrifice'. On this basis, Jutland made a rather greater contribution to the winning of the war than the Somme at a fraction of its cost in men. Some years later, Churchill commented in the context of the Dardanelles:

I marvelled much in those sad days at the standard of values and sense of proportion which prevailed among our politicians and naval and military authorities. The generals were so confident of breaking the line in France that they gathered masses of cavalry behind the assaulting troops to ride through the huge gaps they expected to open on a hostile front. To sacrifice quarter of a million men in such an affair seemed to them the highest military wisdom. That was the orthodox doctrine of war; even if it did not succeed, no error or breach of rules would have been committed. But to lose one hundredth part as many sailors and a dozen old ships ... with the possibility of gaining an inestimable prize – there was a risk before which the boldest uniformed greyhead stood appalled.

As to Bertrand Russell's minimum expense, some headlines are perhaps worth remarking here, impossible as it is to put a precise financial cost on Jutland or the Somme. In 1914 the Army cost the nation around £30 million a year, the Navy about £50 million. By 1919 the tables had been turned, the Navy having doubled in size, the Army expanding more than tenfold. The Army was costing £405 million, the Navy £160 million.

Ultimately, the reality is, of course, that the two services and their work were inextricably intertwined and interdependent rather than autonomous, and that these sort of figures are merely very rough pointers and indicators. Asked Jacky Fisher at the height of the U-boat crisis in 1917, 'Can the Army win the war before the Navy loses it?' Eighteen months later, Haig's chaplain, the Reverend George Duncan, offered the field marshal his congratulations on the Armistice. Haig responded with becoming modesty, 'Oh! You mustn't congratulate me; we have all been in this together, trying our different ways to do our part.'

In the meantime, Asquith's Cabinet was rightly seen as responsible for the stewardship of the resources of a nation, and for the supervision of those more directly expending them. Given the scale of casualties on the Somme it was not surprising that in July 1916 'the powers that be' were uneasy. Lloyd George, who had taken over as Secretary of State for War after Kitchener's death, was appalled. He flailed himself as 'the butcher's boy who leads the animals to slaughter. When I have delivered the men my task in the war is over.' By November, the men in grey suits were so concerned by the failure of Asquith's coalition and its underlings – including the admirals and the generals – to conduct the war with any conviction or success that they took matters into their own hands. It was in Paris on 15 November 1916 that Lloyd George had expressed his pessimism about the war to Maurice Hankey, secretary of the Committee of Imperial Defence. With the failure on the Somme, President Wilson of the United States pressing for a peace conference, and a negotiated settlement with the Central Powers in the air, a cabal was formed. It comprised Lloyd George himself, the leader of the Conservatives, Andrew Bonar Law, First Lord of the

Admiralty Edward Carson, and the Canadian adventurer Max Aitken. They were increasingly taking the French Prime Minister Georges Clemenceau's line that war was far too important a business to be left to generals (or indeed admirals). They proposed what amounted to a civilian general staff, chaired by Lloyd George himself. It has also been called, 'in essence a democratic form of constitutional dictatorship'.

'Either Mr Lloyd George or Sir Edward Carson are fancied for the Premiership, and I think we should do well with either,' wrote Vera Brittain in her diary:

> Undoubtedly where warfare is concerned we want business men rather than politicians to direct affairs, and certainly the only man in the Government of the present who shows real power and strength of mind to us it is Mr Lloyd George. He has consistently from the outbreak of War shown himself a strong man in every sense of the word.

For Churchill, Lloyd George was the only person in the government who possessed, 'any aptitude for war or knowledge of it'. John Buchan adds, 'Of all the civilians I have known Mr Lloyd George seems to me to have possessed in the highest degree the capacity for becoming a great soldier. But he might have lost several armies while he was learning his trade.' The eventual outcome on 7 December 1916 was the resignation of Asquith and the installation of Lloyd George as prime minister.

By this time the Welshman's ebbing confidence in Haig was matched by a belief that – in any case – it was not necessarily in battle that the war would be won. Buchan continued:

> Mr Lloyd George could see small co-ordination in the many desperate allied attacks of the past two years. When he was told that they had a common purpose, the attrition of the enemy, he replied that attrition in the third year of war could not be a serious policy, but a confession of the absence of policy. If we were wearing Germany down we were wearing ourselves out of existence, competing in a futile race towards bankruptcy.

In his memoirs, the prime minister noted that in the absence of a military solution and with the passage of time, other factors were coming into play.

> It was becoming a war of starvation. In the end, meagre and mean feeding at last subdued the spirit that for years of sanguinary battles had proved indomitable on every battle front. Food in all the belligerent countries was therefore at the end of 1916 becoming a growing and, as it turned out, a paramount element in the chances of victory.

At much the same time, Ludendorff remarked that, 'Corn and potatoes are power, just like iron and coal.'

Just before Christmas of 1916 Vera Brittain's brother Edward wrote to her about his Uppingham schoolfellow and friend Roland Leighton, his sister's late fiancé:

> I know it is just a year and you are thinking of him and his terrible death, and what might have been, even as I am too. This year has, I think, made him seem very far off but yet all the more unforgettable. His life was like a guiding star which left this firmament when he died and went to another one where it still shines as brightly but so very far away.

Besides Edward, her two surviving close friends serving overseas in the army were her brother's friend Geoffrey Thurlow and Victor Richardson. Thurlow had been commissioned in the 10th Sherwood Foresters; Richardson, the Royal Sussex Regiment. The painter C R W Nevinson, like Leighton himself and Richardson, an Uppingham boy, recalled that on a pre-war speech day, the school's headmaster had declared, 'If a man can't serve his country he's better dead.'

9

The Kaiser Plays Macbeth

'Our armies might advance a mile a day and slay the Hun in
thousands, but the real crux in whether we blockade the enemy to
his knees or he does the same to us'.

Admiral Sir David Beatty

'This castle,' said the Kaiser, 'hath a pleasant seat. The air nimbly and
sweetly recommends itself unto our gentle senses'. So might Kaiser
Wilhelm have reflected on arriving at the Schloss Pless in Silesia on 8
January 1917. The eastern headquarters of the Oberste Heeresleitung
was constructed in the thirteenth century and remodelled in the
eighteenth and nineteenth in the style of the late baroque; in 2009 it
was voted one of the seven architectural wonders of Poland. Today it
would make a pleasant country retreat for Prince William or Prince
Harry, distant cousins of the Kaiser, should the fancy take them for
hunting wild boar. There again, the 58-year-old Wilhelm, grandson of
Queen Victoria, might have taken the part of Macbeth rather than
Duncan in the Scottish play. For the Kaiser, the Oberster Kriegsherr,
the supreme warlord, was in the throes of a terrible conundrum.
There, at a meeting of the Crown Council at Pless, he would make the
decision he described as the most difficult of his life. It was one which
the German Chancellor Bethmann-Hollweg would describe as, 'A
game of *va banque* [risking everything in a game of cards] whose stakes
will be our existence as a Great Power and our entire national future'.
This was the choice concerning unlimited submarine warfare.
According to Churchill:

The total defeat of Germany was due to three cardinal mistakes: the
decision to march through Belgium regardless of bringing Britain
into the war; the decision to begin the unrestricted U-boat war

regardless of bringing the United States into the war; and thirdly, the decision to use the German forces liberated from Russia in 1918 for a final onslaught on France.

Few historians today would disagree.

With the Somme, Jutland and Verdun, 1916 had been a very difficult year for the Entente. It had been no easier for the Central Powers. General Erich von Falkenhayn's assault on the great French fortress had seen the attackers' casualties put as high as 337,000, almost certainly more; the defence of the Somme something very much the same. On the Eastern Front the Brusilov offensive had eventually cost around 900,000 casualties to Austria–Hungary and a third of a million to Germany herself. These figures were utterly unsustainable. The Central Powers were running out of cannon fodder and peace proposals were being aired in Germany herself, in England and by President Wilson in Washington. On 28 August 1916 Falkenhayn was sacked by the Kaiser as chief of the Oberste Heeresleitung, paying the price for Verdun. He was replaced by Field Marshal Paul von Hindenburg; and – as Erster Generalquartiermeister – Erich Ludendorff. This duumvirate was dubbed the third Oberste Heeresleitung or Dritte OHL, so succeeding the leaderships of Moltke and Falkenhayn himself.

They were a curious couple. Hindenburg was a Prussian aristocrat born in 1847. A career army officer, he had fought in the Austro-Prussian war of 1886 and the Franco-Prussian war of 1870–71, graduating to the famous Kriegsakademie in 1873. Here he worked under Count Schlieffen. He became acquainted with the Kaiser on manoeuvres in 1885. By 1905 he had become a general of the infantry. In 1909, with war clouds gathering, he was recommended by Schlieffen as chief of general staff of the Deutsches Heer. Losing out to Helmuth von Moltke, in 1911 he retired from the army and retreated with his wife and family to Hanover in Lower Saxony. On 22 August 1914 he was abruptly recalled to the colours by Moltke and appointed to the command of the beleaguered 8th Army in Prussia. His wife Gertrud set about hastily altering his old blue Prussian uniform which had shrunk in the wardrobe and no longer quite fitted his striking 6ft 4in frame. At 0400 that morning in Hanover station Hindenburg stood stiffly as a single locomotive and a couple of carriages pulled into the *Hauptbahnhof*, a building as atmospheric as a cathedral in the half-light of dawn. It was a special train, from which stepped a smart 47-year-old dressed in the regulation field grey. Of slighter build but sporting the same waxed moustache and *Pickelhaube* spiked helmet as his new chief, this was Ludendorff.

The younger man was another Prussian aristocrat and graduate of the Kriegsakademie. He, too, had served under Schlieffen; and he had calculated that the Deutsches Heer was short of six army corps for the successful execution of the count's plans. His calculations – he was a gifted mathematician – unfortunately proved correct. A glutton for work, he was friendless and humourless, and in the early days of the war was credited with orchestrating the reduction of the Belgian city-fortress of Liège. Indeed, just hours before setting off for Hanover, he had been awarded by the Kaiser the country's highest military award, rather strangely called *Pour le Mérite*, as though in the gift of the French. This pair – Hindenburg and Ludendorff – had been joined at the hip to harness the seniority and presence of the older man with the greater intelligence and understanding of contemporary war of the younger. Wrote Christopher Clark:

> Hindenburg ... was a towering, charismatic figure with bristling moustaches and an almost rectangular head; he radiated calm and confidence at all times. Ludendorff was the more brilliant tactician and strategist, but Hindenburg was the more gifted communicator. Ludendorff worked like a mule behind the scenes, but was content to see Hindenburg emerge as a figure of national adulation. It was a supremely effective wartime partnership.

As Prussians, the two men exemplified the martial prowess of the greatest of the states that constituted federal Germany.

Having exchanged salutes and handshakes on that Hanover morning more than a century ago, the pair headed east for Magdeburg, capital of Saxony. Within weeks they would mastermind the battle of Tannenberg, taking 92,000 Russian prisoners. For two years they then worked to discredit Moltke's successor Falkenhayn, largely by example of a strategy on the Eastern Front that was more effective than Falkenhayn's in the west; and by proposing the annexation of a handful of eastern European states to the Second Reich. Having supplanted the chief of the general staff in the aftermath of the Verdun bloodbath and formed Dritte OHL, Hindenburg and Ludendorff surveyed their inheritance. They toured the Western Front and were dismayed by their discoveries both at the Somme and at Verdun. France and England had put their economies on a war footing and the Entente was beginning to enjoy growing superiority both in men and military equipment. The two Germans accordingly put in hand the Hindenburg programme. This was intended to increase Germany's output of munitions and weapons, and to address manpower issues by calling up men born in 1898. These 18-year-olds would be sent to reinforce both the Eastern and the Western Fronts. Nevertheless, they remained pessimistic. 'I spoke with Ludendorff,' recorded Generalleutnant Hermann von Kuhl, chief of staff of Prince Rupprecht's Bavarian army, on 8 September 1916. 'We were in agreement that a large-scale, positive outcome is now no longer possible. We can only hold on and take the best opportunity for peace. We made too many serious errors this year.' For Hindenburg, as he prepared for the Crown Council meeting in early 1917, the future was 'darker than ever'. He suffered 'the sense of frightful peril, of increasing pressure, of dwindling resources, of hard-pressed fronts, of blockade-pinched populations, of red sand running out in the time-glass,' that Churchill later said, 'lay heavily upon the leaders of Germany.'

In early 1917 Wilhelmine Germany was indeed facing challenges both on the fighting and the home fronts.

Although Imperial Germany was a military monarchy rather than a parliamentary democracy, the war could clearly not be continued without the support of the German people. It has been remarked that in modern warfare the home front became just as important as the actual fighting since it offered the material and psychological support that soldiers needed to persevere. As John Buchan said of the Great War itself, by this time Germany in 1917 was 'beginning herself to realise that in the long run the home front was the vital front'. At its outbreak the conflict had been greeted with an enthusiasm in Berlin that matched that in Vienna, Budapest, Paris, Moscow and London. In Munich, the young Adolf Hitler declared, 'I was carried away by the enthusiasm of the moment of and ... sank down upon my knees and thanked Heaven out of the fullness of my heart for the favour of having been permitted to live in such times'. Rupert Brooke, not an obvious soulmate of the future Führer, had taken a similar line. 'Now God be thanked who has matched us with His hour.' Neither in the Central Powers nor the countries of the Entente was this mood sustained much beyond the grotesque losses of the late summer and autumn of 1914. These casualties, of course, impinged as much on families at home as soldiers in the trenches. Although in the First World War the civilian populations of the belligerents were largely, though by no means entirely, shielded from direct hostilities, the conflict was brought home to the population of the Central Powers by way of their stomachs. Alexander Watson, the historian of the Central Powers at war, noted that by 1916, 'Not even the high casualties, the intervention of the new enemies or the annexationist war aims did more to destabilise Central European societies than the food shortages'.

In some respects these were the inevitable consequences of war. The despatch of millions of men – and horses – to the Eastern and Western Fronts robbed what were still significantly agrarian societies of their labour forces and, indeed, sources of motive power. At the same time, families at home sent what they could spare of their food to those facing infinitely more difficult and dangerous conditions in the trenches and elsewhere. The demands of war also compromised the system of internal food distribution, never spectacularly efficient in Germany and in wartime compromised by the black market which flourished everywhere. Food prices rose and by 1916 were double their pre-war levels.

As a consequence of the British blockade, particularly the Northern Patrol, supplies from overseas to the Central Powers also plummeted. Like Great Britain, Germany herself was far from self-sufficient in agricultural produce. She imported 25 per cent of her grain and 40 per cent of fats. By 1915, as the noose of the blockade began to tighten, Germany's total imports halved. Agricultural fertiliser was one of the major shortages, with the consequence that livestock brought to market was sometimes half its pre-war weight. Staples including bread were adulterated; wheat shortages saw wheat flour 'stretched' with maize, lentils, peas, soya beans, bran and – illegally – sawdust and sand; war bread, *Kriegsbrot*, eventually became a term of abuse, even when augmented by the delicacy of sausages made of rats' meat, a sort of contemporary 'currywurst'. With the advent in February 1916 of Britain's Ministry of Blockade, which would co-ordinate the multiplicity of efforts to throttle Germany, the situation deteriorated further. Coffee was now unobtainable. In Germany's second largest city, Hamburg on the Elbe, queues of 600 or 800 people would form in anticipation of a delivery of butter. That summer the first of the country's food riots took place: working-class women shouting for bread, raiding bakers, fighting police. By the autumn of 1916 in the aftermath of Verdun, Jutland and the Somme, these shortages seemed to herald the breakdown of law and order. Poor weather, a poor cereal harvest, and an even worse harvest of potatoes eventually forced the German population to subsist on turnips. This root vegetable was normally used as animal feed and was the only major source of carbohydrate widely available that winter of 1916/17. This was dubbed the *Steckrübenwinter*, the Turnip Winter. It was said that 80,000 children died of starvation, tens of millions went ill-nourished, and that female mortality rates soared. When a horse fell dead in a suburban street: 'In an instant, as though they had been lying in ambush, women armed with kitchen knives stormed out of the apartment building and fell upon the cadaver. They screamed and hit one another to get the best pieces as the steaming blood sprayed their faces.'

'The turnip winter of 1916–17,' says Watson, 'was the turning point; it was then that peoples' patience snapped. Disorder and protests before the winter were but a prelude to the ubiquitous, more violent and increasingly political street and industrial unrest that defined urban life in 1917.' German propagandists were certainly clear where the blame lay. They called the British efforts the 'starvation blockade'. Admiral Sir David Beatty, mindful of both the U-boat threat and the Royal Navy's own blockade, commented in January 1917, 'Our armies might advance a mile a day and slay the Hun in thousands, but the real crux is whether we blockade the enemy to his knees or he does the same to us'.

In Germany, the proposed panacea for these troubles had been debated at great length by the Oberster Kriegsherr, Admiralstab, OHL, by the Reichstag and the German public ever since the battle of Jutland on the last day of May and 1 June 1916. This was the resumption of unrestricted submarine warfare, not only against the Entente shipping but neutral merchantmen too. On 22 December 1916 the Admiralstab's C-in-C, Admiral Henning von Holtzendorff, circulated a memorandum updating and buttressing his previous submissions on the issue. The Pless Conference had been called by the Kaiser to discuss and resolve the matter, the final decision lying at least nominally in the hands of the supreme warlord alone. As the Kaiser mulled over Holtzendorff's memorandum, he was also obliged to take into account two recent events.

First, encouraged by Brusilov's success, on 28 August 1918 the Balkan state of Romania had declared for the Entente. The significance of this nation of nine million was partly military, partly because of her possession of the only reserves of oil in Europe and partly because of her plentiful supplies of wheat. It was a decision that horrified German public opinion, striking as it did against Austria–Hungary, the fatherland's vulnerable southern ally. Churchill wrote: 'the apparition in the field of Roumania with twenty-three organised divisions ... and the denial of the Roumanian supplies of corn and oil, seemed both to friend and foe ... one of the most terrible blows which Germany and her reeling partner had yet been called upon to encounter.' On 6 December 1916 German forces nevertheless entered the Romanian capital of Bucharest. Romania's war was effectively over, and what had seemed a fillip for the Entente in August proved at least a respite of some sort for the Central Powers. Yet Romania's defection was a painful reminder of how precarious was Germany's position, how few her friends. It seemed to herald defeat.

Secondly, as Christmas approached, events in Romania were coupled with the rejection by the Entente of German peace proposals. Such schemes had been in the air in all the belligerent capitals for some time, and had been publicly promulgated by Lord

Lansdowne in Britain in November and – more formally – by Germany herself on 12 December 1916. The very existence of these proposals was a recognition of the impasse that the war had reached. Despite terrible sacrifices, neither the Entente nor the Central Powers had gained the upper hand. Not unreasonably, Lansdowne thought that the continuation of the war would 'spell ruin for the civilised world'. For neither side did there seem any prospect of victory. This situation Holtzendorff's memorandum acknowledged: 'The war requires a decision before autumn 1917, lest it should end in the mutual exhaustion of all parties and thus is a disaster for us'.

Given this imperative, the remainder of Holtzendorff's argument was that, given the weakened state of France and Italy, it was England whose energy and resources were sustaining the war; that England herself would be defeated only if her backbone, her merchant fleet, was destroyed; that the exceptionally poor world harvest of grain that year made England peculiarly reliant on imports to feed her people; that the record of the U-boat fleet suggested it could now destroy more merchant tonnage than Britain could replace; and that a U-boat campaign – if it was unrestricted – would therefore force the Entente to negotiate. Holtzendorff argued that if the U-boats sunk 600,000 tons of shipping a month it would take just five months to bring Great Britain to the negotiating table. An armistice would be in force by August 1917, just before the harvest. For good measure, the Admiral concluded by claiming that Germany had no other option and that unleashing the U-boats was the only means of victory at her disposal. The Hochseeflotte had failed to deliver a decisive victory at Jutland and, as a consequence – in the language of *va banque* – was a busted flush. Victory, if it were to be achieved at all, would be won beneath the sea. For 1916, this was quite an idea.

Much as Asquith mulled over the strategic options volunteered by Churchill, Lloyd George and Maurice Hankey over the Christmas of 1914, so too did the Kaiser ponder Holtzendorff's arguments over Christmas of 1916. He was in a quandary. Persuasive though he found the admiral's proposals, he had hitherto always been swayed by the voice of moderation of Bethmann-Hollweg, the chancellor who was the driving force behind the idea of peace talks. His own mind he knew not. As the political creator of the federated Germany, Otto von

Bismarck had said, 'The Kaiser is like a balloon ... If you do not hold fast to the string, you never know where he will be off to.'

Before the war the chancellor had pursued a policy of detente with Britain. Her overwhelming power, especially at sea, he recognised. He had seen little in the two years since 1914 to make him believe that that force was failing. Where was the Hochseeflotte ruling the waves? Admiral von Spee's squadron – led by *Scharnhorst* and *Gneisenau* – lay mouldering at the bottom of the South Atlantic. The actions of Heligoland Bight and the Dogger Bank had both been misfortunes. *Skagerrakschlacht* – Jutland – had flattered to deceive. He had heard that repairs to one of Scheer's battlecruisers had only been completed in November. The fleet spent most of its time in harbour, where morale was said to be poor. The British had put Sir David Beatty in charge of the Grand Fleet, a more pugnacious fellow than Jellicoe, said the Admiralstab. He had moved the Grand Fleet from Scapa Flow to Rosyth in the Firth of Forth to be closer to the Wilhelmshaven bases of the Hochseeflotte. The United States was equally troublesome. As the furore that had followed the sinking of the *Lusitania* in May 1915 had demonstrated all too clearly, neutral nations whose shipping was imperilled by the strategy took unkindly to such atrocities. At the Kaiser's orders, it had been abandoned – other than in the North Sea – at the Crown Council meeting on 31 May 1915. The supreme warlord thought that 'to torpedo huge passenger ships full of women and children was a barbarous brutality without parallel, with which we will bring upon us the hatred and the poisonous rage of the entire world.' This opprobrium was to be avoided, especially – especially – from President Wilson's United States. America, they said, had a population of 120 million, double that of Wilhelmine Germany. If she had a tiny army of 108,000 then, like Great Britain herself, she would doubtless have no difficulty having a much larger one in due course. Her economy was now rivalling that of both Great Britain and of Imperial Germany herself; and it was an economy which, far from being bled dry by the war, had hugely benefited from it. Her net foreign trade from August 1914 until she declared war on Germany in April 1917 lay between $4.5

and $5 billion. Her industrial base, though not on a war footing nor producing a great deal by way of war materiel, was also greater than Germany's; indeed, the chancellor had heard that she now produced more steel than France, Germany and Great Britain combined. Finally, the chancellor argued, if America declared for the Entente, what sort of a signal would this send to their own allies, let alone the rest of the world? Romania had been quite bad enough. Wrote Churchill some time later:

> Suddenly a nation of one hundred and twenty millions unfurls her standard on what is already the stronger side; suddenly the most numerous democracy in the world, long posing as a judge ... hurls itself into the conflict. The loss of Russia was forgotten in this new reinforcement. Defeated movements were strangled on one side and on the other inflamed. Far and wide through every warring nation spread these two opposite impressions – 'The whole world is against us' – 'the whole world is on our side.'

Such had been the Chancellor's objections to Holtzendorff's proposals. The Kaiser found these, too, persuasive; indeed like George Orwell's farmyard animals, he 'listened first to Napoleon, then to Snowball, and could not make up [his] mind which was right; indeed, [he] always found himself in agreement with the one who was speaking at the moment.' In his difficulties, as a final set of advisers the Kaiser also had to bear in mind Ludendorff and Hindenburg themselves: Dritte OHL.

As Voltaire had quipped, Prussia was not so much a country but an army with a state attached, and it was Prussia and her army which had been the catalyst behind the creation of the federal German state in 1871. The army was quite literally the kingmaker. John Keegan talks of, 'the leaders of [Wilhelm's] army, the institution through which the Hohenzollern dynasty had risen to power, and to which it always looked to sustain its dignity and authority.' The Deutsches Heer enjoyed a degree of power the envy of its counterparts in Great Britain and France, strength which could only grow as the country's society and economy became subsumed by war. In August 1916 the Kaiser had formally invested that power in Hindenburg and Ludendorff. Like Lord Kitchener in England in the days of his pomp in the autumn of

1914, the pair symbolised the martial ardour of their country. They were seen as having saved Germany from the armed hordes of Slavs in the autumn of 1914 at Tannenberg, again at the second battle of the Masurian lakes in 1915. They had won plaudits for their imaginative proposals to colonise much of eastern Europe for Wilhelmine Germany. Their promotion by the Kaiser himself to supreme command presented them to the German people as the duumvirate who would deliver victory, victory where Helmuth von Moltke and Erich von Falkenhayn before them had failed miserably. The pair had yet to assume the qualities of a military dictatorship, but in January 1917 that was clearly where they were heading. Their Kaiser, the supreme warlord, was ever more the observer rather than director of events. Perhaps a little uncharitably, Liddell Hart calls him the 'chief puppet'. So it was that when the baggage of Dritte OHL arrived in advance of its owners on 8 January 1917 at the Schloss Pless, the supreme warlord suspected what was coming with it. Hindenburg and Ludendorff were quite well acquainted with the wider aspects of the war, and would have their own well-informed – if not necessarily judicious – views on unrestricted submarine warfare. For the Kaiser, the pair were all too patently the power behind the throne of the Oberster Kriegsherr, behind his own jewelled crown. That wintry January evening he glanced at Hindenburg and then looked again at that massive figure with those striking blue eyes set in that strange square head. He began to regret he had ever read *Frankenstein*.

After breakfast at the Schloss Pless on 9 January 1916 the pair, Dritte OHL, gave a formal verdict. They were, they said, in agreement with Holtzendorff and not the chancellor. The U-boats offered the only realistic prospect of victory for the Second Reich. They would do so rapidly, and they would relieve pressure on the Deutsches Heer while it was rebuilt after the debacle of Verdun and the Somme, while the economy of the country was put on a proper war footing. The threat of the United States should be discounted. Her army was tiny; perhaps contemptible would be a better word; and it was three thousand miles away over the great waters of the Atlantic, an ocean infested with U-boats. Without a means of transport the US Army would be restricted to manoeuvres at home in Texas and other such remote places, still some way from the Western Front. In 1803 Lord St Vincent had famously declared, 'I do not say they [the French] cannot come. I only say they cannot come by sea.' More than a century later in January 1917 his remarks were echoed by Admiral Eduard von Capelle, secretary of state for the Kaiserliche Marine when he assured the Reichstag budgetary committee of the impotence of the American forces. 'They will not even come, because our submarines will sink them. Thus America from a military point of view means nothing, and again nothing and for a third time nothing.' Dritte OHL said much the same to the Kaiser that January morning at the Schloss Pless.

So to the Kaiser himself. The decision lay in his hands, the hardest of his life. He understood that his beloved Hochseeflotte had failed – or at least had not succeeded – at Jutland. He realised that there was little prospect of victory on land, either in the east or to the west. He suffered that 'sense of frightful peril, of increasing pressure, of dwindling resources, of hard-pressed fronts, of blockade-pinched populations, of red sand running out in the time-glass,' that Churchill said, 'lay heavily upon the leaders of Germany.' Only the U-boats offered any prospect of victory; sooner or later unrestricted submarine warfare would surely bring in America on the side of the Entente. It was indeed a gamble, as the chancellor had told him, a game of *va banque*. The stakes could not have been higher. It was the fulcrum of twentieth-century world history. Churchill continued, 'If the Allies had been left to face the collapse of Russia without being sustained by the intervention of the United States, it seems certain that France could not have survived the war, and the war would have ended with a Peace by negotiation or, in other words, a German victory.' Here was the sword of Damocles. Thus the Kaiser, worn down by the arguments of his military and naval advisers, spurned the advice of Bethmann-Hollweg and capitulated. He accepted Holtzendorff's memorandum and recommendation. He would endorse a campaign of U-boat warfare unrestricted by the cruiser rules. The Admiralstab's submarines would have the freedom to destroy Allied and neutral merchantmen without warning and without concern as to the fate of their crews. Bethmann-Hollweg, noting the direction of the wind, acquiesced. The war would – he hoped – be over before America joined the Entente.

Churchill wrote:

However long the controversy may last, there will never be any agreement between the belligerent nations on the rights and wrongs of U-boat warfare. The Germans never understood, and will never understand, the horror and indignation with which their opponents and the neutral world regarded the attack ... To sink [a neutral vessel] incontinently was odious; to sink her without providing for the safety of the crew, to leave that crew to perish in open boats or drown amid the waves was in the eyes of all seafaring peoples a grisly act, which hitherto had never been practised deliberately except by pirates ... But the Germans were newcomers on salt-water [and] cared little for the traditions of seafaring folk.

Later that month of January 1917 the Kaiser gave vent to his resentment at what he felt was Germany's sanctimonious and hypocritical treatment by the United States. This was a country which he regarded as exploiting the miseries of the old world under the guise of what President Wilson would soon be calling a campaign 'to make the world safe for democracy'. Democracy indeed, said the Kaiser. 'The war,' he explained, 'is a struggle between two world views: the Teutonic-German of morality, right, loyalty and faith, genuine humanity, truth and real freedom; against the Anglo-Saxon [world view], the worship of Mammon, the power of money, pleasure, land – hunger, lies, betrayal, deceit and – last but not least, treacherous assassination!' On 31 January 1917 Germany officially informed the United States of her decision. Three days later President Wilson announced to Congress the severance of diplomatic relations with Germany. 'At the meeting in Pless,' concludes Christopher Clark, 'Wilhelm had presided over a decision of world-historical moment ... if Germany had not embarked on unrestricted submarine warfare against merchant shipping and the United States had stayed out of the war, a German defeat at Allied hands seems highly unlikely.'

10

The Plague Bacillus

'The endurance of Russia as a prime factor, until the United States
had entered the war, ranked second only to the defeat of the
German submarines as a final turning-point in the war.'

Winston Churchill

On 9 April 1917 a train steamed out of Zurich railway station straight
into the pages of history.

It carried the revolutionary firebrand Vladimir Lenin, leader of the
Bolsheviks, and thirty-two of his Communist brothers in arms.
Imperial Germany had promised Lenin safe conduct over its railway
system on his way to Petrograd (now once again called St Petersburg),
the capital of Imperial Russia. Here, thought the Kaiser and the
German chancellor, Lenin's presence would reignite the glowing
embers of the February revolution of 1917 that had seen the abdication
of Tsar Nicholas II and the installation of Prince Georgy Lvov's
provisional government. Chancellor Bethmann-Hollweg had also
thoughtfully provided Lenin with the stupendous sum of – reputedly
– 50 million marks. This would buttress his oratory, spread the word
of Marx, foment a Bolshevik revolution that would unseat the tepid
provisional government, cause Russia to withdraw from the war, and
rend asunder the Entente. When the February Revolution was duly
followed by an October Revolution of 1917, the storming of the Winter
Palace, the overthrow of the provisional government, the institution
of the Bolshevik administration, and – later – the Treaty of Brest-
Litovsk that saw the formal end to fighting on the Eastern Front, this
seemed to the Kaiser a wise decision and to the chancellor money very
well spent. When the proletarian revolution spread to Germany herself
with the mutiny of the Kaiserliche Marine in Kiel in October 1918, the
scarlet infection of the remainder of the country, the abdication of

Kaiser Wilhelm and the collapse of the Second Reich, it seemed less so. Michael Pearson wrote:

> It is one of the great ironies of history that without the help of the German Emperor – the arch-proponent of the imperialist capitalist system that Lenin was dedicated to destroy – Lenin could never have achieved what he did. His establishment of a socialist state, the first stage of which he hoped would be a world communist system, was made possible only by German co-operation, a German train, and the massive German finance that followed it.

The revolution which Lenin was to foment was one of the chief factors in the downfall of Wilhelmine Germany, and it was a pestilence which would infect the rest of the twentieth century and beyond.

The war had begun as a consequence of dissatisfaction felt by the ruled for their rulers: the assassination of Archduke Franz Ferdinand by a Bosnian Serb who took exception to Habsburg rule over his country. Amongst all the other principal belligerents – Imperial Germany, republican France, Great Britain and Russia herself – socialist ideas of one hue or another had taken root in the second half of the nineteenth century. Many of them found inspiration in the works of Karl Marx and Friedrich Engels – both native Germans – not to mention the reactionary politics of the rulers of Europe. Few Victorian monarchs, presidents, chancellors or prime ministers welcomed the rise of an intelligent, well-educated and articulate populace schooled in such pernicious documents as *The Rights of Man, The Communist Manifesto* or *Das Kapital*; even less desirable were reckless experiments like the Paris Commune and the First and Second International. Germany was in the forefront of the movement. 'No political development in Europe between the Franco-Prussian war and the first world war was more striking than the rise of the German Social Democracy,' wrote the historian A J Ryder. 'It is difficult ... to realise the strength of the hopes and fears aroused by this party, which by 1890 received more votes than any other party.' The advent of the twentieth century and the widespread industrialisation it brought had fuelled further calls for change. The workers were finding their voice. The Labour Party in Great Britain won its first seats in Parliament in 1902, Australia elected a Labour prime minister at much the same time, the nascent kibbutz movement took its inspiration from Zionist socialism, and in Russia the revolution of 1905 was essentially a socialist one. The war itself was a still more powerful catalyst, nationalism and patriotism morphing into political radicalism throughout Europe.

When Erskine Childers volunteered to fight in the Boer War, he wrote to his sister Dulcibella, 'Don't you think it would be splendid to do something for one's country?' In 1914 it was a sentiment cheered to the rafters through much of Europe. *Dulce et decorum est pro patria mori*, might Dulcibella have replied. For Horace, 'How sweet and honourable it is to die for one's country.' There again, like Vera Brittain, she might have had reservations about her brother risking his life for his fatherland. By 1915 the playwright Berthold Brecht had pointed out that it was sweeter and more fitting to live for one's country rather than to die. At much the same time, Sir Edward Grey told the Canadian Prime Minister Robert Borden that the burdens of war imposed on the people of Europe 'must result in the overthrow of all existing forms of government.' For John Buchan, 'Ancient constitutions began to crack, old faiths to be questioned, potent, undreamt of powers to be released.' By 1917, for Wilfred Owen, *pro patria* had become 'the old Lie'. As the casualty lists lengthened, the numbers of widows and orphans multiplied, as the circumstances of daily life deteriorated, and as strikes, civil disobedience and food riots broke out, particularly in the Central Powers, it was not surprising that those who had plunged Europe into its catastrophic war – not to mention the generals and admirals – should take the blame. Wrote Siegfried Sassoon:

> 'Good morning: good morning!' the General said
> When we met him last week on the way to the line.
> Now the soldiers he smiled on are most of 'em dead,
> And we're cursing his staff as incompetent swine.
> 'He's a cheery old card,' grunted Harry to Jack
> As they slogged up to Arras with rifle and pack
> But he did for them both by his plan of attack.

In England, in the wake of the Dardanelles fiasco and the resignation of the First Sea Lord, Jacky Fisher, Asquith's Liberals had first been replaced by a national coalition; Asquith himself was dismissed in favour of Lloyd George in December 1916. Fisher, prescient as ever and hopeful of a return to office, declared in August 1917, 'A revolution is coming along and the new Cromwell may want me!' The French had five leaders between June 1914 and November 1917, each discarded in favour of someone who appeared to know better how to win the war. In Russia the Tsar had been forced to abdicate. The end of the war would see the collapse of the Russian, Ottoman, Habsburg and Germany's own empires. If the people of Europe had lost faith in their political, naval and military leaders, who could these leaders blame but themselves? 'Dear child,' Vera Brittain's brother Edward had written to her on hearing of the death of her fiancé. 'There is no more to say; we have lost almost all there was to lose and what have we gained? Truly as you say has patriotism worn very threadbare.'

Lenin was born Vladimir Ulyanov in 1870 in Simbirsk, five hundred miles east of Moscow. Russia then was a country that stretched from the Baltic to the Pacific, in terms of surface area she was the world's largest state, boasted a population of 120 million, had an excellent secret police force, and was an acknowledged world power. She was also the home of Tolstoy, Turgenev, Dostoyevsky, Tchaikovsky and Mussorgsky. She had been drawn into the war by her alliance with Serbia, where Archduke Franz Ferdinand had, of course, been assassinated in June 1914. She had at her disposal huge numbers of men of military age, relatively little of the militarism of Germany, little equipment and – with the exception of General Aleksei Brusilov – not much by way of military leadership.

Son of an inspector of schools, Lenin was a highly intelligent, well-read and observant youth who soon became critical of the police state that was Tsarist Russia under the reactionary Tsar Nicholas III. At sixteen he was radicalised by the execution of his elder brother Alexander for plotting the Tsar's assassination. As a student at Kazan University he discovered Marx's *Das Kapital*, which argued that capitalism proceeded by the exploitation of labour, posited the class struggle between capital and labour, and anticipated a world revolution. Much taken by these ideas, Lenin became a revolutionary.

He graduated from St Petersburg University, plotted against the government, was arrested and found guilty of sedition. Following a period of internal exile in 1900 he went abroad. The following year he adopted the pseudonym Lenin. He pursued his studies of socialism in Geneva, Munich and London, becoming an ardent Marxist. In 1903 he founded the Bolshevik party, dedicated to world revolution. Switzerland, at the time a relatively welcoming country for those seeking political asylum, eventually became his home; here he developed a fondness for alpine walks and for cats. In 1915 he was living in the capital of Berne in extreme poverty when he attended the international socialist conference in nearby Zimmerwald. This famously declared, 'Either the war will kill the revolution or the revolution will kill the war.' Moving to Zurich, in February 1917 Lenin heard the spellbinding news of the spring revolution. His reputation in Russia, and indeed in Europe as a whole, was such that he was seen as the obvious man to take the events of that month to their logical, Bolshevik, conclusion. The provisional government in Russia ran counter to proletarian principles by still engaging in the war on the Eastern Front – a war which to Lenin was imperialistic, bourgeois and had caused around two million Russian deaths. Not least at the hands of Ludendorff and Hindenburg at Tannenberg and the Masurian Lakes.

For Wilhelmine Germany and the Third OHL, for Hindenburg and Ludendorff, for the Kaiser and the chancellor, Lenin represented opportunity. The idea of Schlieffen's plans had been to avoid war on two fronts, simultaneously against France and Russia. Their failure had committed Germany to just such a war. The February Revolution and Lenin seemed heaven-sent opportunities to remove Russia from the war. This would enable around fifty divisions of Germany's forces on the Eastern Front to be moved west: indeed, eventually for Ludendorff to deploy 192 divisions against 178 of the Allies. There they could deliver a knockout blow to the two remaining original members of the Triple Entente: England and France. It was true that the unrestricted submarine warfare of February and March 1917 had already shown most promising results. It was also true, though less happily, that on 6 April 1917 the United States had finally declared war on Germany. It was not surprising that just twenty-four hours earlier, the British ambassador in Berne had telegraphed the Foreign Office in London with the warning that Lenin's representatives were negotiating a safe passage of the revolutionaries through Germany – the Allies naturally debarring his passage. When Lenin and his party reached Russia, the ambassador expected that they would be commissioned by Germany 'to make violent propaganda among the working classes and among troops at the front.' For Imperial Germany, this was sufficiently familiar a policy to have spawned a word to describe it: *Revolutionierungspolitik*. The move would make assurance doubly sure. It was though, as Churchill remarked, a sombre if not desperate move. 'Ludendorff refers to it with bated breath.'

At around 50 million marks, it was also expensive, but then revolutions are. This was the sort of sum that would have bought the Kaiserliche Marine SMS *Bayern*, the newest of the Hochseeflotte dreadnoughts, the equivalent of Admiral Beatty's flagship, *Queen Elizabeth*. As it was, the money would be spent in Russia on the relatively new medium of propaganda. Mark for mark, this was arguably more cost-effective than *Bayern*, though not in the way anticipated. Writing to the Kaiser on 3 December 1917, the minister of foreign affairs Richard von Kühlmann explained, 'It was not until the Bolsheviks had received from us a steady flow of funds through various channels and under varying labels that they were in a position to be able to build up their main organ *Pravda*, to conduct propaganda to enlarge the originally narrow base of their party'. The ultimate implications of this German generosity forms a good if rather unhappy example of the law of unintended consequences. At Dritte OHL, claimed Generalmajor Max Hoffman, not necessarily truthfully, and if so, rashly, 'We neither knew nor foresaw the danger to humanity of this passage of the Bolsheviks to Russia.' Consequences, though, this journey would have.

The practical arrangements for the excursion were that a party of thirty-two revolutionaries – including women and children – would be transported in a sealed train. This was a legal designation which allowed the train to pass through a country without formally entering it, like transit passengers at an airport. It was a precaution devised by Lenin – a trained lawyer – with a view to preventing the seizure of the party by those unsympathetic to the great cause. 'They transported Lenin,' wrote Churchill famously, 'in a sealed truck like a plague bacillus from Switzerland into Russia'.

The party left Zurich at 1510 on 9 April 1917, the train first heading for the border town of Singen. It was not a very impressive train, comprising a single green carriage of eight compartments. Lenin had brought – or perhaps caused to have obtained – a kerosene stove and stores of food and drink to sustain the party. At first there was no restaurant car, Lenin himself, in any case, being abstemious. At Gottamadingen on the border itself the party was met by two German officers who had been briefed personally by Ludendorff. Under this escort the revolutionaries headed north for Karlsruhe, Frankfurt, Berlin and Sassnitz. Here they would take a steamer, *Queen Victoria*, for Sweden, thence north and east right round the Gulf of Bothnia to Finland and Russia. En route, though, trouble arose. According to one of Lenin's companions, Karl Radek:

There was a constant conflict between the smokers and the non-smokers about a certain location in the carriage. We could not smoke in the compartment, because of the little four-year-old Robert and because of Ilyich, who would not tolerate it. Hence the smokers tried to convert a room which normally served other purposes [the lavatory] into a smokers' lounge. Hence outside this room there was a permanent crowd of bickering people. So Ilyich cut a piece of paper in two and distributed permits. For every three tickets of category A for the legitimate use of the premises, there was one smoker's ticket. This naturally evoked further discussions about the value of human needs, and we acutely regretted that comrade Bukharin was not with us, as a specialist in Böhm Bawerk's theory about marginal utility.

On 16 April 1917, after a journey of a week and some two thousand miles, Lenin's Bolsheviks reached Finland station in Petrograd, Catherine the Great's 'window on the west'. Here, with the sort of stage management at which the Soviets later became adept, the party was greeted by a thronging crowd of thousands, a reception committee from the local workers' council or 'Soviet', and a booming rendition of the Marseillaise, the soundtrack of the French Revolution. 'To arms, citizens!' Clasping a bouquet and looking rather the worse for his trip, the 47-year-old Lenin donned a workers' flat cap and declared:

> Dear Comrades, soldiers, sailors, and workers! I am happy to greet in your persons the victorious Russian revolution, and to greet you as the vanguard of the worldwide proletarian army ... The piratical imperialist war is the beginning of civil war throughout Europe ... The hour is not far distant when at the call of our comrade, Karl Liebknecht, the German people will turn their arms against their own capitalist exploiters ... The worldwide Socialist revolution has already dawned ... Any day now the whole of European capitalism may crash. The Russian revolution accomplished by you has prepared the way and opened a new epoch. Long live the worldwide Socialist revolution!

Now what had originally been a war about territory – mainly French territory – became one of ideology. Not far off were the ten days which shocked the world.

In Austria–Hungary, Emperor Franz-Joseph had been succeeded in November 1916 by his great-nephew Carl, nephew of the assassinated Archduke Franz Ferdinand. He, at least, recognised that his ally Germany was playing with fire. As Lenin was arriving in Petrograd, Carl wrote to the Kaiser, 'We are fighting a new enemy which is even more dangerous than the Entente – the internal revolution. I implore you not to disregard this fateful side of the question.' Carl, presiding over the fragile dual monarchy and fighting both the Russians and the Italians, watched the events which unfolded in Russia over the summer of 1917 with dismay. For the men of the Kaiserliche Marine, though, these proceedings spelt hope. On 2 August 1917 the crew of *Prinzregent Luitpold* mutinied over the poor quality of rations. For Imperial Germany, it was first symptom of Churchill's plague.

11

Lloyd George's *Coup de Théâtre*

'The struggle between the British sailor-men, Royal and Mercantile – for both played an equally indispensable part – and the German U-boats stands among the most heart-shaking episodes of history, and its declared result would for generations be regarded as a turning-point in the destiny of nations. It was in scale and in stake the greatest conflict ever decided at Sea.'

Winston Churchill

God moves in a mysterious way his wonders to perform and much the same might be said of politicians. Still, David Lloyd George's stratagems and manoeuvres to defy the high command of the Royal Navy, save his premiership, and rescue the country from starvation and defeat by the U-boats threatened to put him – if not in the class of the supernatural – certainly in one entirely his own; that is, until 1940, Winston Churchill and the fighting on the beaches. Having consistently rejected professional advice from the Navy's high command, Lloyd George had junior naval officers smuggled into Downing Street to ascertain the real state of affairs at the Admiralty and the true facts of the case for convoys to defeat the U-boats – and much else besides. In the light of another catastrophic failure on the Western Front in the earlier part of April 1917, one offensive under General Robert Nivelle and its counterpart under Field Marshal Sir Douglas Haig, on 30 April the great radical pounced. In the company of Nathaniel Curzon in his capacity as member of the War Cabinet and Leader of the House of Lords, the prime minister struck out south from Downing Street and charged down Whitehall, a posse from the sally port of Number 10.

Most of April had been unusually cold, the temperature at the beginning of the month barely above freezing. The last week of the month was brighter and drier, temperatures in London – in Whitehall

– reaching 16°C. At the Admiralty, though, the atmosphere remained decidedly chilly. On the prime minister's arrival at the epicentre of the Royal Navy's power, Lloyd George recounted in his memoirs how he sat down in the First Lord's own chair at the head of the Admiralty Board and ordered the Navy to institute a system which it had bitterly resisted: the use of convoys to protect the ocean-going merchant ships that were the country's lifeline. According to A J P Taylor, this was 'the only occasion in British history when a prime minister had directed a great department of state in the teeth of the minister responsible for it.' Taylor further suggested that 'convoys were due to Lloyd George alone'. This is an overstatement: indeed, Lloyd George's own account of his *coup de théâtre* is a caricature. Yet the introduction of convoys as the decisive instrument to defeat the threat posed by the U-boats is undisputedly one of the main reasons the Entente won the war.

The spring of 1917 was a time of crisis for the Allies. The Triple Entente of Great Britain, France and Russia was soon to be shorn of its eastern component, with Lenin preaching Russian withdrawal from the war in his April theses and the country on the brink of another revolution. In France, Generalissimo Joffre's replacement, Robert Nivelle, had proved no more competent than his predecessor. In the month of April he masterminded the joint French and British attacks to the north and south of the Somme basin, the scene of Haig's bloodbath of the previous year. Despite the success of the Canadians at Vimy Ridge on 9/10 April 1917, the battle of Arras eventually ended with 150,000 British casualties to 100,000 German. To the south, Nivelle's great attack on the Aisne also failed at the cost of another 187,000 French casualties – a defeat already apparent by the time of Lloyd George's naval *coup d'état*. As to the submarine war itself, in that month of April, the cruellest of months, more than a million tons of British and neutral shipping was lost.

If the bright spot on the horizon was America's declaration of war on Germany on 6 April, the United States Navy was aghast at what it discovered in London about the Royal Navy's assessment of the U-boat campaign being perpetrated by Admiral von Holtzendorf of the Kaiserliche Marine. On 10 April 1917 Admiral William Sims of the US Navy had paid an unofficial visit to Admiral Sir John Jellicoe. Sims had travelled incognito from the United States on the steamship *New York*. The liner was mined just outside the Mersey. Rescued and taken ashore to Liverpool, Sims was met by Rear Admiral Hope of the Royal Navy, and rushed by special train to London for audiences with the American ambassador Walter Page and then Jellicoe himself.

A few months earlier the commander-in-chief of the Grand Fleet had been promoted rather against his will to the position of First Sea Lord. He replaced Admiral Sir Henry Jackson, who had himself succeeded Jacky Fisher. Like other fighting admirals before – and after – him, Jellicoe found the corridors of power little to his liking and ill-matched to his talents. Neither was his principal task of combating the U-boat campaign much to his taste. Sims, who was only just beginning to grasp the magnitude of the U-boat successes and who had been led to believe by the press that the losses were a quarter of the real figure that Jellicoe now disclosed, was aghast. He cross-questioned the First Sea Lord on the steps that might be taken to stem the tide. Their exchange, as recorded by Sims himself in *The Victory at Sea,* has gone down in history:

'It looks as though the Germans are winning the war,' I remarked.

'They will win, unless we can stop these losses – and stop them soon,' the Admiral replied.

'Is there no solution for the problem?' I asked.

'Absolutely none that we can see now ... It is impossible for us to go on with the war if losses like this continue.'

What with one thing and another, and despite the promise of future American aid, April 1917 really did look like defeat for the Entente, for Great Britain, for the Empire. There was more talk of a negotiated peace in the air and renewed fears in England that – with Russia wavering – France might make a separate peace. The hour was getting late. Jellicoe himself described the submarine campaign as 'the gravest peril which ever threatened the population of this country, as well as the whole Empire.' For Churchill, 'The hour was tragic. The U-boat sinkings to April, surpassing all previous records, had reached the total of 800,000 tons. The fatal curve was still rising and in British minds it dominated everything. "Let the armies fight while time still remained." Or in Lord Fisher's challenging phrase, "Can the Army win the war before the Navy loses it?"'

As Churchill himself had noted, at the beginning of the war neither the Central Powers nor the Entente had any real idea of the importance submarines would play in its course. The sinking by *U-9* of the British cruisers *Aboukir*, *Cressy* and *Hogue* on 21 September 1914, the exploits of British submarines in the Dardanelles in the spring of 1915 and in the Baltic thereafter, the sinking of the *Lusitania* by *U-20* on 7 May 1915, showed the shape of things to come. For a country as dependent as was Great Britain on overseas supplies for so much of what she needed to feed herself, let alone to make war, the advent of these craft made her remarkably vulnerable. As Admiral Reinhard Scheer had put it very simply to the Kaiser on 4 July 1916 in the aftermath of Jutland, 'England can only be injured by a war on her trade.' With Imperial Germany's surface commerce raiders like *Scharnhorst* and *Gneisenau* at the bottom of the South Atlantic and the Hochseeflotte unable to break out of the North Sea, the U-boats were now the only means by which this damage could be inflicted on sufficient scale. According to Holtzendorff, 600,000 tons a month would do the trick of bringing the British to the negotiating table. Following the 9 January meeting of the Crown Council at Schloss Pless, on 1 February 1917 the Kaiser had finally given his permission for the resumption of the campaign. Losses in January 1917 to the U-boats had amounted to 298,000 tons. They rose to 468,000 tons in February, to 500,000 tons in March, and to an astonishing 849,000 tons in April. It was a campaign against which the Royal Navy seemed powerless, and – certainly in the person of Jellicoe and his senior colleagues – peculiarly resistant to any imaginative attempt to counter the offensive. Despite a huge expansion of the British ship-building programme, the launch of replacement vessels could not keep pace with the losses; indeed the rate of loss was four times that of replacement. Hence Jellicoe's assessment to Sims: 'It is impossible for us to go on with the war if losses like this continue.'

Yet although the scale of the attacks was unprecedented, the essential nature of the campaign was not. From the beginning of the war the Admiralty had developed means of combating the U-boats. This comprised the mining of passages and channels used by the craft, the use of netting to entrap them like flies in amber, the arming of merchant ships – some disguised – and the deployment against the marauders of Royal Navy vessels, including its own submarines. These measures were developed by Churchill during his days at the Admiralty. They were moderately effective against what began as a modest campaign, but of the beginning of 1917 Churchill later conceded that 'the problem of actually attacking and destroying U-boats was still in a rudimentary stage'.

On his promotion to First Sea Lord in November 1916, Jellicoe's principal task was to develop a strategy to counter the U-boats. As the losses mushroomed in early 1917 following the Kaiser's lifting of the restrictions on his U-boat flotilla, the system of convoy was in some naval circles increasingly advocated. Rather than sailing singly and alone, groups of merchant vessels would be shepherded together by Royal Navy warships. This practice, introduced by Churchill himself at the beginning of the war for troopships, commonplace during the Napoleonic Wars and dating back to classical times, was vehemently rejected by Jellicoe and the Admiralty. It would rob the fleet of destroyers – escort vessels already in desperately short supply; the number – supposedly thousands – of ships leaving and arriving at British ports every week was far too large to permit such a strategy; the merchant vessels were incapable of keeping station within the convoy; the convoy itself merely formed a bigger target for the U-boats; and the convoy would steam only as fast as the slowest vessel. 'The highest professional opinion,' summarised Churchill, 'remained opposed to convoy as a defence against U-boats'. That of course included Jellicoe himself; also the director of the new Anti-Submarine Division (ASD) Jellicoe had established, Rear Admiral Sir Alexander Duff.

As the shipping losses rose and their consequence became all too apparent in England, Lloyd George was bound to interest himself in the matter. His own future, as well as that of country, was at stake. Like Churchill, he was a man of great independence of mind and was far from unquestioning of the professional advice he was given on a whole range of subjects with which he was concerned. His term as Minister of Munitions had been a bravura performance in which he had made hay with the ways, means – and people – with which the British government normally discharged its duties. He had become prime minister because the existing system and the existing men had failed to deliver the victory the country so desperately needed. He went so far in his disdain of the professional civil service to establish his own doppelgänger staff in a series of huts set up in St James's Park. These were dubbed the 'garden suburb'.

In the course of 1916, the year at the end of which Lloyd George became prime minister, the Somme debacle had caused the Welshman to lose faith in Field Marshal Sir Douglas Haig. Similarly, Jutland had tarnished the reputation of his opposite number in the Royal Navy, Jellicoe himself. Hence his replacement in November 1916 by the 45-year-old Admiral Sir David Beatty as C-in-C of the Grand Fleet. 'As War Secretary,' wrote the naval historian Dan van der Vat, 'Lloyd George had notably failed to change the attritional thinking of the generals, who continued to immolate the British Army in the mud of the Western Front. As Prime Minister he was determined to shake up the Admiralty.' Judging by Beatty's comments it needed it. The new C-in-C of the Grand Fleet visited the Admiralty on 17 April 1917, finding the institution in a state of 'chaos and indecision', finding himself 'worn out with their vacillation and hopeless condition of uncertainty about anything and everything.'

In his new guise as First Sea Lord, Jellicoe had assured Lloyd George in early December 1916 that convoys did, indeed, present too large and too easy a target for the U-boats. Lloyd George was sceptical. As the losses mounted he cast around for more constructive counsel. Maurice Hankey, another – essentially – civilian strategist, wrote to the prime minister in early February 1917 calling for the introduction of 'scientifically organised convoys'. In the course of a breakfast meeting with the prime minister on 13 February 1917 Jellicoe agreed to reconsider the matter and conduct a couple of low-key trials. He remained half-hearted and still the losses rose. The British reserve of wheat fell to six weeks' supply; the supply of oil for the fastest of Beatty's dreadnoughts dwindled from six months to eight weeks; the complete cessation of the cargoes of pit-props from Norway meant that coal production was on borrowed time; a scheme of voluntary rationing of food had already been introduced. Wrote Churchill, 'It seemed indeed that Time itself, hitherto counted as an incorruptible Ally, was about to change sides ... in April the great approach route to the south-west of Ireland was becoming a veritable cemetery of British shipping ... it was calculated that one in four merchant ships leaving the United Kingdom never returned.'

It was fortunate that that the Royal Navy, though a disciplined body of men, was not entirely rigid in its doctrine or thinking.

In the spring of 1917 the service was under the political direction of the First Lord of the Admiralty Sir Edward Carson and the professional guidance of the First Sea Lord – Jellicoe himself – the pair heading up the Admiralty Board. To many, Jellicoe seemed as inflexible in his thinking about maritime matters as Haig was about the trenches. One of his junior colleagues commented that he was 'a brave, patriotic and devoted man, though apparently incapable of agreeing to a new strategy and adept at finding unanswerable reasons to any change proposed.' Carson was a political appointee who by his own admission knew next to nothing about naval affairs and – by way of a dramatic contrast to his most prominent predecessor in the post, Winston Churchill – left the admirals largely to their own devices. On first meeting Tyrwhitt, the latter had written, 'He has brogue you can *see* ... He was very pleasant and told me he knew nothing about his job and wanted to know more.' A barrister by profession, the Dubliner had made his name as Queensberry's counsel in the Oscar Wilde libel case; he also chaired the Ulster Unionist Council determined to resist the long-standing cause of Irish Home Rule. Neither equipped him to tangle with the Senior Service. For Fisher, nuanced as ever, 'Carson is a tired, unfit, elderly lawyer, totally unfit to his position.'

Still, some other officers and officials did have ideas of their own. From very early in the war, men like Keyes and Tyrwhitt had acted as far as possible in the Nelsonian tradition of engaging the enemy more closely. As the war stretched from days into weeks, weeks into months and months into years, a body of men emerged in the service who railed against what they saw as the Admiralty's muted and passive prosecution of the war at sea – especially after the abrupt departure of Churchill and Fisher in May 1915 and the Navy's equivocal performance at Jutland a year later. Known as the 'Young Turks', one of these was a junior officer in the Admiralty War Plans Division, subsequently a Liberal MP, Commander Joseph Kenworthy. 'We were a group in mental revolt against the policy of the Board of the Admiralty ... and included officers in all ranks from the most senior downwards.' Amongst them were Beatty himself, Keyes, Tyrwhitt and Rosslyn Wemyss, who would go on to be the senior naval officer at the Armistice negotiations in November 1918. There was also Commander R G H Henderson, a man regarded as unusually numerate for a naval officer of the time. To this group, wrote Kenworthy, the 'British Admiralty appeared smitten with paralysis ... a huge bureaucratic machine ... designed only for day to day operations and administration ... with Sir Edward Carson as First Lord and Admiral Jellicoe as First Sea Lord ... seemed unable to readapt their strategy to the new conditions.' In the months after Jutland in the autumn of 1916, this group openly criticised the Admiralty's efforts. As the merchant shipping losses to the U-boats rose, so too did the degree of their winter's discontent. According to Kenworthy, they advocated three things. The introduction of the convoy system to better protect merchant ships; the prevention of the hostile submarines reaching the open sea; the use of the Navy's superior strength to regain the strategic initiative. After all, Beatty now commanded, in his own terms 'the greatest array of naval might ever assembled.'

Kenworthy himself, though, went further. As the son-in-law of the Liberal politician Sir Frederick Whitley-Thomson, he was familiar with the world of politics in a way unusual for naval officers. He also had some understanding of the levers of power. He recognised the symbiotic relationship between Lloyd George and the press, then at the height of its power in the days before radio and television. In the early spring of 1917 Kenworthy inveigled himself into the good graces of Lord Northcliffe. Proprietor of *The Times*, the *Daily Mail* and a clutch of evening papers, Northcliffe was the greatest press magnate of his age and a fearless proponent of the more vigorous prosecution of the war. Kenworthy found Northcliffe sufficiently receptive to the ideas of the Navy's unofficial opposition as to ask the commander to draft a written summary to be passed to Lloyd George and the War Cabinet. This Kenworthy duly did:

> On my next visit ... Northcliffe asked me if I dared go with him to Downing Street and tell the Prime Minister himself some of the things we had been discussing, face to face. He was good enough to warn me that the visit would be known and reported to the Admiralty, that there were spies everywhere, and that the arm of the Board was long.

A few days later, Kenworthy was smuggled into Downing Street by the back door into Horse Guards Parade, through the 'garden suburb' of other unofficial advisers, and into the Cabinet Room, a room in disarray in the aftermath of a War Cabinet meeting. It was not the usual way for a British prime minister to proceed. Kenworthy's account of the meeting opens:

> Northcliffe: 'Here is an officer, Prime Minister, who is not afraid to tell you the true state of affairs at the Admiralty.'
> Prime Minister: 'I am very glad you have been brought to me, Commander Kenworthy. It is not too much to say that everything now depends on the Navy. Sit down, and speak to me quite frankly.'
> Commander Kenworthy: 'I first of all want to tell you, sir, that the majority of officers in the Navy are very disappointed with the conduct of the naval war to date. They feel that the Germans are always given the initiative. We wait for them to make a move, and then try to counter it. We never seem to look ahead. The Navy so far has played a feeble part in the war.'

On this basis, it looked as though Lord Fisher's question was a reasonable one. 'Can the Army win the war before the Navy loses it?'

In the spring of 1917 this was the crux. Fisher himself had called this the 'VITAL QUESTION' in a letter of 23 April to Maurice Hankey. The secretary to the War Cabinet had replied:

> Your letter is the truest thing I have ever read. The question you pose sums up the whole thing in a nutshell. I feel my personal responsibility to be clear because from the very first day of the war, when I went to my chief on the announcement of the first of the 'K' [Kitchener] armies being formed and uttered a solemn warning against putting our faith in land forces. 'We may win on land, but lose on sea' I said, as it must inevitably react on our sea power. Now all our strength, all our material, all our men, all our manufacturing resources have been diverted to the military side of the war.

Meanwhile, Lloyd George's hopes – the hopes of the nation – of progress on the Western Front had certainly been raised by the advent of General Robert Nivelle.

Joseph Joffre's prodigal and largely unprofitable expenditure of Frenchmen's lives – quite a few English, too – had rendered him surplus to requirements. In December 1916 he was promoted to where he could do less harm, his dismissal disguised and dignified by the conferment upon him of the title Marshal of France. He soon discovered that he had been robbed of power. He complained, as others have done since, 'This is not what they promised me.' Still, the Marne in 1914 was his, albeit not his alone; and his appetite remained.

Nivelle was born in 1856 in Tulle in southwestern France and joined the French army in 1878. He at once specialised in artillery, of which he became an expert exponent and proponent. A veteran of the Boxer Rebellion, he was one of the most effective artillery officers on the Marne in 1914; and he developed an interest in the welfare – and survival – of his men that largely distinguished him from both Joffre and Haig. Nivelle, whose mother was English, was in fact for Lloyd George everything that Douglas Haig and Joseph Joffre were not. Articulate, charming, persuasive and – having made his name as an artilleryman at Verdun with the reduction of Fort Douaumont – apparently the possessor of the key to victory. Abandoning the war of attrition that had proved catastrophic for the Allies on the Somme and for the Germans at Verdun, Nivelle preached a new philosophy. It comprised a rolling barrage of artillery and a single rush, pierce or 'rupture' of the defending trenches. Less of a wave, more of a punch, this would break the deadlock. 'The artillery conquers; the infantry occupies,' he would declare. Like Churchill, Lloyd George was strangely reluctant to embark on another offensive against one of the Kaiser's Western Front strongpoints. His preference lay on the Italian front, where the Entente forces faced the less formidable opponents of Austria–Hungary. Nevertheless, the prime minister met Nivelle briefly at the Gare du Nord in Paris in the early days of January 1917 and was bewitched. Invited to meet the War Council in Whitehall a few days later on 15 January, Nivelle created a most favourable impression. Explained Churchill, 'The British Ministers had never met before in Council a general who could express himself in forceful and continuous argument, and they had never met before a French general who they could understand. Nivelle not only spoke lucidly, he spoke English. He had not only captured Fort Douaumant, he had an English mother.'

Nivelle planned to break through the German defences on the Aisne in forty-eight hours. Fifty miles to the north, the British were to provide a diversionary attack around the town of Arras, capital of the Pas de Calais *département*. The main British task was to recapture the Vimy Ridge, eight miles to the north of the historic centre of Artois; then to divert German reserves away from the French front. The French and British forces would meet behind the German lines and chase the opposing forces of Erster Generalquartiermeister Erich Ludendorff and Kronprinz Wilhelm – the Kaiser's eldest son – back to the German border. Casualties were expected to be in the order of 10,000; that is, just a sixth of those of British forces alone on the first day of the Somme. In Churchill's words it was a 'doctrine of the sudden general onslaught culminating in victory or defeat within twenty-four, or at the most, forty-eight hours.' For Lloyd George, the scheme also had the advantage of placing Nivelle in command of the man in whom he had lost faith, Field Marshal Haig. The Nivelle offensive which attracted such high hopes was set for early April, just as the U-boat sinkings soared. On it much depended.

꩜

It was regrettable that, not for the first time, the Germans also had plans. In the aftermath of Verdun, Falkenhayn's replacement Hindenburg and his Erster Generalquartiermeister Ludendorff had toured the Western Front. Dismayed by what they saw and heard, they determined to make changes.

In the course of the battle of the Somme, two bulges or salients in the line had been created. They lay between Arras and St Quentin, and between St Quentin and Noyon in the Hauts de France *département* to the southeast of Arras. They were the shoulders of the Somme battlefield. Ludendorff decided to withdraw from these salients to a line further east, easier to hold, and altogether more substantial. He called it the Siegfriedstellung or Fortress Siegfried; the Allies, when they discovered its creation and name dubbed it the Siegfried or Hindenburg line. By shortening his line by twenty-five miles, Ludendorff reduced the number of troops necessary to defend the front by thirteen divisions. This was quite a stroke. To this the Erster Generalquartiermeister added by applying a scorched earth policy to the land over which Nivelle's forces would need to advance towards the new line. Wells were poisoned, roads broken up, buildings booby-trapped, drainage systems destroyed. In early February 1917 the Germans withdrew. Ludendorff buttressed this advantage by capturing the plans of Nivelle's offensives, by straightforward observation of the French preparations for battle, and by virtue of the terrible weather of that spring of 1917 in northeastern France: wind, rain, sleet, mist, snow.

At first, though, all went well for Nivelle. The preliminary attacks by the French Third Army at St Quentin in the early days of April saw the successful seizure of defences in front of the Hindenburg line. On 9 April 1917 the British 3rd Army attacked to the east of Arras, achieving the biggest advance made since the institution of trench warfare of 6000yds. To the north the 1st Army attacked from Ecurie to Vimy Ridge in an advance of 4000yds, all four divisions of the Canadian Expeditionary Forces fighting together for the first time. 'The success of the Canadians was sensational,' commented John Keegan. The much-heralded breakthrough seemed at hand, and the main French offensive on the Aisne opened on 16 April.

Yet then, it seemed as ever, the offensive lost momentum. Despite significant tactical gains on the Chemin des Dames and in Champagne, the intelligence failures, the weather and the German defences all played against Nivelle. The first day alone saw 100,000 casualties; the French casualty clearing-stations, instructed to expect a tenth of that figure, were overwhelmed. No major breakthrough was achieved:

> The headlong pace of the advance was nowhere long maintained. There was a perceptible slowing down, followed by a general halt of the supporting troops which had been pressing heavily forward since zero hour. German machine guns, scattered in shell holes, concentrated in nests, or appearing suddenly at the mouths of deep dugouts or graves, took fearful toll of the troops now labouring up the ragged slopes of the hills.

On 25 April 1917 the main offensive was suspended. Four days later, Nivelle – refusing to resign – was sacked. The losses included not only 29,000 irreplaceable French lives out of a total of 187,000 casualties, but a virtually complete loss of fighting spirit. The late spring mutinies of 1917 followed. This saw fifty-one French divisions refusing to obey orders, 100,000 *poilus* court-martialled, thousands deserting. Despite the Canadian success at Vimy Ridge, despite Nivelle's offensive achieving greater advances with fewer casualties than hitherto, no breakthrough, no decisive battle, not even real tactical advantages had been achieved. The British casualty list was 160,000 strong. Commented Martin Gilbert, 'A dent of four miles had been made along ten miles of German front line.'

Vera Brittain's brother Edward wrote of one of the casualties of the offensive, his Uppingham schoolfriend Victor Richardson. 'Victor got a bullet right through the head behind the eyes. I'm afraid the sight has gone entirely; the left eye had to be removed in France and a specialist here thinks there is no hope for the right eye; the optic nerve is severed. It is a tragedy which leaves one stupefied and he had such beautiful eyes.'

On 30 April 1917 as Lloyd George closed the door of Downing Street behind him and headed up Whitehall for the Admiralty, he was not in

a good mood. The answer to Fisher's question seemed to be 'no'. The Army couldn't win the war and there seemed every prospect of the Navy losing it. The convoys must be instituted before it was too late. Lloyd George wrote in his memoirs:

> It was clear that the Admiralty did not intend to make any effective moves in the direction of convoying. After first discussing the matter with Sir Edward Carson, I informed the Cabinet that I had decided to visit the Admiralty and there take peremptory action on the suggestion of convoys. Arrangements were accordingly made ... that I should attend a meeting to investigate with them all the means at present in use in regard to anti-submarine warfare. I reserved the right to send for any officers, whatever their rank, from whom I desired information ... Apparently the prospect of being over-ruled in their own sanctuary galvanised the Admiralty into a fresh inquisition, and by way of anticipating the inevitable they further examined the figures which Commander Henderson had prepared in consultation with Mr Norman Leslie of the Ministry of Shipping.

Contrary to the Admiralty's own belief, around 140 ocean-going vessels a week would need to be escorted, rather than 2500. The former was a manageable number; the latter derived from the Admiralty's original estimates which included coastal shipping, Thames barges and even ferries on the Solent. The Ministry of Shipping had been able to put the Admiralty right. 'Accordingly', continued Lloyd George, 'when I arrived at the Admiralty I found the Board in a chastened mood. We discussed the whole matter in detail and agreed to conclusions which I thus reported to the Cabinet.' He wrote that 'I was gratified to learn from Admiral Duff that he had completely altered his views in regard of a system of convoys, and I gather that the First Sea Lord shares his view.'

Lloyd George's memoirs – like Churchill's and virtually everyone else's – are, of course, self-serving. The Admiralty's about-face was undoubtedly more considered and complex than as represented by the prime minister. Carson, the First Lord of the Admiralty, with the sort of rhetorical flourish not entirely unknown among QCs and politicians, called the PM's account 'the biggest lie ever told'. Moreover, the sudden and recent availability of United States Navy destroyers to serve as escort vessels undoubtedly made the convoys markedly more practicable. Nevertheless, the notion that Lloyd George was the driving force behind the institution of convoys that April is difficult to deny. Commented the prime minister's biographer John Grigg:

> The idea that he went to the Admiralty, sat in the First Lord's chair, and imposed the convoy system on a still implacably hostile board is in a strict sense mythical; and it is also a myth that his visit was the culmination of a sustained and unrelenting struggle on his part. But myth is often an exaggeration or oversimplification of truth, and it was something of both in this case.

The convoy system was started for inward-bound ships on 10 May 1917, extended to outward-bound in August 1917. Entirely contrary to the Admiralty's belief, the convoys were no easier for the U-boats to find than a single ship, and they were far better protected. Even the official history concedes 'the chief objections urged against the system before it was tried had one and all proved to be unfounded.' Reflecting the piecemeal way in which convoys were introduced, the sinkings fell gradually. Worldwide shipping losses in May were down to 600,000 tons, of which 345,000 were British. They rose marginally in June, then fell again to 550,000 in July, 500,000 tons in August. Losses by the end of the year fell to half their April peak. The attrition rate had fallen from 25 per cent to 1 per cent. Wrote Churchill, 'By the end of October 1917, 99 homeward convoys, comprising steamers of deadweight capacity 10,656,000 tons, had been brought in with a loss of only 10 ships torpedoed while actually in convoy, and of 14 which had become separated'. This, as Churchill again pointed out, was a triumph both of the Royal Navy and the British merchant marine. 'By the end of the year,' concluded Churchill, 'it was certain we should not succumb.' As to the significance of the victory, Lloyd George, again, had his views. 'The great Allied triumph of 1917 was the gradual beating off of the submarine attack. This was the real decision of the war, for the sea front turned out to be the decisive flank in the gigantic battlefield'. For Churchill, 'Its declared result would for generations be regarded as a turning-point in the destiny of nations.' John Grigg described it as 'A victory analogous to that of the Battle of Britain a generation later.'

Haig had not been best pleased by Lloyd George's attempt at the beginning of 1917 to place him under Nivelle's overall command; moreover, he had misgivings about the whole philosophy of Nivelle's 'rupture'. Still, in the end he had acquiesced. Credit for such success as was obtained at Arras was largely given to his subordinates General Sir Hubert Gough and Lieutenant General Sir Julian Byng – not to mention the latter's Canadian Army Corps. Now the mutinies which left the French army in crisis left the battlefield open to Haig. Asked Fisher: 'Can the Army win the war before the Navy loses it?' With the Navy now gaining the upper hand over the U-boats and prosecuting the blockade with greater success than before, as the autumn of 1917 drew on the tables seemed to be turning. It was the Army's turn under the microscope. The focus was now on another major British offensive on the Western Front. It would go down in history as Third Ypres, popularly for its final phase as Passchendaele. In John Keegan's phrase, Britain's 'most notorious land campaign of the war'.

As for Vera Brittain's friend Victor Richardson, blinded by a machine-gun bullet at Arras, on 9 June 1917 he had died.

12

Don't Do it Again

'The theatre was crowded with generals and officers ... I could not even get a seat, but stood at the wings of the stage. Tom [Colonel Tom Holland] spoke very well but his tale was one of hopeless failure, of sublime heroism utterly wasted and of splendid Scottish soldiers shorn away in vain ... with never a ghost of a chance of success. 6000 killed and wounded out of 10,000 in this Scottish division alone. Alas, alas. Afterwards they asked what was the lesson of the lecture. I restrained an impulse to reply, "Don't do it again." But they will – I have no doubt.'

Winston Churchill, 17 January 1916

On 20 June 1917 the British Cabinet effectively made a decision that sent 70,000 infantrymen to their deaths. It did so at Field Marshal Haig's behest, aided and abetted by the First Sea Lord, Admiral Sir John Jellicoe. Five weeks later on 30 July 1917, on the eve of the series of battles that would become known as Third Ypres, rather better by their notorious final phase of Passchendaele, Haig pronounced this was 'the critical moment of the war'.

The concurrence of Army and Navy was unusual. The Royal Navy was the Senior Service, the shield of the nation, the embodiment and expression of national pride. In late Victorian times the British Army was seen as an imperial police force of less moment, certainly by comparison with the million-strong forces of France and Imperial Germany. 'To every right-thinking Englishman,' wrote Jan Morris, 'the Army was only a second shield. The Pax [Britannica] was primarily a peace of the sea, and the little land wars of the Empire were only picturesque asides.' Despite skirmishes like the Anglo-Zulu War and the Boxer Rebellion, the Army had hardly covered itself in glory during the two Boer wars. Colenso, Magersfontein and Stormberg were national embarrassments, albeit misfortunes later redeemed by the relief of Ladysmith and Mafeking. The naval race between England and Germany that dominated the reign of Edward VII largely eclipsed the story of the army reforms of that age. The outbreak of war, the recall of Lord Kitchener, the despatch of the BEF to France, the raising of the great Kitchener armies, the fiasco of the Dardanelles and the absence of a decisive battle at sea saw the two sister services develop into rivals for the increasingly scarce resources of manpower, Cabinet confidence, public funding and public goodwill. Both had grown as a consequence of what had become a voracious, unquenchable and all-consuming conflict. The Navy almost doubled in size from 200,000 towards an eventual 400,000; the Army from a similar figure to around ten times that size – 4,000,000. Hugely to Jacky Fisher's annoyance, the Navy had become what Sir Ivor Philipps MP would refer to as a 'subsidiary service'. It was not surprising that the public came to believe that the war was being mainly fought on land, indeed on the Western Front. When forced to co-operate in the Dardanelles, the two services did so with success only when it came to the evacuation of January 1916. In 1903 Erskine Childers had written, 'We have no theory of national defence, and no competent authority whose business it is to give us one ... co-operation between army and navy is not studied or practised.' Even by 1917 little had changed, despite the Navy acting as the Army's lifeline, not only on the Western Front but in supporting armies of three-quarters of a million in Macedonia and more than a million in Palestine. The military historian Allan Mallinson recently described Jellicoe as Haig's 'unlikely ally' in his attempts to win over Lloyd George to the 1917 offensive of Third Ypres.

After the catastrophes of Haig's Somme offensive of 1916 and of Robert Nivelle's great 'rupture' of the spring of 1917 on the Aisne, there were many English and Frenchmen who questioned the need for any fresh land offensive whatsoever. With the United States of America now allied with the Entente as an 'Associated Power', her multitudes would in due course be at the Allies' disposal in France and Belgium. Indeed, the pioneer forces of General John Pershing's American Expeditionary Force were already on their way, largely courtesy of the Royal Navy. In the House of Commons on 10 May 1917 Churchill asked a critical question. 'Is it not obvious that we ought not to squander the remaining armies of France and Britain in precipitate offensives before the American power begins to be felt on the battlefield?' Answer came there none, so Haig was recalled from France to explain his enthusiasm for a new offensive. With the field marshal, Lloyd George took a similar line to that of Churchill. The Cabinet, he told Haig in a letter that followed the field marshal's meeting with the newly formed War Policy Committee (a subset of the Cabinet) on 19 June 1917, 'must regard themselves as trustees of the country's servicemen'. It must ensure that they were 'not sacrificed on mere gambles'. The prime minister was more than mindful that he had backed the wrong horse in the outwardly plausible and highly articulate Nivelle. He was determined to avoid repeating his mistake. He had got the best of Jellicoe at the end of April 1917 over the matter of the convoys. Now Haig – the Chief of Imperial General Staff Sir William Robertson, too – was in his sights. John Buchan wrote carefully:

Mr Lloyd George had never believed in the dogma of his military advisers that the Western Front was the only decisive area. He did not greatly believe in soldiers, since he distrusted all hierarchies and was constitutionally disinclined to submit to the dictation of experts. He thought, not without reason, that, since they were engaged in a new kind of war, the ordinary staff officers had little to their credit except a certain familiarity with an out-of-date technique.

To Lloyd George, Third Ypres seemed a gamble.

In Flanders fields, close to the town of Ypres, the British occupied a salient. It suffered under both the scrutiny and the gunfire of the German armies on the higher ground, the half-moon of low hills to the south and the east. Haig envisaged a campaign that would first wrest control of the ridges, then to open the way for a drive towards the Belgian North Sea ports of Zeebrugge and Ostend. Here the Kaiserliche Marine based some of its U-boats. Should it succeed, the offensive might – might – not only roll up the whole of the northern end of the German front, but cripple the U-boat campaign too. For John Buchan, it was 'a scheme which promised the most profound and far-reaching of consequences'. So ran Haig's argument. It might also win the war before the advent of large numbers of American troops.

A J P Taylor commented uncharitably that Haig 'preferred an unsuccessful offensive under his own command to a successful one under someone else's'. It should be added that Buchan – writing much earlier – thought such vanity improbable.

From the very beginning the plan attracted sceptics. Their objections were fourfold. The Deutches Heer, recognising the strategic importance of the Ypres ridges, had, in Churchill's words, fortified them 'with every resource of German science and ingenuity'. There were nine layers of defence in what Erster Generalquartiermeister Ludendorff called 'the Flanders position'. Given the extent to which the heights commanded the salient below, there was no possibility whatsoever of surprise. With the French still *hors de combat* and deeply demoralised in the aftermath of the Nivelle catastrophe, the onus of the offensive would fall on the British virtually alone. Their forty divisions were scarcely stronger than those serving under one of the Kaiser's best commanders, Crown Prince Rupprecht of Bavaria. Finally, three years of fighting round the largely ruined town of Ypres – the last major Belgian town in Allied hands – had destroyed all the vegetation and drainage of the battleground and turned it into a quagmire. Robertson himself, other British generals, Haig's own intelligence staff and their counterparts in London were more than mindful of these problems; seemingly more mindful than Haig himself. General Henri Pétain, who had replaced Nivelle as C-in-C of the French armies in May 1917, declared that 'Haig's attack towards Ostend was certain to fail'. Ferdinand Foch, his superior as the French chief of the general staff, said 'the whole thing was futile, fantastic and dangerous'.

It was true that the doubts of the French and those of Haig's own colleagues were concealed from the War Policy Committee. Yet at their meeting in the Privy Council Office on 19 June 1917, the committee still hesitated. With something like parity in infantry and artillery, why would the offensive succeed? Were not the defences in Flanders amongst the strongest on the Western Front? What was the precedent for reaching Zeebrugge and Ostend? Could the ports be taken at the end of long communication lines? Unimpressed by Haig's answers, arguments and retorts, Lloyd George wrote to him the evening of 19 June 1917 that deferring any offensive until the arrival of the Americans in force and the recovery of French fighting spirit should be carefully considered. So, too, the possibility of reinforcing the Italian army against the Austro-Hungarians in the Dolomites, another front of current concern and always appealing as a theatre to Lloyd George. Like the rest of the committee – indeed the Cabinet as a whole – he had little appetite for the casualty lists that had been despatched from the Somme. Why, the committee wondered above all, should this campaign succeed when – despite all Haig's assurances – the Somme had failed? It was at this point in the two days of discussions in the Privy Council offices, on 20 June 1917, that Admiral Jellicoe intervened.

By the end of 1917 it had become apparent that the Royal Navy had largely mastered the U-boat campaign. Losses had fallen from the April peak of 849,000 tons to considerably less than half that figure. Yet at the time of the debate on Third Ypres in June 1917, sinkings still stood higher than the 600,000 tons a month that the Admiralstab in Berlin believed would force Britain to the negotiating table. The convoy system, though instituted, had yet to take much effect. The possibility of being blockaded into defeat remained very real. Jellicoe, too, was a worrier and a pessimist. He abruptly told Lloyd George's meeting that it was 'improbable that we could go on with the war next year for lack of shipping'. The U-boats could not be tamed at sea, he said. The solution lay in seizing their bases on the Belgium coast. This, Haig's great 'northern offensive' would achieve. Wait for the Americans? 'There is no good discussing plans for next spring,' declared the First Sea Lord. 'We cannot go on.'

This was misleading. Although the Flanders flotillas played a part in the U-boat campaign, the main German U-boat forces were based in the ports on the German North Sea coast and the island of Heligoland. The seizure of the Flanders bases would have been of tactical, not strategic significance. (Indeed, so it proved when Admiral Roger Keyes pulled off his great stroke of the war, the Zeebrugge Raid of April 1918). This was a point of which Jellicoe was perfectly well aware. He felt that something was better than nothing; probably, too, that the Flanders U-boats tied up British light forces best spent guarding the vital communication lines with France, the umbilical cord without which the BEF would have collapsed. As it was, though, Jellicoe's intervention tipped the balance in favour of the offensive. The Cabinet eventually agreed to Haig's proposals a month later on 25 July 1917.

The caveat was that it should proceed – as Haig duly promised – step by step. 'It must on no account be allowed to drift into a protracted, costly, and indecisive operation as occurred in the offensive on the Somme.' The prime minister's doubts remained, though as a civilian he felt that he could scarcely 'impose my strategical views on my military advisers'. Not that such scruples had stopped him with Jellicoe and the convoys.

The consequences were momentous. On 16 June 1917 Churchill had returned to the government as Minister of Munitions, rescued from the wilderness by Lloyd George. He commented:

> Whatever influence this erroneous argument may have had upon the Haig–Robertson decision to launch a new offensive, it certainly contributed to baffle the objections of the Prime Minister and the War Cabinet. It seemed to throw the army into the struggle against submarines. It confused the issue, it darkened counsel, it numbed misgivings, overpowered the dictates of prudence, and cleared the way for a forlorn expenditure of valour and life without equal in futility.

It was just at this time that Vera Brittain's brother Edward returned to the Western Front, now invested with the Military Cross.

To be fair to Haig, what clearly was a gamble was attended by ill-fortune. Though summer in Flanders often broke in very early August, three days of downpour on a surface that had already endured fifteen days of bombardment stopped his offensive in its tracks on 4 August 1917. Sir Hubert Gough's 5th Army had reached the Pilckem Ridge, but Prince Rupprecht's forces still held much of the high ground; Sir Herbert Plumer's 2nd Army had largely failed. Initial French and British casualties amounted to 35,000. Haig reported to the War Cabinet that the offensive 'had been highly satisfactory and losses slight'. When it was resumed on 16 August in the face of determined German counter-attacks, progress was slow. Gough described the battlefield:

> ... battered, beaten and torn by a torrent of shell and explosive ... such as no land in the world had yet witnessed – the soil shaken and reshaken, fields tossed into new and fantastic shapes, roads

blotted out from the landscape, houses and hamlets pounded into dust so thoroughly that no man could point to where they had stood, and the intensive and essential drainage system utterly and irretrievably destroyed. This alone presents a battleground of tremendous difficulty. But then came incessant rain. The broken earth became a fluid clay; the little brooks and tiny canals became formidable obstacles, and every shell-hole a dismal pond; hills and valleys alike were but waves and troughs of a gigantic sea of mud. Still the guns churned this treacherous slime. Every day conditions grew worse. What was once difficult now became impossible. The surplus water poured into the trenches as its natural outlet, and they became impassable for troops; nor was it possible to walk over the open field – men staggered wearily over duckboard tracks. Wounded men falling headlong into shell-holes were in danger of drowning. Mules slipped from the tracks and were drowned in the giant shell-holes alongside. Guns sank till they became useless; rifles caked and would not fire; even food was tainted with the inevitable mud. No battle in history was ever fought in such conditions as Passchendaele.

The village which gave its name to the last battle was one of the first objectives of the campaign. It was just four and a half miles beyond the British trenches. In 1914 this was perhaps ninety minutes' walk. Ostend and Zeebrugge lay beyond, quite a lot beyond, both ports lying about forty miles to the north. As autumn drew on and the evenings drew in, the ports and the U-boat bases were mentioned by Haig less frequently in his despatches to the Cabinet. Lloyd George attempted to halt the operation to cut the Allied losses, took advice from other British generals – Wilson and French – who recommended its abandonment, thereby courted Haig's resignation, and despaired over the casualty lists. Passchendaele, though, remained. It was a vantage-point which certainly commanded the gruesome scene below, though a site only. All that existed by October 1917 was, in Keegan's evocative phrase, 'the smear of the brick that represented all that remained of the village.' This was indeed duly captured on 11 November 1917 after a campaign that lasted almost two months and provided some of the Commonwealth forces – notably the New Zealanders and Canadians

– with the worst days in their military histories. The capture of Passchendaele nevertheless allowed Haig – in Allan Mallinson's words – 'to call off the offensive while claiming success.'

It would be charitable to Haig to call this a moot point. A J P Taylor commented:

> Then Haig stopped. The 'campaign had served its purpose'. What purpose? None. The British line stuck out in a sharper and more awkward salient than before the battle began. All the trivial gains were abandoned without a fight in order to shorten the line when the Germans attacked again the following year. The British casualties were something over 300,000; the Germans under 200,000 – a proportion slightly better than the Somme.

Martin Gilbert called the seven weeks it took to seize the ridge, 'seven of the most terrible weeks in the history of British warfare'. As for Keegan:

> The point of Passchendaele, as the Third Battle of Ypres has come to be known, defies explanation ... what is unarguable is that nearly 70,000 of [Haig's] soldiers had been killed in the muddy wastes of Ypres battlefield and over 170,000 wounded. The Germans may have suffered worse ... statistical disputes make the argument pointless – but, while the British had given their all, Hindenburg and Ludendorff had another army in Russia with which to begin the war in the west all over again. Britain had no other army. On the Somme [Haig] sent the flower of British youth to death or mutilation; at Passchendaele he had tipped the survivors into the slough of despond.

Leaving aside the human cost – if that is at all possible – the initial bombardment of 4.5 million shells cost £22 million. This sum would have given the Grand Fleet another ten dreadnoughts. The United States Navy when it joined forces with Admiral Beatty's Grand Fleet in 1917 provided five.

When Reginald Blomfield's great memorial to the fallen of Ypres at the Menin Gate was unveiled in 1924, Siegfried Sassoon wrote that the dead of the Ypres salient would 'deride this sepulchre of crime'. Its barrel-vaulted 'hall of memory', on which the names of those Commonwealth soldiers who died in the salient but who have no known graves, was found to be too small for the task. It carries the names of 54,395 men; the remaining 34,984 are to be found in the nearby Tyne Cot cemetery. The sounding of the Last Post at the Menin Gate, a ceremony undertaken continuously since 2 July 1928 – except during German occupation in the course of the Second World War – remains the most moving of memorials to the fallen of the Great War.

In England such promise as 1917 had ever possessed was very largely dispelled by December. It was true that the U-boat campaign was at least in check, partly due to the convoy system and partly due to a multiplicity of other measures introduced by the Navy – mines, submarines of its own, surface forces and netting. It was also true that the Hochseeflotte barely ventured out of Wilhelmshaven and was no longer regarded by the Admiralty as a significant threat. Increasingly, the Kaiserliche Marine seemed subdued. Yet the two great land offensives of the war – Nivelle's in the spring, Haig's in the summer and autumn at Ypres – had both been catastrophes. At Ypres, dead and injured on both sides amounted to around half a million, never more than an approximate figure because of numbers of bodies never found, consumed as they were either by shellfire or the mud, indifferent as these agents were to the nationality of their victims. Such was the prodigal expenditure of manpower that there was little hope of an Allied offensive in 1918. Few volunteered for the Army any longer. Conscription, introduced in January 1916, was broadened to include men of forty-five.

Dritte OHL could be marginally more optimistic, despite the losses it had suffered at Third Ypres, and despite the increasing threat of food riots and famine on the home front. Alongside Ypres, Ludendorff had ventured to support his Austro-Hungarian ally on the Italian front. The battle of Caporetto in late October 1917 saw the Italians pushed back seventy miles, losing 200,000 men. In Russia, Lenin's Bolsheviks were edging towards an armistice, and it was apparent to Ludendorff that soon he would no longer have to fight a war on two fronts. The Russians, long incapable because of the morale of their troops of mounting an offensive themselves, were really already out of the war. Dozens of Ludendorff's divisions from the Eastern Front would be transferred to the West, perhaps thirty-five in all and, according to Churchill, one million men. The Kaiser's forces on the Western Front would soon for the first time since 1915 outnumber those of the Allied powers by 191 divisions to 178. Though the first of Pershing's US troops had landed in France on the fitting date of 4 July – Independence Day – 1917, it would be summer 1918 before any substantial number of them would be ready for battle. Colonel Albrecht von Thauer, one of Ludendorff's general staff officers, declared, 'Since the start of the year our situation was never really so good'. For Churchill, 'Russia [was] down, Italy gasping, France exhausted, the British armies bled white, the U-boats not yet defeated, and the United States 3000 miles away.' For Dritte OHL, the early months of 1918 represented a window of opportunity before the United States could exercise its will, perhaps its last chance. As the U-boat campaign was not delivering Holtzendorff's promise, the Deutsches Heer would have to have the last word. Dritte OHL still believed in an Imperial German victory.

So too did Lloyd George. His faith in his military and naval advisers, never high, had been eroded, if not entirely dissolved, by the events of the year that had passed since he came to power. He correctly assumed that Dritte OHL – Ludendorff and Hindenburg – was planning a knockout blow on the Allies. In the light of the events of 1917, he was understandably sceptical as to whether the Entente could withstand it. He had at his disposal the wrong men. 'Haig,' he declared, 'does not care how many men he loses. He just squanders the lives of these boys'. Jellicoe, guilty as charged over the matter of the convoys in April and then his support for Haig's 'northern offensive' in June, fared scarcely better. In the aftermath of the taking of the Passchendaele ridge, the prime minister sought alternatives to both his C-in-C on the Western Front and his First Sea Lord, the leading lights respectively of the Army and the Navy. 'We have won great victories,' the prime minister noted ironically to the Supreme War Council on 12 November 1917. 'When I look at the appalling casualty lists I sometimes wish it had not been necessary to win so many ... When we advance a kilometre into the enemy's lines, snatch a small shattered village out of his cruel grip, capture a few hundred soldiers, we shout with unfeigned joy.' He had clearly been studying his Pyrrhus: 'One more such victory and we are undone.' This was not a vote of confidence in Haig. A little earlier in the year, Fisher had written brightly to Rear Admiral William Sims, commanding the United States naval forces in European waters – Jellicoe's April visitor – 'We have not shot a single General or Admiral in the war. WE'VE PROMOTED THEM.'

Finding no one better to replace the field marshal, perhaps lacking the ultimate political power or will to remove him – for Liddell Hart the 'moral courage' – the PM attempted to circumvent the issue by trying once again to place Haig under the overall command of the French. In this he would succeed. Ferdinand Foch became the de facto head of the Allied forces when Ludendorff launched his great offensives on the Western Front in the spring of 1918; on 14 April 1918 he became 'commander-in-chief of the Allied armies in France'. Sir John Jellicoe, lacking Haig's Tory support and royal connections, and surrounded by some more plausible replacements, was dismissed on Christmas Eve 1917. It was poor treatment of a man who as C-in-C of the Grand Fleet had done the country great – and insufficiently recognised – service. 'This plain, unassuming figure did great things for the Navy and the nation,' wrote Richard Hough. Of the two, Haig was patently more culpable than Jellicoe. Many men in the field marshal's position would have fallen on their swords. His counterparts – Falkenhayn and Nivelle – were sacked. Such were the consequences or otherwise of Third Ypres.

In a sense, Haig was quite right when he called the battle's opening phase the critical moment of the war. It was certainly one which proved once and for all that attacking the enemy where he was strongest, eschewing any element of surprise, and assuming that the infantry was very largely proof against bullets and shells – not to mention mud – was no way to win the war. It was a pity that General Aleksei Brusilov had already demonstrated several of these points in June 1916 in Galicia on the Eastern Front; a pity, too, that men of the vision and power of Churchill and Lloyd George had been unable or unwilling to restrain Haig and the Chief of Imperial General Staff, General Sir William Robertson; a pity too that a strategy that had failed several times before should be thought worth repeating. For Churchill, the lesson of the first use of the Kitchener armies at Loos in the autumn of 1915 had been, 'Don't do it again.' He continued, 'But they will – I have no doubt.' They did, Haig in particular sticking to the strategy of the offensive; in his own words attacking 'whenever possible'. Given the advantage in the trench warfare of 1914–1918 of the defender over the attacker, it should be pointed out that – as was often observed – it would have been entirely possible for the Kitchener armies to be used in an essentially defensive role. Efforts to force a decision in the war would be made elsewhere, an approach Lloyd George dubbed 'knocking away the props'. As it was, Third Ypres ended as a tragic – the word is paltry and inadequate – rerun of the Somme. In his own assessment, Churchill quoted Sir William Robertson's note to Haig on 27 September 1917:

> My own views are known to you. They have always been 'defensive' in all theatres but the West. But the difficulty is to *prove* the wisdom of this now Russia is out. I confess I stick to it more because I see nothing better, and because my instinct prompts me to stick to it, than because of any good argument by which I can support it.

Churchill concludes, 'These are terrible words when used to sustain the sacrifices of nearly four hundred thousand men.'

That Christmas of 1917 Vera Brittain's brother Edward wrote from the Italian front, where he had now been posted. The letter, wrote his sister, 'came out of a snowstorm to remind me that love still existed, quick and warm, in a world dominated by winter and death.'

13

One Flew Over the Cuckoo's Nest

'We now come to one of the most important decisions of the war. Hindenburg and Ludendorff's all-out offensive in the west in the spring of 1918 opened the endgame. Its failure wrecked the German army, and made possible an Allied offensive that would have been delayed at least another year and possibly would not have come at all.'

David Stevenson

It was the day on which Ludendorff's aides sent for the men in white coats. Oberstabsarzt Hochheimer was an old colleague of the Erster Generalquartiermeister. On 4 September 1918 the psychiatrist – 'nerve specialist' as they were then called – arrived at Dritte OHL head-quarters in Spa, German-occupied Belgium. He found his 53-year-old patient a broken man, sleeping only an hour a night, a martyr to desk and to bottle. Hochheimer diagnosed gross overwork and extreme depression brought about by the continuous pressure under which the warlord had been operating – not to mention the death of two of his stepsons – and the dire circumstances of the war. He prescribed a reduction in his patient's formidable consumption of schnapps, daily walks, roses in his room, and the recital of soothing German folk songs 'to soften a soul hardened by the weight of war'. It was to no avail. Despite the flowers and the folk songs, on 28 September 1918 Luddendorff suffered a nervous breakdown. According to some accounts he foamed at the mouth; according to others he chewed the carpet in his office; according to yet others he launched into a terrible diatribe 'against the Kaiser, the Reichstag, the navy and the home front'. In any case, the outcome was the same. The following morning he and his alter-ego Hindenburg prevailed on the new German Chancellor Georg von Hertling to seek an armistice.

The paradox was that the fortunes of Dritte OHL and Imperial Germany had turned so swiftly. In March 1918 Russia had been finally and formally lost to the Entente as the upshot of the Treaty of Brest-Litovsk, and Pershing's American Expeditionary Force (AEF) was just about to be branded by Lloyd George as 'the worst disappointment of the war'. By late May Ludendorff's forces had pushed the Allies back further west than their positions in 1916. By early June Paris was in peril, Clemenceau and Lloyd George both thought defeat imminent, and on 15 June the Kaiser could declare, 'If a British parliamentarian comes to sue for peace, he must kneel before the Imperial Standard, for this is a victory of monarchy over democracy.' That was yesterday. Today, quite suddenly, after years of deadlock and after the sacrifice of countless young lives, Foch, Pétain and Haig seemed to have discovered the keys to success, to breaking the stalemate on the Western Front. The logjam of the trenches had been smashed, and the war once again became what it had been in the autumn of 1914, one of mass, movement and manoeuvre – albeit in reality more on account of Ludendorff than Foch himself. Like Paul McCartney, Ludendorff might have been forgiven for believing in yesterday.

On 21 March 1918 Ludendorff had launched his great offensive in the West. From Douai in the north to Laon in the south, along a front of around fifty miles that included the Somme battlefield of happy memory, seventy-six German divisions struck out against the British 5th Army less than half that number. Operation Michael, said Churchill, 'must be regarded as the greatest onslaught in the history of the world.' It seemed an immediate and resounding success. Despite widespread and accurate intelligence of the impending attack, both the French and British forces were ill-prepared. The British had been decimated at Passchendaele and 88,000 troops had been sent on leave on the eve of the attack; most of Haig's forces were concentrated in the north in Flanders rather than the south where the attack came. Using novel tactics – some of Brusilov's – Ludendorff's forces pierced three layers of defence, in places pushed General Sir Hubert Gough's 5th Army back forty miles, and threatened to drive a wedge between the French and British forces. When the Erster Generalquartier-meister called off the operation on 4 April 1918 he had netted 90,000 prisoners, 1300 guns, killed or wounded 212,000 Allied troops and, it seemed, destroyed the reputations of both Haig and Pétain – such as they were in the spring of 1918.

On 7 April 1918 Ludendorff's next operation – Georgette – opened against the British further north in Flanders, an attempt to capture Ypres and cut off the 2nd and 3rd Armies from the Channel Ports. Haig issued his famous order:

> Every position must be held to the last man: there must be no retirement. With our backs to the wall, and believing in the justice of our cause, each one of us must fight on to the end. The safety of our Homes and the Freedom of mankind alike depend upon the conduct of each one of us at this critical moment.

It was said to have been met in the trenches with derision, though acclaimed by those at home, like Vera Brittain. For the Deutsches Heer the whole time recalled the heady days of August 1914 when the Kaiser's five great armies debouched from their railheads and executed Schlieffen's plans, a seemingly unstoppable tide surging inexorably towards Paris and the Channel, carrying all before it towards a Western Europe dominated by the Second Reich. Huzzah! Next would come Operation Blücher which, opening on 27 May 1918, would surely – surely – see the collapse of the Allied powers on the Aisne, the river to which Helmuth von Moltke's armies had retreated from the Marne in September 1914. In Whitehall, so serious did matters seem that on 5 June 1918 the Cabinet considered evacuating the BEF to England, leaving the French to fend for themselves. For once, thought Lloyd George, Haig – brilliant to the top of his boots – was right. The Allies really did have their backs to the wall. 'I shall never forget the crushing tension of those extreme days,' wrote Brittain. 'Nothing had quite equalled them before – not the Somme, not Arras, not Passchendaele – for into our minds had crept for the first time the secret, incredible fear that we might lose the War.'

It was a pity for Ludendorff that all was not as it seemed. It was true that the Allies had sustained casualties of 212,000. It was equally true that Operation Michael had proved no exception to the rule on the Western Front that – Verdun excepted – offensives were more costly than defensive operations. On the Somme, 600,000 Allied casualties tallied with 400,000 German defenders, at Third Ypres around 300,000 to 200,000. Operation Michael had cost Ludendorff 239,000 casualties. Come July 1918, after Blücher and Georgette, this figure had soared to 430,000, alongside some 340,000 taken prisoner by the Allies.

In some respects, it was the latter figure that Ludendorff and Hindenburg found so telling. History taught that although casualties and ground lost or gained were obvious enough pointers to an army's success or failure in the field, prisoners were more so. What had concerned Erster Generalquartiermeister Helmuth von Moltke in the heady days of late August 1914 was the absence of French prisoners in any great numbers. Conversely, for Dritte OHL, the story for almost the very first time was of the German army losing its will to fight. Michael had been flagged by Hindenburg and Ludendorff as the offensive that would win the war. Consumed around St Quentin were many of the Deutsches Heer's best remaining officers and men, not least the storm troopers (*Sturmtruppen*) used with great effect during Operation Michael. The survivors were aghast that the war had not been won, that the British had not been forced back to – or over – the Channel, that the French were still fighting, that the Allies seemed as far as ever from the negotiating table. The Americans, too, were coming; coming, too, in substantial numbers. By July there would be a million in France, most brought by the Royal Navy and by German ships interned in US ports at the beginning of the war. As the Blücher offensive unfolded against the French between Soissons and Reims in very late May, Ludendorff's officers noted a marked diminution in the morale and combat effectiveness of their men. This was coupled with an equally marked inclination to surrender.

Dritte OHL was also obliged to remember another simple lesson of military history. That an army marches on its stomach. Not only were the troops operating at increasing distances from the railheads from which their rations – and munitions – were supplied, but in over-running Allied positions they discovered that while the enemy had been feeding like the fighting cocks they were, Ludendorff's own men were limited to iron rations. 'Notoriously,' writes David Stevenson, 'the advancing Germans were disheartened by the food and drink they discovered in British depots.' John Keegan amplified: 'The British rear areas, stuffed with the luxuries enjoyed by the army of a nation which had escaped the years of blockade that in Germany made the simplest necessities of life rare and expensive commodities, time and time again tempted the advancing Germans to stop, plunder and satiate themselves.' Seductive Allied propaganda leaflets dropped from the air by the newly formed Royal Air Force detailed sample menus enjoyed by German POWs.

The front-line troops were also demoralised by their letters from their loved ones on the home front, where conditions were worsening rapidly. The Northern Patrol of Admirals Tupper and de Chair had done sterling work in the first three years of the war; in David Beatty's words, it had been 'the squadron ... which could win us the war.' Now the blockade, A J P Taylor's 'silent noose', had tightened sufficiently to allow into Wilhelmine Germany a figure perhaps as small as a fifth or even – according to some sources – a tenth of its pre-war imports. These efforts had told. German imports of livestock fell from 356,229 animals in 1914 to 130,643 in 1918, bread grains from 240,350 tonnes to 42,598, meat and meat products from 119,913 to 8005. The meat ration was down to about 12 per cent of its pre-war equivalent. The consequences were catastrophic. A report in May 1918 from Erzegebirge on the borders of Saxony and Bohemia noted:

> There is a degree of hardship here that I had never imagined. In districts with a predominately industrial population they receive over ten days 1kg of potatoes – that is, two potatoes a day, very little bread, the people are gradually starving ... crowds of beggars go through agricultural villages. There are many cases of people falling dead in the streets.

In the country as a whole, the German authorities estimated that as many as three-quarters of a million people died of starvation as a direct or indirect result of the blockade – though later academic studies place the figure between 400,000 and 600,000. Many more suffered from diseases such as tuberculosis and dysentery brought on by malnutrition.

This happy news was carried to the distant front in what the Germans called 'letters of lament'. An agricultural labour force – both horses and men – decimated by drafts to the front, and the incompetence of government policy on food distribution, were certainly significant factors alongside the blockade itself; so too were the co-ordinating efforts of the Ministry of Blockade; so too was American pressure on neutrals to curtail their trade with the Central Powers, notably Holland and Denmark. Whatever the cause the result, though, was the same. Food riots, starvation and despair. Disturbances broke out in Vienna and Berlin as early as 1915, again in Berlin and in Leipzig in 1917, and in January 1918 more than a million took to the streets in the Kaiser's capital. At times, Ludendorff told Colonel Walther Nicolai of the military intelligence service Abteilung IIIb, he was more concerned by the situation at home than on the front; he felt he was fighting 'a two-front war against inner and outer enemies'. Haig himself thought at this time that the war would be over before the end of the year, 'because of the internal state of Germany. She could not continue ... because her population was degenerating so fast'. Wrote Martin Gilbert, 'Hunger and privation at home were as much an influence for war weariness as the killing.' Beatty had been right.

The Allies then helped the Germans on their way to dissolution, on land, in the air, and at sea.

For quite some time now the 'young Turks' of the Royal Navy had been champing at the bit. Since the 45-year-old Sir David Beatty had taken over the Grand Fleet from Sir John Jellicoe in November 1916, it had been hoped that the Senior Service would follow the prime minister's example of providing a more energetic and enterprising prosecution of the war. The swashbuckling huntsman Beatty was temperamentally more aggressive than Jellicoe and he is generally held to have adopted a more offensive stance. He certainly shifted the Fleet from Scapa Flow in Orkney to Rosyth in the Firth of Forth to be closer to Scheer and the Hochseeflotte in Wilhelmshaven. Opportunities, though, were few. With the Kaiserliche Marine now concentrating on U-boat warfare, the Hochseeflotte was used less as a force in its own right than as a quarry for crews for the U-boats, notably the best junior officers and engineers. Beatty, often supported by Tyrwhitt's light forces from Harwich, swept the North Sea for his counterparts from the Kaiserliche Marine, but Admiral Scheer seemed strangely reluctant to co-operate in his own fleet's destruction. Raids on the Dover Straits in February and April 1917 and actions off Lerwick in October and Heligoland Bight in November were modest affairs undertaken by Scheer's light forces; the Hochseeflotte remained notable by its absence. In Whitehall, the Admiralty focused on the U-boat threat. Besides the belated adoption of the convoy system in April 1917, it ordered extensive minelaying operations in the Heligoland Bight and off the Flanders coast. It also concerned itself with the Northern Barrage. Principally a US Navy initiative, this was a field of 70,000 mines stretching 180 miles from Orkney to Norway. Under Roger Keyes – now an admiral – the Dover Patrol became much more successful in denying the Straits to U-boats, forcing them to go round Scotland and therefore diminishing the time spent on active patrol in the Western Approaches, sinking merchantmen. These were amongst the measures that saw the gradual and steady diminution of Allied merchant shipping losses. By December 1917 they had fallen to 350,000 tons, down from the April peak of 850,000. Eventually, too, in January 1918, the Admiralty accepted Beatty's recommendation that the Grand Fleet should 'no longer ... endeavour to bring the enemy to action'. The fleet had done its job in neutering the Hochseeflotte and the Kaiser's creation was no longer regarded as a real threat. Those in the Navy enthusiastic to engage the enemy more closely began to look elsewhere.

To Tyrwhitt himself, the Flanders ports were certainly as tempting as they had been to his superior, Sir John Jellicoe. In fact, well before the former First Sea Lord's ill-fated support of Haig's 'northern offensive' in June 1917, Tyrwhitt had had his eye on Ostend and Zeebrugge. These ports, as we have seen, were used by the Kaiserliche Marine as bases for its light forces which harried Allied shipping in the Channel, and which threatened the endless chain of troops, munitions and victuals across the seaway to the BEF. Bruges, ten miles inland and linked by canals to both Zeebrugge and Ostend, was the heavily fortified U-boat base. Tyrwhitt had long hankered after an amphibious operation attacking these bases. In 1916 he had proposed a plan to land a force of marines on the huge Zeebrugge breakwater, seize the town and advance on Antwerp. This could threaten the northern end of the German Western Front. It was rejected by the Admiralty as too hazardous. The idea was revived by Tyrwhitt's comrade-in-arms Roger Keyes when he was appointed head of the plans division of the Navy in October 1917. Keyes proposed a more modest operation which would block both Ostend and Zeebrugge, stopping up the Kaiserliche Marine's surface and undersea forces like ships in a bottle. To do so it would use block-ships in the form of obsolete cruisers. The operation would be launched at night and would be preceded by artillery bombardment from the sea. A diversionary attack would be made on the breakwater, where a German garrison was quartered – as Tyrwhitt had originally proposed.

In January 1918 volunteers were requested from the Grand Fleet for a hazardous operation of an unspecified nature. The Zeebrugge Raid was first set for 19 March, as it so turned out just two days before Ludendorff's Operation Michael. In practice, the right combination of conditions – tide, moon, wind direction and weather – did not materialise until 23 April. Fittingly enough, this was St George's Day – by which time General Gough's 5th Army was on its knees, its line broken over forty miles. On the evening of that day, seventy-five ships and 1700 men attempted an operation that would result in three block-ships being sunk in the channel; a viaduct linking the break-water to the town was destroyed by a Royal Navy submarine packed with explosives, so isolating the garrison. St George had slayed the dragon. The cost, though, was high: around 200 dead and 300 wounded; and the results were decidedly equivocal. The channel was certainly not entirely blocked and the U-boats threaded their way round the obstacles. Taylor, acerbic as usual, called Zeebrugge, 'one of the most daring operations of the war, though quite pointless'. The raid, though, did much to restore morale in the Navy, it electrified the nation at a time when it was horrified by the events not far inland from Zeebrugge, and it did something to puncture what remained of the confidence of the Deutsches Heer and the Kaiserliche Marine. As Tyrwhitt wrote to Keyes, 'A thousand congrats on the success of your great venture. I think it was splendid and, by Jove, I do think the fellows who did the business deserve all they can be given, including yourself.' Keyes was feted as a naval hero and created Knight

Commander of the Bath; eight Victoria Crosses were won. For Churchill, 'It may well rank as the finest feat of arms in the Great War, and certainly as an episode unsurpassed in the history of the Royal Navy.' Coincidentally, on the same day as Zeebrugge, the Hochseeflotte made its last sortie of the war in search of an Allied convoy off the Norwegian coast. It proved fruitless.

At much the same time as this the Royal Air Force had been created. It constituted an amalgamation of the Royal Flying Corps and the Royal Naval Air Service, the two senior services hitherto having had at their disposal their own airborne divisions. Air power, though peripheral to this story, played an ever-increasing role through the war. It was aircraft of the RFC that had alerted Sir John French to Kluck's armies lying in his path at Mons in the early days of the deployment of the BEF in August 1914. Thereafter, the task of both the RFC and the RNAS grew from simply reconnaissance at land and on sea to more complex and aggressive aspects of warfare, including artillery spotting, attacks on communications, munitions dumps and barracks, then on ground troops and – late in the war – on German civilians. The formation of the RAF on 1 April 1918 was testament to the contribution that British airmen made to the war, and it was also one that heralded the far greater role they would play twenty-one years later and beyond. Before the beginning of the war, Foch had remarked of a flying display, 'That is good sport but for the Army the aeroplane is useless.' Unlike Jacky Fisher, Foch was no visionary.

Having expended something approaching half a million men and seriously eroded the morale of the Deutsches Heer, in the high summer of 1918 Ludendorff's forces were ripe for plucking. The Allies had regrouped and both Haig and Pershing – and, of course, the Frenchman Pétain – had agreed to work under the overall command of Ferdinand Foch. 'The appointment of a single commander,' noted Keegan, 'with the absolute authority to allot reserves ... wherever they were most needed, was essential in such a crisis.' The Allies duly launched a series of daring and successful counter-attacks, the British in Flanders and the French and Americans on the Soissons front further south. On 15 July 1918 OHL was still expecting Allied peace proposals before the end of the summer. 'That was on the 15th,' wrote Chancellor Georg von Hertling. 'On the 18th even the most optimistic among us knew that all was lost ... The history of the world was played out in three days.' When the Kaiser visited OHL advance headquarters at Avesnes on the Belgium border to be briefed on the latest Allied advance, he was not so much downcast as aghast. In his misery he declared, 'I am a defeated war lord, to whom you must show consideration.'

On 24 July 1918 a conference was held by Foch, with Haig, Pétain and Pershing in attendance. Following a successful defence – or at least a retreat that was not a rout and had certainly been fought with great gallantry – the time had now come for a major counter-offensive, indeed a general offensive. A grand plan for the entire encirclement of the Germany army was conceived. 'The general concept of the great battle rested with Foch,' wrote Churchill. 'The intervention of supreme control was decisive. Neither Haig nor Pétain, with their intense pre-occupations, could have achieved the general view.' The British would attack in the north near Ypres, the Americans in the south close to Verdun, the French in the centre would stay on the defensive. Held at Bombon in the Seine-et-Marne *département*, this conference was the first and only meeting ever held between the Allied commanders. Here Foch was radiant and confident: '*L'édifice commence à craquer. Tout le monde à la bataille,*' yet not *too* confident; he anticipated victory at some point in the next twelve months. It would certainly be September before the preparations would be completed for the offensive, and that was close to the end of the campaigning season. Churchill commented, 'General Headquarters, Sir Henry Wilson, the Imperial War Cabinet, the Prime Minister, all proceeded rigorously upon the belief that another most severe campaign would be necessary in 1919.'

In the meantime there came a succession of short successful, tactical attacks by the British, notably at Amiens using tanks, and – later – by the Americans in the Saint-Mihiel salient at Verdun. The day of the great British massed tank success at Amiens, 8 August, saw an advance of seven miles against what the Generalquartiermeister himself called 'six battle-worthy divisions'. Wrote Liddell Hart, 'Hitherto [man] could not fire if he wished to move, and could not move if he wished for cover.' The tank combined 'in one agent ... fire power, movement and protection – an advantage until then enjoyed in modern warfare only by those who fought at sea ... an antidote to the machine-gun which, in alliance with barbed wire, had reduced warfare to stagnation and generalship to attrition.' For Buchan, Amiens was 'the most brilliantly conceived and perfectly executed of any British action on the Western Front.' The result was an episode later described by Ludendorff as 'the black day for the German Army in the history of this war ... the 8th of August opened the eyes of the staff on both sides; mine were certainly opened ... The Emperor told me later on, after the failure of the July offensive and after 8 August, he knew the war could no longer be won.' It was the beginning of what would later be called the Allies' Hundred Days Offensive, in homage to Napoleon.

'The real effect of 8 August was psychological,' wrote A J P Taylor. 'It shattered the faith in victory which, until that moment had carried the Germans forward. The German soldiers had been told they were fighting the decisive battle. Now they realised that decision had gone against them. They no longer wanted to win. They only wanted to end the war.' Ludendorff recorded in his memoirs, 'men were beginning to say, "better a terrible end than terror without end."' Trains carrying men returning from leave were festooned with red flags. Hundreds of thousands of men – perhaps nearly a million – refused to rejoin their units. Around half a million German troops were also laid low by the influenza epidemic sweeping the world. This was a figure far higher than that suffered by the better-fed men of the Entente.

The situation on the Home Front was also now deteriorating fast. W G Max-Müller worked for the British Foreign Office collecting intelligence reports from Germany. Between July and September 1918 he recorded a dramatic drop in morale:

Germany would endure intolerable hardships if cheered by hopes and victory, but now such hope is gone and the whole machinery of national life is running down ... I have all along insisted that the enemy would endure privations as long as they were buoyed up by the assurance of ultimate victory, but that once that had gone the powers of resistance would collapse, and that is the situation in Germany today.

On 26 September 1918 Foch's counter-attack began. 'Everyone to battle!' cried the little generalissimo. This in itself might have been cause sufficient for Germany to seek an armistice, but in itself it was not. The offensive had, indeed, opened towards the end of the campaigning season; and like Ludendorff's own attack earlier in the year, it involved cripplingly long lines of communication. Although the British did outstandingly in finally over-running the Hindenburg Line on the St Quentin canal, Pershing's AEF suffered 100,000 casualties further south in the Argonne. Soon it became apparent that the Germans would not be pushed back to their own frontiers before winter, that it was the Allies who were now losing momentum. It was in fact the collapse of another front that forced Ludendorff's hand. What amounted to no more than a tactical attack by the French in Salonika led to Bulgaria suing for peace. This opened the way for the Allies to reach the Danube and with it Vienna, the seat of the Austro-Hungarian empire; it also robbed the Central Powers of the oil vital to continue the war.

This news from Salonika reached Ludendorff on 28 September 1918. Dritte OHL now had no forces to spare from the west to support Wilhelmine Germany's southern ally. It was the last straw. 'You don't know Ludendorff,' Bethmann-Hollweg had warned the Admiralstab earlier in the war. 'You don't know Ludendorff, who is only great at a time of success. If things go badly he loses his nerve.' Now he did just that. Perhaps he chewed the carpet, perhaps he foamed at the mouth, almost certainly he fell into a terrible diatribe against the Kaiser, the Reichstag, the navy and the home front. His staff locked him in his office and sent for a straitjacket. The roses had been to no avail. Eventually he calmed down. John Keegan continues:

At six o'clock he emerged to descend one floor of headquarters to Hindenburg's room. There he told the old field marshal that there was no alternative but to seek an armistice. The position in the west was penetrated, the army would not fight, the civilian population had lost heart, the politicians wanted peace. Hindenburg silently took his right hand in both of his own and they parted 'like men who had buried their dearest hopes'.

The following morning Ludendorff made his call to his political masters – if masters they were – for an immediate armistice. He could not guarantee to hold back the onrush of the Allied armies for more than twenty-four hours. This was not entirely an act of desperation. An armistice, by no means the same thing as a surrender, would perhaps enable the Deutsches Heer to regroup behind Germany's own frontiers: 1919 could then be left to look after itself.

On 30 September 1918 Chancellor Georg von Hertling resigned. He was replaced by the liberal Prince Maximilian of Baden, a cousin of the Kaiser, who accepted the post only on the condition that in future the Reichstag alone would have the power to seek peace or declare war. This was the thin end of the wedge of revolution, albeit from above. On 4 October 1918 Germany formally sought an armistice on the basis of Wilson's Fourteen Points. The request was addressed to President Wilson himself; the two other principal belligerents, France and Great Britain, were ignored. Germany declared that she accepted the Fourteen Points, principles which neither Hindenburg nor Ludendorff had read, and which Clemenceau and Lloyd George disdained. Clemenceau remarked, 'The Lord God has only ten.' The pair were not consulted by Wilson, who replied with some enthusiasm to Prince Maximilian on 8 September 1918. Once again, the New World had been brought in to redress the balance of the Old.

This brief account of the climactic closing months of the war on land does not square very closely with some commonly held ideas about the Allied victory. It would certainly be easy to imagine that the prodigious slaughter of Loos, Arras, the Somme and Passchendaele eventually bore fruit and that the sacrifices made by so many in the five great Kitchener armies were not in vain. It would certainly be pleasant to suppose that in the end Field Marshal Haig led the Allies – Foch, Pétain, Pershing – to victory, so following in the footsteps of

Marlborough and Wellington. There is, of course, more than a grain of truth in these ideas and many people do so believe. As Haig's biographer Gary Mead puts it, 'For the general public ... the victory in 1918 was a British-led victory, won by the biggest British Army ever to take part in a continental war.'

It is certainly true that many military historians acknowledge the progress in the expertise of the novice Kitchener armies, garnered from their experience in the field over the three years since they were set to task by Haig. It is true, too, that by supplementing the infantry and artillery with tanks and aircraft in large numbers the Allies made great strides in the last months of the war. It is true that in administration and logistics the British, in particular, had made great strides. True, too, that they were learning to co-ordinate these forces. General Sir John Monash, who commanded the Australian forces at Amiens whose success had so disillusioned Ludendorff, declared, 'A modern battle plan is like nothing so much as a score for a musical composition, where the various arms and units are the instruments, and the tasks they perform are their respective musical phrases. Each individual unit must make its entry precisely at the proper moment, and play its phrase in the general harmony.' Still, the fact remains that the One Hundred Days was masterminded by Foch, not Haig. Mead tells us that, 'in truth he [Haig] bore little responsibility for the changes of this period, which enabled steady progress towards victory.' The Americans and the French played major parts in the success alongside the Kitchener armies. Pershing's AEF accepted a level of casualties unseen since 1914, and at Saint-Mihiel in mid-September launched the first wholly US offensive of the conflict. The French lost half a million men between July and September 1918. Equally important was the extent to which the Deutsches Heer was demoralised by the constant winnowing of its own men and the prospect of the ever-gathering strength of the Americans: in 1919 there would be two million of the 'doughboys' at the Allies' disposal. In so far as the Armistice was brought about by events on the battlefield, it was indeed more on the Salonika front rather than in the west that the decision was actually achieved. The Western Front was the main theatre of operations but Salonika was – for Churchill – 'the final blow.' Perhaps above all, historians from Churchill to David Stevenson attribute the German debacle on the Western Front more to OHL and its great warlords than to the Allies themselves. Says Churchill:

> It was their own offensive, not ours, that consummated their ruin. They were worn down not by Joffre, Nivelle and Haig, but by Ludendorff ... But for Operation Michael and its successors, OHL would have been able to confront the Allies with an unbreakable front on the Meuse or on the Rhine, and have made self-respecting terms for abridging the slaughter.

For A J P Taylor, 'Joffre, Haig and Nivelle had nearly lost the war by their repeated offensives ... Now Ludendorff was imitating them.' For Allan Mallinson, 'Only when ... the German army obligingly abandoned their strong defences – because the Royal Navy's blockade was rapidly destroying Germany's very cohesion, and because by the end of the year the American troops would give the allies over-whelming superiority – did the Entente have the opportunity to mount successful offensives.' Accordingly, Ludendorff's decision on the auspicious day of 11 November 1917 to execute Operation Michael was as important as the Kaiser's decision at Pless ten months earlier to resume unrestricted submarine warfare. Between them, the pair pulled down the House of Hohenzollern on their own heads.

In any case, on 9 October 1918 Ludendorff decided that his precipitate demand ten days earlier on 29 September for an armistice had been premature. He had been having a turn and now he had regained his nerve. He told a rather surprised chancellor as much, assuring Prince Maximilian that the Deutsches Heer could and would hold Germany's frontiers for the time being. The problem lay not there but at home where the genie of revolution was just slipping out of the bottle. As Erster Generalquartermeister Ludendorff and the German chancellor both appreciated, the mood in the German cities was such that if Germany's rulers failed to deliver '*Frieden und Brot*' – peace and bread – very soon, the ruled would take matters into their own hands.

14

Freedom and Bread

'The end of the war came more emphatically and completely than anyone had foreseen ... the Germans defeated themselves, and by the autumn they had no alternative but to attempt desperate damage limitation.'

David Stevenson

Grand Admiral Reinhard Scheer was a man of ideas, not all of them good.

After the battle of Jutland – Skagerrak to the Kaiserliche Marine – it was Scheer who had broken the unwelcome news to the Kaiser that the operation which had been celebrated in Germany as a great victory was, in fact, a defeat. This was percipient. Altogether less so was his plan to force one final encounter between the Hochseeflotte and the Grand Fleet, just as Ludendorff's battalions reeled back towards the borders of Germany in the face of the Allied offensive of the late summer and autumn of 1918. The Naval Order of 24 October 1918, despite its cancellation within forty-eight hours of promulgation, led to the Kiel Mutiny. This was the spark that ignited the November Revolution, the collapse of the Wilhelmine monarchy, and the institution of a republic. *Frieden und Brot* – peace and bread – was the slogan of the Kiel mutiny, quite clear pointers of the revolutionaries' motivation. With Kiel the end really was nigh, both for the war and Wilhelmine Germany.

In August 1918, just as the failure of Ludendorff's great spring offensive on the Western Front was becoming apparent, just as the great Deutsches Heer suffered its 'black day' at Amiens, Reinhard Scheer was promoted chief of naval staff. He replaced Admiral Henning von Holtzendorff. This was the man who had successfully urged the Kaiser at the Crown Council meeting at the Castle of Pless in

January 1917 to adopt unrestricted submarine warfare. Although the U-boat campaign had signally failed to deliver its promise of bringing Great Britain to the negotiating table, Germany had nothing else to hand, no other weapon in her arsenal. On the day following his appointment, 12 August 1918, Scheer held a meeting with Hindenburg and Ludendorff. The mood was sombre. The duumvirate could see no prospect of anything other than retreat on the Western Front. Although Allied shipping losses to U-boats that month of 280,000 tons stood at only a fraction of those at the peak of the Admiralstab's campaign in April 1917, there was no other prospect or means of victory.

Scheer called for a redoubling of the U-boat building programme to create a fleet of around 400. This plan was overtaken by events. On 4 October Chancellor Prince Maximilian had requested President Wilson to act as an intermediary in the armistice negotiations. The discussions were to be based on the Fourteen Points, circulated to a startled world in January 1918. These were intended as a counterblast to Bolshevism and as a doctrine – modest indeed – intended to make further wars impossible. A J Ryder commented, 'Lenin promised a millennium through revolution. Bolshevism would destroy the economic roots of war and inaugurate, after much turmoil, the reign of social justice and proletarian brotherhood. Wilson, President of a bourgeois republic, offered popular government, the self-determination of peoples and the League of Nations to settle international disputes.' As a pre-condition to an armistice, Wilson demanded the withdrawal of the Deutsches Heer from foreign soil, the abdication of the Kaiser and the cessation of the unrestricted U-boat warfare. Despite Scheer's objections, the latter concession was made by Prince Max on 20 October 1918. The following day, the U-boats were ordered back to base.

On reflection, Scheer realised that the submarine flotilla might still come in useful. For some weeks he had been planning what seemed likely to be the final sortie of Admiral Franz von Hipper's Hochseeflotte. He would lure Admiral David Beatty's Grand Fleet into battle, supported by the U-boats. This might actually prove the decisive operation – *Entscheidungsschlacht* – that had eluded both Scheer himself and Jellicoe at Jutland two years previously. The plan was to mount two simultaneous raids by light forces on the plentiful Allied merchant shipping on the Flanders coast and in the Thames Estuary. The Hochseeflotte would then ambush the Grand Fleet as it steamed south from Rosyth to the rescue; the U-boats would lurk beneath the waves unseen as an additional surprise.

There were, however, some oddities about this plan. First, it did not meet with the formal approval of the Dritte OHL, of Hindenburg and Ludendorff. Ludendorff alone had been informed, and told to keep the matter quiet. It had also been concealed from those who were nominally the political masters of Scheer in the shifting sands of Wilhelmine statesmanship: of the Kaiser and the chancellor. It was virtually a freelance naval operation conceived by Scheer in collusion with Hipper. This secrecy raised the suspicions that the thinking behind the plan was more political than purely naval. Scheer, indeed, suspected that Ludendorff would sacrifice the navy to get an armistice on the best possible terms for the Deutsches Heer on land. Clearly, this had to be circumvented. Hipper himself volunteered, 'A battle for the honour of the fleet in this war, even if it were a death battle, would be the foundation of a new German Fleet.' Neither as it turned out, did the plan meet the approval of the crews of the great dreadnoughts of the Hochseeflotte. Like Scheer himself, many of the men had been less than convinced that the Grand Fleet had been entirely and permanently vanquished at Jutland. Since that historic day, the Grand Fleet had been augmented, not least by five dreadnoughts from the US Navy. Four had joined in December 1917, later joined by a fifth. The Grand Fleet had always substantially outnumbered the Hochseeflotte, both in battleships and battlecruisers. That, amongst other things, was its problem. In October 1918 the Grand Fleet boasted thirty-five battleships to the Hochseeflotte's eighteen; eleven battlecruisers to five of the Kaiserliche Marine. It was true that American gunnery was poor, but this infirmity had naturally been kept from the Admiralstab. The balance was roughly two to one ships in favour of the British, markedly better than at Jutland. Morale, too, favoured the Grand Fleet. Beatty's men were out to avenge Jutland, a battle in which they supposed they had not done themselves justice. Hipper's crews were demoralised by those good men siphoned off to the U-boats, those playing much more prominent parts in fighting for the Fatherland on the Western Front, by their ever poorer rations, and by the strange allure of events in Russia.

As has been remarked, the teachings of Marx and Engels had always found some favour in their homeland. The Social Democratic party (*Sozialdemokratische Partei Deutschlands*), founded in 1875, predated Britain's Labour Party by a quarter of a century. By 1912 the SPD was the largest political party in the country. Although it initially supported the war, the catastrophic losses on the Western Front, culminating in those incurred at Falkenhayn's failed offensive at Verdun in 1916, had tipped the balance. The SPD was increasingly of the view that this was a capitalist war being fought for the benefit of the bourgeoisie at the very considerable expense of labour. Events in Russia, culminating in the February and October revolutions of 1917, whetted appetites. Paradise was within reach. Power really might lie in the hands of the people. Poor people were going to rise up, and take what was theirs.

The devil made work for those idle hands. In the Wilhelmshaven barracks where the crews of the Hochseeflotte had largely lain idle since Jutland, the poor rations predicated by the British naval blockade were fortified by a rich diet of revolution. On 2 August 1917 mutiny had broken out on *Prinzregent Luitpold*. A third of the dreadnought's thousand-strong crew had staged a revolt, two hundred had been arrested, many had been imprisoned and two of the ringleaders had been shot. This had done nothing for morale. As the war ground on, as rations shortened further, and as the Treaty of Brest-Litovsk on 3 March 1918 brought the promise of both peace and bread to the beleaguered Russian comrades of the crews, the sailors on the ships of the Hochseeflotte set up their own councils or 'Bolsheviks'. Some bought red flags. Having little better to do, they followed the course of Ludendorff's great offensives of the spring of 1918 with considerable interest, the subsequent retreats of the imperial armies in the late summer in Flanders and Soissons with dismay. The literate amongst them were familiar with reading between the lines of the propaganda peddled by Dritte OHL through the German newspapers.

In late July 1918 the news broke of the murder of the Romanovs in Yekaterinburg. The Tsar and his family had been shot and bayoneted, their bodies mutilated, doused in sulphuric acid and thrown into a pit. Some crews applauded the execution, undertaken in the euphemistic phrasing of the Soviet regime, 'without bourgeois formalities but in accordance with our new democratic principles'. Lenin, whom the Germans themselves had, of course, despatched to Russia in the 'sealed train', was implicated in the deaths. These events, of the ruled getting the better of their rulers, were thought-provoking. As the prospect of defeat loomed ever larger, so too did the crews' realisation that the Hochseeflotte might be used as one last desperate throw of the dice, of *va banque*. The once proud Kaiserliche Marine – or at least its officers – would not surrender without a fight.

What would Lenin have made of that? What about the incident that the Bolshevik leader called the dress rehearsal for the revolution of October 1917, the mutiny in 1905 on the battleship *Potemkin*?

Hipper's plan for the raids on the Flanders coast and Thames estuary shipping was drafted on 24 October 1918. On 27 October it was approved by Grand Admiral Scheer. The order was promulgated in outline to the Hochseeflotte crews under the transparent guise of a routine training sortie. The High Seas Fleet was ordered to assemble at Schillig Roads, just outside their Wilhelmshaven and Brunsbüttel bases, on 29 October 1918. On hearing these orders many of the crews decided they had little taste for battle so close to what might well be the end of the war. They correctly assumed that Scheer and Hipper were prepared to sacrifice their lives for the honour of the Kaiserliche Marine, justifying the very existence of the Imperial Navy, and in the hope of influencing the armistice negotiations. It was the end. Whatever the high motives of the leadership, the sailors' councils had little taste for a Wagnerian death-ride into the sunset in the face of the Grand Fleet's 15in shells. Not all of them even liked Wagner.

On the night of 29/30 October 1918 crews on ships from both the 1st and 3rd Navy Squadrons refused to obey orders. With the Hochseeflotte mutinous, Scheer was obliged to cancel the order of 24 October. It was too late. The centre would not hold. Ludendorff had just been sacked by the Kaiser. Having discarded his distinctive *Pickelhaube* spiked helmet, he had flown the country disguised in blue-tinted spectacles and a false beard. The following day, forty-seven mutineers from the dreadnought *Markgraf* were arrested and imprisoned in Kiel. Over the next forty-eight hours, two mass meetings of the crews were held. 'We do not put to sea,' the sailors crowed. 'For us the war is over.' They demanded the release of the mutineers. On 3 November the slogan '*Frieden und Brot*' was raised on a banner. A crowd of sailors moved off towards the military prison to the effect the mutineers' release. A military patrol opened fire, killed seven of the demonstrators and seriously injured twenty-nine. On 4 November the governor of the Kiel naval station, Admiral Wilhelm Souchon, requested military assistance. The red flag was raised on the battleship *Kaiser*. This was the great dreadnought launched on the Kaiser's birthday in 1911. Six infantry companies were brought to Kiel. They, too, refused to obey orders; some joined the revolutionaries. The mutineers were freed. By evening that day, Kiel was in the hands of the Bolsheviks. In an echo of Wilson's Fourteen Points, they issued fourteen demands. Above all, they refused to put to sea. Such was the once proud Kaiserliche Marine. 'My dear Admiral,' said the Kaiser tartly to one of Scheer's colleagues, Admiral Paul von Hintze, 'the Navy has left me in the lurch very nicely!' For the naval historian Andrew Lambert, 'the Kaiser's Fleet ... brought down his empire.'

In the following seventy-two hours, sailors and soldiers' councils on the Soviet model were set up all over Germany. In the cities they seized both military and civil power. By 7 November 1918 the revolution had spread like wildfire as far south as Bavaria. Law and order were breaking down. The red flag was flying over Germany, the plague bacillus had come. On 9 November in Berlin, the leading German socialist, Karl Liebknecht, declared Germany a free socialist republic. The rule of capitalism, which had turned Europe into a graveyard, was shattered. He appealed to his audience to join him in completing the world revolution, begun in Russia and now continued in Germany. Three years earlier, in 1915 Maurice Hankey, secretary to Asquith's war committee and much else besides, told the prime minister that 'when the psychological moment arrives and the cumulative effects [of blockade] reach their maximum and are perhaps combined with crushing defeats of the enemy, the results may not be merely material, but decisive'. Which came first, the collapse of the home or of the

Western Front? 'Military defeat set the collapse in motion, but internal upheaval completed it,' wrote David Stevenson. So which came first, the chicken or the egg? In reality, the two were inextricably linked, converging forces which destroyed Wilhelmine Germany, the yin and yang of its collapse. Churchill commented that 'When the great organisations of this world are strained beyond breaking-point, their structure often collapses at all points simultaneously.'

Three days later, on 10 November 1918 at Rethondes in the Compiègne forest clearing, there were Secretary of State Matthias Erzberger, Count Alfred von Oberndorff, Major General Detlov von Winterfeldt and Captain Ernst Vanselow. These were the German civilian, foreign office, military and naval delegates gathering in railway wagon 2419 to continue the armistice negotiations. It was Sunday morning. Along with croissants and coffee, they were handed by their French and British hosts the newspapers from Paris. The Kaiser had abdicated. Prince Max had been replaced by the Social Democrat Friedrich Ebert. A republic had been declared. Wilhelmine Germany was no more. As in Russia, the leadership had paid the price of failure. The following day, 11 November 1918, at just after 0500, the truce was signed. Erzberger made a formal protest that the terms dictated would precipitate in Germany anarchy and famine. The Armistice came into force at 1100. Back in England, Lloyd George informed the House of Commons of the terms of the truce, concluding, 'I hope we may say that thus, this fateful morning, came to an end all wars.'

Wrote Vera Brittain, 'When the sound of victorious guns burst over London at 11 a.m. on November 11th, the men and women who looked incredulously into each other's faces did not cry jubilantly: "We've won the War!" They only said: "The War is over."' Five months earlier she had opened a telegram which read, 'Regret to inform you Captain E.H. Brittain MC killed in action Italy June 15th.' This was her brother. In Shrewsbury, on 11 November Wilfred Owen's mother heard the church bells pealing in celebration of the Armistice just as another telegram arrived. It announced the death a few days earlier of her eldest son. 'For the first time I realised,' continued Brittain, 'with all that full realisation meant, how completely everything that had hitherto made up my life had vanished with Edward and Roland, with Victor and Geoffrey. The War was over; a new age was beginning; but the dead were dead and would never return.'

Four days later, at 1430 on the foggy afternoon of 15 November 1918 Admiral Hugo von Meurer steamed the German light cruiser *Königsberg* under Royal Navy escort into Rosyth. That evening he was to meet Admiral Sir David Beatty in the Grand Fleet's flagship *Queen Elizabeth* – late of the Dardanelles. He was to be told the punitive terms of the naval armistice. These he took badly. To Beatty he said, 'I do not think the Commander-in-Chief is aware of the condition of Germany'. Then, recounted Beatty, Meurer:

> began to retail the effect of the Blockades. It had brought Revolution in the North which had spread to the South, then to the East and finally to the West, that anarchy was rampant, the seed was sown, it remained for the harvest of human lives to be reaped in the interior of Germany as well as on the frontiers. Men, women and children under six were non-existent, that Germany was destroyed utterly.

The naval historian Richard Hough echoed:

> It is no reflection on the prodigious and continuing effort and glorious courage of the armies in France and the numerous other theatres of war, or of the airmen who gave such valuable assistance, to say that the Royal Navy provided the greatest contribution to victory by its perpetual and mainly unseen and soundless pressure. It was the blockade that finally drove the Central Powers to accept defeat. At first mild in its application, the blockade's noose gradually tightened until, with the American entry, all restraint was cast aside. Increasingly deprived of the means to wage war or even feed her population, the ultimate response was insurrection, apathy and demoralisation, the mute consequence of dashed hopes and thin potato soup.

We have been taught – or at least have perhaps assumed – that the history of warfare is the story of battles lost or won, rather like a football or a rugby match. These are battles which Churchill in 1918 defined as 'a succession of climaxes on which everything is staked, towards which everything tends and from which permanent decisions are obtained.' Eye-catching, earth-shattering events that change the course of history. In 1923 he cited Blenheim, Rossbach, Austerlitz, Waterloo, Gettysburg, Sedan, the Marne and Tannenberg. To these might now be added – say – the Battle of France in 1940, the Battle of Britain in the same year, El Alamein in 1942, Stalingrad in 1943, Berlin in 1945, the Arab-Israeli war of 1967 and both the Gulf Wars. In the Great War, the Entente won the battle of the Marne that eviscerated Schlieffen's schemes; the Central Powers, Tannenberg – Ludendorff's victory that largely destroyed the Russians' will to fight. The One Hundred Days in 1918 was a series of operations conducted jointly by British, US, Belgium and French forces which petered out short of Germany's borders. In Churchill's terms these actions do not really constitute a battle, lacking unity of time, place and indeed outcome – as the name by which they are called partly suggests. At sea, Jutland was inconclusive in so far as neither fleet was destroyed, but the Royal Navy certainly mastered the U-boat threat by destroying around half the Kaiserliche Marine's submarine flotilla. That was a battle, and a battle decisively won.

However, as the naval strategist Sir Julian Corbett – amongst others – pointed out, this reading of history is misleading. Decisive battles ('permanent decisions') either on land or at sea are the exception rather than the rule. Trafalgar was a blue moon conjured up by the sort of magician who illuminates the night sky once a century. Churchill himself actually took the same line, pointing out that though there were in fact 'real battle crises of the Great War' – notably the Marne and Tannenberg – they stood out from a 'long series of partial, though costly operations'. Verdun, the Somme and Passchendaele were actions etched into the history of the armies and into the consciousness of the nations concerned, killed hundreds of thousands of men. Yet although they were epics, they were not watersheds. 'The human mind,' observed John Buchan, 'loves a dramatic finale, and asks for ostensible signs of victory.' Neither the British nor the Germans could look to dramatic finales or curtain calls on the Somme or at Passchendaele; nor could the French or the Germans at Verdun. They just ebbed away, operations abandoned and called off rather than completed with the trumpet call of victory that brought down the walls of Jericho. Nobody lost and nobody won – other than the units, battalions, divisions and the hundreds of thousands of men concerned – along with those crafting coffins, headstones and memorials. In terms of grand strategy, they were draws. Of ostensible signs of victory there were none.

Yet this hardly to say that they were all without importance or that – if significant – they were equally so. In the course of this book I have described fourteen turning-points of the war. Of these I have said that the Marne, Heligoland Bight, Jutland and Ludendorff's 1918 March offensives really were watersheds in the sense that they were instrumental to the Allied victory. Loos, Arras, the Somme and Passchendaele were not pivotal in the same way; though the Somme helped pave the way for unrestricted U-boat warfare; and if it had not been fought, the French might well have made a separate peace with Imperial Germany. This would not have been good news. I have also suggested that turning-points other than battles were critical to victory: the sinking of the *Lusitania*, the Kaiser's decisions in 1917 to endorse unrestricted U-boat warfare and to back Lenin's return to Russia, Lloyd George's insistence on convoys to combat the U-boats, and Scheer's decision to order the Hochseeflotte to sea in October 1918. I have also proposed that the British decisions to send the BEF to France in August 1914, to attach it at that time to the French left wing, and to prosecute the Dardanelles so half-heartedly were all own goals – or at the very least represented major opportunities missed to shorten the war and to lessen the monstrous loss of life on the Western Front and elsewhere. Finally, I have argued that the Royal Navy's blockade, as was generally believed at the time, was almost as important as military methods in obtaining victory. These were Lloyd George's words. Both the Central Powers and the Allies realised from 1916 onwards that, in John Buchan's terms, 'in the long run the home front was the vital front.'

This argument is an attempt, therefore, not to belittle the Army, its sacrifices, its great gallantry and, indeed, the achievements of its men, its junior and middle-ranking officers, or even much of its high command. It indubitably made a major contribution to the Allied victory, starting with the Marne and ending with the One Hundred Days. Without its presence on the Western Front from 1916 onwards, the war on land would have been lost. Rather, it is to place the Navy rather closer to centre stage in achieving the Armistice of 1918. Without the Navy, the Empire and everything it meant to the nation and the Entente in terms of money, material and men would have dissolved like an insubstantial pageant faded. Without the Navy, the nation would have been invaded; or if not invaded, starved into submission by the U-boat campaign. Without the Navy, the Army on its way to France and the other four theatres in which it was operational would have settled in fairly spacious lodgings in Folkestone and Dover to gaze wistfully over the grey waters of the Channel; if Kitchener's great volunteer armies had been wafted overseas by magic carpets, without the Navy they would have been starved of food, drink, shells, bullets, horses, motor transport, tanks and, indeed, orders. Without the Navy, half of Pershing's AEF would have been left playing checkers on the docksides in New Jersey and New York. Without the Navy and its blockade, Germany's home front would have survived largely unscathed, and what would – or would not – have happened then? For John Buchan, the Royal Navy was 'the weapon on which all others depended'. For Lloyd George, 'The sea front turned out to be the decisive flank in the gigantic battlefield'. For Basil Liddell Hart, the 'Navy was to win no Trafalgar, but it was to do more than any other factor towards winning the war for the Allies.'

Today, David Stevenson quotes Sir Halford Mackinder, a thinker whose ideas greatly influenced US strategy during the Cold War. A Conservative politician and academic – one of the founders of the London School of Economics – he was the father of the academic discipline of geography and of the very idea of geopolitics and geo-strategy. This is the study of the effects of human and physical geography on politics and international relations. Said Mackinder, 'We have been fighting in the close of the war a straight duel between land-power and sea-power, and sea-power has been laying siege to land-power.' Stevenson himself continues, 'This was an unspectacular struggle, fought out away from the public gaze in a myriad of encounters across the expanses of the Mediterranean and the Atlantic. Yet the outcome was emphatic and underlying every other Allied achievement.' Hew Strachan, another admirer of Mackinder, took a similar line in his inaugural Rothermere Lecture in 2016, arguing that 'So much of our understanding of the First World War focuses on the conflict on land and yet the nation who controlled the seas also controlled the flow of resources, so critical in such a long and attritional war.' 'Naval power,' he concludes, was 'critical to the outcome'. Yet he also cautioned that, 'The war was simply too complex, and embraced too many moving parts and too many states and nations for a mono-causal explanation.'

Epilogue
Pictures at an Exhibition

On 11 November 2017, the ninety-ninth anniversary of the Armistice, I paid a visit to the National Portrait Gallery. It was established in 1856 by the 4th Earl Stanhope and the two Thomases: Macaulay and Carlyle. In the Age of British Confidence, the Trafalgar Square gallery was intended to display 'portraits ... of those persons who are most honourably commemorated in British history as warriors, as statesmen, or in arts, in literature or in science'. On that Saturday morning I was going to see the fruits of a commission made by the South African financier Sir Abraham Bailey. Shortly before the Armistice in 1918 he had decided to contract two paintings by the masters of the day. One would recognise 'the great soldiers who have been the means of saving the Empire'; the other 'the gallant sailors who have taken as great a share in the victory'. The chairman of the trustees, Lord Dillon, declared that the proposal was 'the most important of its kind ever made to the Gallery.' The trustees also suggested to Bailey that a third painting should be added to honour the statesmen who had overseen the military and naval achievement. Clausewitz had said that war was merely a continuation of politics by other means. To this the baronet agreed, dashing off three cheques for £5000 apiece.

Sir Arthur Stockdale Cope was duly commissioned to produce what is now called *Naval Officers of World War I*; John Singer Sargent, *General Officers of World War I*. Sargent is better known for *Gassed*, his searing portrait of blinded and blindfolded victims of a mustard gas attack near Arras. Both artists refused to paint the politicians. According to Sir Michael Howard, they were 'so reflecting widespread public attitude of the time, namely, "that the politicians had made a hash out of the war."' Sir Douglas Haig himself commented, 'I despise the Politicians, or Statesmen as they would like to be called! They would have lost the war if it had been possible to do so.' The commission and the £5000 was eventually accepted by Sir James Guthrie. It took the form of *Statesmen of World War I*. On completion – Guthrie took twelve years – all three paintings were presented to the gallery. There they hang to this day. There, too, from time to time I had noticed but had not studied them. It came to me one day – not really in a vision – that seeing the pictures would help me draw together the strands of this book which I had been weaving rather incontinently for a couple of years, and to tie up some loose ends. If you live in north Norfolk as I do, a visit to the capital is also an outing for a country mouse. Despite, rather than because of, the railway system, that bright November morning I was one of the first of the visitors to the shrine of our great and good.

What intriguing questions about the Great War are begged by these three relics of another country! Of the war to end war, of the conflict which for John Keegan, I remembered:

> ended the lives of ten million human beings, tortured the emotional lives of millions more, destroyed the benevolent and optimistic culture of the European continent and left, when the guns at last fell silent four years later, a legacy of political rancour and racial hatred so intense that no explanation of the causes of the Second World War can stand without reference to those roots.

Of what the German historian Wolfgang Mommsen called, 'the great seminal catastrophe of the twentieth century'.

I went first to James Guthrie's politicians, for the original intention was for the statesmen to be flanked on either side by the warriors: the generals and the admirals.

Given his South African background – given, too, the contributions made by the Dominions to the war effort – Bailey specified that the portrait should feature Dominion statesmen alongside their Westminster counterparts. Accordingly, amongst the seventeen figures are Louis Botha, prime minister of the Union of South Africa; Sir

Joseph Cook, prime minister of Australia; Sir William Massey, prime minister of New Zealand; and Robert Borden, prime minister of Canada. From closer to home are Edward Grey, Winston Churchill and David Lloyd George. 'The finished painting', I read in the Gallery's commentary:

> presents the seventeen men gathered at conference in a vast hall flanked by Doric columns, in the shadow of a sculpture of Nike, the winged victor of Samothrace [which] ... becomes the centrepiece and dominant motif in the finished picture. She watches over the group of statesmen and conveys a sense of action and triumph, transforming the piece into an allegory of imperial victory.

Yes, I thought, standing in front of what many regard as Guthrie's masterpiece. What had Churchill said? 'Victory was bought so dear as to be almost indistinguishable from defeat'. Well, by the time of the Armistice around three million British and Empire men had been wounded, were missing or were dead. One in three British households had lost someone: either dead, wounded or taken prisoner. No family, hamlet, village, town or city in the land was untouched. Hundreds of thousands were mutilated sufficiently to be debarred from living any productive, happy or rewarding life thereafter. In England's once green and pleasant land – in the Dominions, too – there lived hundreds of thousands of orphans and war widows, hundreds of thousands of young women who would never become brides, wives, mothers or grandmothers, and who in this way would miss much of what life has to offer. Vera Brittain called her generation 'depleted' and 'condemned'. The country herself began the war with a national debt of £651 million and ended it with a deficit of £7171 million. She was virtually bankrupt. The war precipitated her imperial, industrial and cultural decline. For Correlli Barnett, the war left the country 'psychologically crippled'. For Martin Gilbert, the war changed 'the map and destiny of Europe'. In his essay on his Cabinet colleague John Morley, who in 1914 had resigned rather than commit Britain to the war, Churchill wrote of the 'long era of peace, prosperity and progress which filled Queen Victoria's famous reign', of the 'brilliant and hopeful' world which Morley inhabited and enjoyed; and how 'He lived to see that fair world shattered, its hopes broken, its wealth squandered'. Victory bought so dear as to be almost indistinguishable from defeat.

With Churchill's words ringing in my ears, it did cross my mind to wonder whether those statesmen merited worthy and honourable commemoration or whether they had indeed made a mess of the war. Had Morley been right? Were his colleagues in 1914 ill-advised to take the Empire into the European conflict, and to despatch the BEF to the Continent and to order it to fight alongside the French? Were they right to let Kitchener build an army on a Continental scale with barely a by your leave? Deadlock having been reached on the Western Front before the year of 1914 was out, were they sensible in seeking alternatives to chewing barbed wired in Flanders? How well did they oversee the naval and military operations in the Dardanelles? How completely did they subsequently develop a framework of policy within which to direct the Royal Navy and to approve the various expeditionary forces on land, mainly on the Western Front? Were they right in 1916 to repudiate the several American and German feelers and more formal proposals for a negotiated peace? And in their endorsement of various offensives, including those on the Somme and at Passchendaele? It is all too easy to pass judgement on others whose difficulties you have never faced, and in whose times you do not live, but might they reasonably have acted otherwise? Ultimately, how well had they discharged what Basil Liddell Hart described as their 'heavy responsibility of being trustee for the lives of the nation'? Readers may well have their own views.

From the statesmen I passed to Sargent's *General Officers of World War I*. By common consent, this is the worst – aesthetically – of the three paintings. The twenty-two subjects, including of course Sir Douglas Haig, Sir John French and Sir Henry Wilson, are painted full length against a background – in Sargent's own words – of a vacuum. Clad in khaki, flanked by plinths and Doric columns, the generals stare out at the viewer apparently unaware of their companions. The critic Arthur Clutton-Brock thought that Sargent was more interested in the columns than the generals, that he had produced an accomplished collection of individual likenesses, 'but not, unfortunately, a picture'. Still, as the gallery's commentary suggests, 'As a statement about military leadership, the picture is perhaps very effective. The generals appear like a set of puppets waiting for someone to pull the strings, or as Charteris [Evan Charteris, Sargent's biographer] described them, like a chorus about to advance to the footlights.'

'Great soldiers who have been the means of saving the Empire.' These were Bailey's words. Again, you might be forgiven for wondering. There was Sir Henry Wilson, who conspired with the French to support them in the event of a German attack, largely without the imprimatur of the politicians, let alone the public; there on the far right was Sir John French, who would have fled to the Channel ports with the BEF in September 1914 if it hadn't been for Kitchener's stiffening trip to Paris. There, just to the right of centre, was Sir Douglas Haig himself, he of the moustache, wielding his field marshal's baton. The man who had doubted the wisdom of sending the BEF to the Continent in August 1914, the man who – even in the words of one of his more charitable biographers – was a slow learner, Haig who alongside the One Hundred Days, must forever bear the crosses of the Somme and Passchendaele. Still, Haig has his defenders. An army – like a navy – is a great deal more than its leadership, and leadership itself has many faces. What had John Buchan said of his country? 'Her armies had grown to be the equal of any army in the world, alike in training, discipline and leadership.' From a standing start, facing the great Prussian war machine, wasn't that something? And what of Liddell Hart, 'Without [Britain's] army, to take over the main burden of the struggle from 1916 onwards, defeat would have been inevitable.' During the course of the war, its men won 628 Victoria Crosses. Noel Godfrey Chavasse won two.

Cope's *Naval Officers of World War I* is perhaps the most appealing of the three paintings. The wood-panelled Admiralty boardroom with its wind dial and naval paintings is an effective setting; the arrangement of the twenty-two officers in groups, some sitting, some standing, some in animated conversation, is more effective dramatically than Sargent's chorus line. Nelson, stage right, presides fittingly over the scene. The inclusions are obvious enough: amongst them Sir John Jellicoe, Sir David Beatty, Sir Reginald Tyrwhitt, Sir Roger Keyes and Sir Rosslyn Wemyss. The exclusions are intriguing and rather unfortunate: the two commanders of the Northern Patrol which prosecuted the blockade, Admiral Sir Reginald Tupper and Admiral Sir Dudley de Chair; the sometime First Sea Lord Admiral Sir Henry Jackson, and his predecessor in the post, the great beast himself, Jacky Fisher, 1st Baron Fisher GCB, OM, GCVO. Hidden away on his Norfolk estate, the 77-year-old had refused to have anything to do with Cope's painting. He had taken umbrage. The others were not asked.

So those naval officers, for Bailey, 'the gallant sailors who have taken as great a share in the victory.'

What had Commander Kenworthy of the naval 'young Turks' told Lloyd George in that clandestine meeting in the Cabinet Office at the height of the U-boat crisis in 1917? 'The Navy so far has played a feeble part in the war'. It was certainly true that the Senior Service had more than once let the Hochseeflotte bombard the east coast, had failed to force the Dardanelles, had supposedly achieved nothing very decisive in Heligoland Bight in 1914 and the Dogger Bank in 1915, and that in the saga of the U-boats and the convoys its leadership had been its own worst enemy. Above all, it had failed to deliver a second Trafalgar at Jutland in 1916. It was Georges Clemenceau who, in November 1917, not long after Verdun and the crisis of the French mutinies, who declared '*La guerre! C'est une chose trop grave pour la confier à des militaires.*' Usually glossed as 'war is too important to be left to the generals', the return to power of '*Le Tigre*' found him as enthusiastic as his British counterpart, Lloyd George, to rattle some cages. Looking at the second and third of those pictures, at the admirals and the generals, I have to say I was momentarily inclined to think that the admirals should be included in the French prime minister's indictment. What would have happened if Lloyd George had left Jellicoe to his own devices in the Royal Navy's efforts to defeat the U-boats?

So I made way back to Guthrie's *Statesmen of World War I* and had another look at the puppeteers. On reflection, it was better than I had first thought. Certainly, the use of Nike of Samothrace was more imaginative than the other pair. There was also Churchill. As the gallery points out, a slanted ray of sunlight falls like a spotlight on his face, an emphasis which was 'almost prophetic'; and he alone of the subjects dares to look you in the eye. Churchill! What a difficult man to escape! Churchill. Churchill and the Navy. Churchill and the Army. Winston Spencer Churchill.

In July 1916, just after his escape from the trenches, Churchill published a thoughtful article in the *Sunday Pictorial*. In this he described Britain as 'the great Amphibian'. If her natural home was 'the broad seas', she could 'wade or even dart ashore – first a scaly arm with sharp claws' then 'a head with teeth, and shoulders that grew even broader'. Or this monster might 'return again to the deep, and strike anew now here, now there, and no one can guess where the next attack will fall'. Although amphibious warfare dates back at least to classical times, in so far as there was anything new in Churchill's concept, it perhaps lay in seeing the nation as intrinsically amphibious. It was an idea that recognised the supremacy of the Navy of the island nation, and her consequent ability to move the point of application of her force – the Army – to anywhere that wasn't landlocked. It was an idea that played to the nation's intrinsic strengths. It also played more topically to those of 1916, a time at which the Royal Navy was still the largest in the world and Lord Kitchener's volunteer armies had grown to the size – if not, as yet, of the skill – to challenge the great Continental forma-tions. Churchill's thinking had developed in the wake of the failure in the Dardanelles, a hesitant naval operation that had segued into a poorly planned and badly executed amphibious attack. It perhaps suggested that Churchill had learned from his mistakes, from errors, oversights and omissions that dated from well before Gallipoli. The ultimate expression of this idea lies in the D-Day landings of June 1944, an operation of breath-taking ambition, the like of which – as Baron Dannatt has recently remarked – we will never see again. I looked again from Churchill to Kitchener, the magisterial figure who might perhaps have appeared in Bailey's commissions either as a statesman or as a general. Between them, above all, between the pair of them, perhaps the puppeteers *had* made a hash of it.

I was thinking of that meeting in Downing Street on 5 August 1914 when that group of men 'mostly entirely ignorant of their subject' made the most important British strategic decision of the war. Led by Churchill and Kitchener, had they got it wrong? They sent the BEF to Flanders and they attached it to the French left wing. Wasn't that a decision made very largely against the grain of history and of Great Britain as a sea power, against the argument of the overwhelming strength of her Navy at the time and what the Kaiser supposedly called her contemptible little Army? It is difficult to say that Britain should have resisted the temptation to involve herself in a European war which was likely to have left Germany in control of western Europe – though plenty of people did so at the time and have done so since. It's easier to argue that she should have recognised where her strengths lay and have done one of two things. Either, in Churchill's own words, to have participated 'by naval action alone'; or to have held back the BEF and thrown it ashore at such a place and at such a time that would have been decisive: in France, Belgium, Germany's North Sea or Baltic coasts. An amphibious offensive. At that meeting, of the two weapons at the grandees' disposal, hadn't they chosen to place the emphasis on the weaker?

I recalled that these notions were widely discussed at the time. What had Northcliffe said, Northcliffe who, of all people, had his finger on the pulse of public opinion, who wielded as great a power over the public as the prime minister himself? 'What is this I hear about a British Expeditionary Force in France? It is nonsense. We have a superb Fleet, to which we shall give all the assistance in our power, but I will not support the sending out of this country of a single British soldier.' It took the failure of the Mediterranean Expeditionary Force at the Dardanelles for Churchill to formulate and articulate what perhaps should have been at least the headlines of Britain's combined naval and military strategy in 1914. As it was, wasn't it the case that strategy was made largely on the hoof of one of Haig's chargers, probably the one from which the King was thrown in November 1915? Again, readers may have their own ideas.

In *The Riddle of the Sands* Erskine Childers had asserted, 'We have no theory or doctrine of national defence, and no competent authorities whose business it is to give us one ... co-operation between army and navy is not studied or practised'. The Committee of Imperial Defence, created in 1902, had power merely to advise and had, in any case done little, certainly not until Maurice Hankey became its secretary in 1912. In 1914, surely, Childers' remarks remained very largely true. No theory or doctrine of national defence worthy of the name existed. 'Now we have a war,' said Churchill on that sunny August day, rather like someone who has just won the lottery. 'Now we have a war, the next thing is to decide is how to carry it on.' The Germans and the French had been planning for years – though, of course, they both had had a lot of recent practice, what with one thing and another. As I remembered, A J P Taylor had put it perfectly fairly. The imperial grandees on 5 August 'speculated in a void'. Hadn't they largely forgotten about the Navy on which quite a lot of money had been spent, forgotten about sea power, and sent a BEF of four divisions to play second fiddle to the French – with eighty-five – against a Deutsches Heer of 110? The rest was history, particularly in Flanders fields where the poppies grow. 'A better strategy,' says Niall Ferguson, 'would have been to wait and deal with the German challenge later when Britain could respond on its own terms, taking advantage of its much greater naval and financial capability.'

If war was too important a business to leave to the generals and admirals, then it was perhaps too important to leave to the politicians. For Allan Mallinson, 'Asquith had surrendered Britain's voice in strategy too easily.' If he had waited 'to field as many troops on the Western Front as the French ... the debilitating offensives of the war's middle years could have been avoided.'

As for French and Haig, Jellicoe and Beatty, was it fair to say that all four seemed as fallible as their political masters? What was Fisher's great phrase? 'Admirals who wouldn't fight and Generals who fought too much.' Yet if they were all flawed, human beings not admitting of perfection, some were perhaps more flawed than others. Of Haig, that anecdote of Churchill's came to mind. On 17 January 1916, the month after the field marshal took over from Sir John French as C-in-C of British forces on the Western Front, Churchill went to a lecture on the lessons of the Battle of Loos:

The theatre was crowded with generals and officers ... I could not even get a seat, but stood in the wings of the stage. Tom [Colonel Tom Holland] spoke very well but his tale was one of hopeless failure, of sublime heroism utterly wasted and of splendid Scottish soldiers shorn away in vain ... with never a ghost of a chance of success. 6000 killed and wounded out of 10000 in his Scottish division alone. Alas, alas. Afterwards they asked what was the lesson of the lecture. I restrained an impulse to reply, 'Don't do it again'. But they will – I have no doubt.

I remembered that the conventional defence of Haig was that the offensives at Loos, Arras, the Somme and Passchendaele had been necessary steps along the road that produced an army capable of winning the war on the Western Front in the summer and autumn of 1918. True, I supposed, but perhaps not the whole truth. Haig's armies in 1918 were better led, better equipped and more experienced than in 1916, more adept at co-ordinating their assets and activities, Haig a more competent C-in-C. Yet, of course, Ludendorff lost as much as the Allies – Belgian, French and American as well as British – won the One Hundred Days, and Imperial Germany's collapse was brought about by the naval blockade and precipitated by the Kiel mutiny, not to mention the Kaiser's endorsement of U-boat warfare. As Lloyd George had said and Haig himself very clearly implied, 'Germany has been broken almost as much by the blockade as by military methods.' She collapsed in the late autumn of 1918 because the Western Front offered the prospect only of defeat and the home front only of revolution – a revolution in itself precipitated by Germany's munificence towards Vladimir Lenin. As Haig's steps go, each of which cost, say, the lives of 200,000 of his men, they seemed rather costly. 'The casualties are mounting up,' I recalled General Sir Henry Rawlinson telling Haig a month into the Somme, and the 'powers that be ... are wondering if we are likely to get a proper return for them.'

In the course of the whole war the Army suffered about 750,000 missing or dead, twice that figure – 1.6 million – wounded; according to some accounts I have read, more than 2 million. If you include the Empire the death toll rises to one million. By 1919 its costs were running at £405 million a year. 'A fundamental difference between the higher naval and military leadership in the [First] World War was that the Admirals would not give battle unless sure of an initial advantage, and perhaps not then, whereas the Generals were usually ready to take the offensive whatever the disadvantages,' noted Liddell Hart in a fulsome echo of Fisher. 'In this attitude, the Admirals were true to their art, the Generals were not ... the custom of employing a professional is based on the idea that through art he will be able to obtain more profit at less cost.' More profit at less cost.

> They shall grow not old, as we that are left grow old:
> Age shall not weary them, nor the years condemn.
> At the going down of the sun and in the morning
> We will remember them.

If Haig squandered the Kitchener armies in 1916 and 1917 – the opinion of Churchill and Lloyd George – then how much better did the Admiralty, Jellicoe and Beatty do with Fisher's Navy? 'I've spent thirty years preparing for this day,' cried Fisher in the aftermath of Jutland, 'and they've failed me.' Certainly, Sackville Carden and de Robeck made a hash of the Dardanelles, Beatty and Jellicoe failed to deliver a second Trafalgar, and Jellicoe was manifestly culpable over the U-boat strategy and his support for Third Ypres – Haig's 'northern offensive'.

Still, despite the fumbling of the Admiralty, I remembered that the Navy had had its successes. It had broken the Kaiserliche Marine's naval code. It had safely delivered the BEF to France, kept it supplied for the 1571 days of the war, swept the Imperial German Navy's surface fleet of commerce raiders from the high seas before the end of 1914, castrated the Hochseeflotte by frightening the Kaiser in Heligoland Bight in August 1914 and the Dogger Bank five months later, then penning it into the North Sea, sidestepped losing the war at Jutland on the afternoon of 31 May 1916, eventually beat the U-boats, brought many of the two million American troops to France in 1917 and 1918 and – strangely overlooked by the National Portrait Gallery and Sir Arthur Cope – prosecuted the blockade that eventually did much to destroy the home front of Wilhelmine Germany. Jutland was also the proximate cause of the Kaiserliche Marine adopting the unrestricted U-boat strategy which tipped the balance by bringing the United States into the war. Overall, wasn't it true that the Navy did precisely the job that the naval strategist Sir Julian Corbett identified as the *sine qua non* for the service? It had maintained the maritime communications on which Great Britain and the Empire's survival, prosperity and ability to fight the war depended; ultimately, that of the Entente as a whole as well. In prosecuting the blockade it did more: it precipitated Germany's self-immolation. At 34,642 its war dead – many of whom were Royal Naval Brigade men fighting alongside the Army – were around 4 per cent of those of its sister service. It was hardly cheap, but by 1919 its costs were £160 million or around 40 per cent of those of the Army. How many British and Empire lives might the more rigorous application of Bertrand Russell's austere formula of 'maximum slaughter at minimum expense' have saved?

At the height of the U-boat crisis, Fisher had asked the question that was on everyone's lips, 'Can the Army win the war before the Navy loses it?' It was a compelling question but – I thought that day in the Portrait Gallery – maybe it begged another. It was even simpler, certainly simplistic, but the sort of question that was nevertheless asked at the time of the Armistice by the likes of Beatty and Haig and has been asked quite often since. Did the Army or the Navy win the war? I wondered. Was Jacky Fisher, the sometime First Sea Lord, justified in having inscribed with characteristic flamboyance on his gravestone, 'Organizer of the Navy that WON the Great War'? In so far as either side won anything, in so far as the Allies won rather than the Central Powers lost the war, in so far as any individual state or nation was pivotal, and in so far as the services acted as independent not interdependent agents, did the service whose story is that of the tragedies of Arras, Loos, the Somme and Passchendaele, those maelstroms etched into the national consciousness, do most to win the war? Or was it the service whose story is less spectacular, more elusive and much more fragmentary, whose story culminates in the noose of the blockade and of Mahan's 'far distant, storm-beaten ships, upon which the Grand Army never looked, stood between it and the dominion of the world'? The Great War might have been fought on land, but it was won at sea. Not so, for both the Army and the Navy manifestly made major contributions to the winning of the war. Yet was this not closer to the truth than is widely believed and understood? I pondered. Was it fair to conclude that the Navy was as great a contributor to victory as the Army – as Sir Abraham Bailey had suggested in commissioning his paintings – at a fraction of the financial and, above all, the human cost?

I had a last look at those three pictures before walking out into the sunlight on that brisk, sunny November day and turning south across the esplanade to Trafalgar Square, towards the Admiralty and the War Office in Whitehall. Up flew the pigeons like the doves of peace. It was approaching eleven o'clock. Although the commemoration was to be held on the Sunday as usual, I stood still. As Big Ben struck the hours that marked the ninety-ninth anniversary of the Armistice, as I stood in silence for those two minutes at the eleventh hour of the eleventh day of the eleventh month, as I stood in sight of the statue of Earl Haig and – too – of the Cenotaph in Whitehall, and as I thought of Sir Fabian Ware's calculation that if the Empire's dead were to march past Lutyens' great memorial it would take three and a half days for them all to file past – as I paid my respects – I glanced at Jellicoe and Beatty in their niches on the north side of the square. There was the ghost of a smile on Beatty's face, perhaps on Jellicoe's, too. Then I looked up at Nelson on his column, one hundred and sixty feet above, a silhouette of a figure against the azure sky, his sword and empty sleeve quite clear to the naked eye. He looked down from his eminence and gave me a nod. It was as much as to say that it was.

Sources and Acknowledgements

In writing this book I have done little other than to patch together into a sort of quilt the scholarship of others, many of whom have written tangentially, a few more directly on my theme.

Those to whom I am most indebted lived through or, indeed, were themselves principals in the events I describe. Although Churchill was a politician first and an historian second, I have been much enlightened by *The World Crisis* and *Great Contemporaries*. 'History will be kind to me for I intend to write it,' as perhaps the great man did not, in fact, say. John Buchan, too, was close to the centre of events. As an MP, war correspondent, army intelligence officer, speechwriter for Field Marshal Haig and propaganda chief, his *History of the Great War* and *The King's Grace* are rather more even-handed and less self-serving than Churchill's works. *These for Remembrance* is a unique tribute to six of his friends who died in action in the war, one of whom was the prime minister's eldest son, Raymond: Winchester, Balliol, All Souls, Grenadier Guards. Asquith himself, Beatty, Fisher, Haig, Hindenburg, Jellicoe, Keyes, Kitchener, Lloyd George, Ludendorff, Scheer, Tyrwhitt and Kaiser Wilhelm all have something instructive, revealing, incisive or entertaining to say, either in their memoirs or in private papers. Like Churchill, Lloyd George says what he says uncommonly well; explosive hardly does justice to Fisher's exhilarating memoirs and correspondence; Vera Brittain's account of life on the home front remains an incomparably moving chronicle.

The scholarship of a century has, of course, added a great deal of context, insight, information and fresh understanding to these contemporary accounts. Not least are Basil Liddell Hart's classics of military history, A J P Taylor's iconoclastic works on the period and his wider-ranging collected essays, Arthur Marder's *From Dreadnought to Scapa Flow*, Robert K Massie's two fine works on the *Dreadnought* era, John Terraine's *Douglas Haig: the Educated Soldier*, Paul Kennedy's *The Rise and Fall of British Naval Mastery*, Paul Fussell's *The Great War and Modern Memory*, John Keegan's finely judged *The First World War*, Martin Gilbert's characteristically comprehensive work of the same title, Jan Morris's dazzling caprice *Fisher's Face*, Richard Hough's *The Great War at Sea* and Barbara Tuchman's *The Guns of August*. Of more recent works, I have found most helpful those of Brian Bond, Christopher Clark, Niall Ferguson, Max Hastings, Andrew Lambert, Allan Mallinson, Robert Massie, Gary Sheffield, David Stevenson and Hew Strachan. Alexander Watson's *Ring of Steel* tells the story from the Teutonic perspective outstandingly – and rather conveniently in a language with which I am tolerably familiar. It has also been a privilege to talk to the descendants of Admiral of the Fleet Sir Roger Keyes. Finally, there are good biographies of most of the major players, not least Stephen Roskill's studies of David Beatty and Maurice Hankey, John Grigg's works on Lloyd George, Roy Jenkins on both Churchill and Asquith, and Gary Mead on Haig.

Of those who read the book in manuscript, I am particularly grateful to Brigadier Allan Mallinson and Lieutenant Colonel Tony Slater for holding my feet to the fire of an early draft. Of those who saw something marginally more finished, I must thank my wife Kate Faire, my editor Rob Gardiner, the scholars Clive Jenkins and Anne Ockwell, Professor Peter Sinclair, the naval scholar Mike Tapper and twentieth-century historian Dr Chris A Williams for a plethora of insight, correction and advice. As usual, the point of view, interpretation and the remaining errors and omissions are my own; as is the title.

Select Bibliography

Aspinall-Oglander, C F, *Roger Keyes* (1951)

Asprey, Robert B, The *German High Command at War: Hindenburg and Ludendorff and the First World War* (1991)

Asquith, H H, *Letters to Venetia Stanley* (1985)

Bacon, Admiral Sir Reginald Hugh, *The Life of Lord Fisher of Kilverstone* (1929)

——, *The Life of John Rushworth, Earl Jellicoe* (1936)

Barnett, Correlli, *The Sword Bearers: studies in supreme command in the First World War* (1963)

——, *The Lords of War* (2012)

Beatty, Charles Robert Longfield, *Our Admiral* (1980)

Beatty, David, *The Beatty Papers* (ed B McL Ranft, 1989)

Bell, A C, *A history of the blockade of Germany and of the countries associated with her in the Great War, Austria–Hungary, Bulgaria, and Turkey, 1914–1918* (1937)

Bell, Christopher M, *Churchill and Sea Power* (2013)

Benedictus, David, *Lloyd George* (1981)

Bennett, Geoffrey, *The Battle of Jutland* (2015)

Bilton, David, *The Home Front* (2016)

Blake, Robert, and Roger Louis (eds) *Winston Churchill: A Major New Assessment of His Life in Peace and War*, (1993)

Blythe, Ian, *The Making of an Industry* (2005)

Bond, Brian, *War and Society in Europe, 1870–1970* (1984)

——, *Britain's Two World Wars against Germany* (2014)

Brittain, Vera, *Testament of Youth*, (1933)

Broadbent, Harvey, *Gallipoli: The Fatal Shore* (2005)

Brogan, Hugh, *The Life of Arthur Ransome* (1984)

Brown, Ian Malcolm, *British Logistics on the Western Front, 1914–1919* (1998)

Buchan, John, *These for Remembrance* (1919)

——, *A History of the Great War* (1921)

——, *The King's Grace 1910–1935* (1935)

——, *Memory-hold-the Door* (1940)

Cassar, George H, *Kitchener's War* (2004)

Chalmers, William Scott, *The Life and Letters of David, Earl Beatty* (1951)

Chatterton, E Keble, *The Big Blockade* (1930)

Chickering, Roger, *Imperial Germany and the Great War, 1914–1918* (2014)

Childers, Erskine, *The Riddle of the Sands* (1903)

Churchill, Winston, *The World Crisis* (1923–1931)

——, *Great Contemporaries* (1937)

Clark, Alan, *The Donkeys* (1961)

Clark, Christopher M, *Kaiser Wilhelm II* (2000)

——, *The Sleepwalkers* (2012)

Corbett, Julian, *Some Principles of Maritime Strategy* (1911)

Conquest, Robert, *Lenin* (1972)

de Chair, Dudley Rawson Stratford, *The Sea is Strong* (1961)

Dixon, Norman, *On the Psychology of Military Incompetence* 1976)

Dorling, Taprell, *Endless Story* (1931)

Domville-Fife, Charles W, *Evolution of Sea Power* (1939)

Dunn, Steve R, *Blockade* (2016)

Ekins, Ashley, *1918 The Year of Victory* (2010)

Ferguson, Niall, *History: Alternatives and Counterfactuals* (1997)

——, *The Pity of War* (1998)

Fisher, John Arbuthnot, *Memories, by Admiral of the Fleet Lord Fisher* (1919)

——, *Fear God and Dread Nought. The Correspondence of Admiral of the Fleet, Lord Fisher of Kilverstone* (1952)

Floud, Roderick, *The Economic History of Britain since 1700* (1994)

Foot, Michael, *Armistice 1918–1939* (1940)

Freeman, Richard, *Unsinkable* (2013)

Fussell, Paul, *The Great War and Modern Memory* (2000)

Gibbs, Norman Henry, *The Origins of Imperial Defence* (1955)

Gilbert, Martin, *Churchill: A Life* (1992)

——, *The First World War* (1994)

Goldrick, James, *Before Jutland*, (2015)

Gordon, Andrew, *The Rules of the Game; Jutland and British Naval Command* (1996)

Grainger, John D (ed), *The Maritime Blockade of Germany in the Great War* (2003)

Gray, Edwyn A, *The Killing Time. The U-boat War 1914–18* (1975)

Greenhalgh, Elizabeth, *Foch in Command* (2011)

Grigg, John, *Lloyd George, the Young Lloyd George* (1997)

——, *Lloyd George, War Leader* (2002)

Halpern, Paul G, *A Naval History of World War I* (1994)

Hamilton, C I, *The Making of the Modern Admiralty* (2011)

Hampshire, Arthur Cecil, *The Blockaders* (1980)

Hankey, Maurice Pascal Alers, *Politics, Trials and Errors* (1950)

——, *The Supreme Command 1914–1918* (1961)

Harris, J P, *Douglas Haig and the First World War* (2008)

Hart, Peter, *Gallipoli* (2011)

Hart, P, and N Steel, *Passchendaele: the Sacrificial Ground* (2001)

Hardach, Gerd, *The First World War, 1914–1918* (1977)

Hastings, Max, *Catastrophe* (2013)

Hazlehurst, Cameron, *Politicians at War* (1971)

Heathcote, Tony, *The British Admirals of the Fleet*, 1734–1995 (2002)

Holborn, Hajo, *A History of Modern Germany, Volume 3: 1840–1945* (1982)

Hough, Richard, *Fisher, First Sea Lord* (1969)

——, *The Great War at Sea 1914–1918* (1986)

Hull, Isabel V, *A Scrap of Paper. Breaking and Making of International Law during the Great War* (2014)

James, Robert Rhodes, *Churchill: A Study in Failure, 1900–1939* (1970)

Jellicoe, John Rushworth, *The Crisis of the Naval War* (1920)

——, *The Grand Fleet, 1914–16* (1919)

Jenkins, Roy, *Asquith* (1988)

——, *Churchill* (2001)

Johnson, Boris, *The Churchill Factor: How One Man Made History* (2013)

Keegan, John, *The First World War* (1998)

——, *Battle at Sea: From Man-of-War to Submarine* (2004)

Kelly, Patrick J, *Tirpitz and the Imperial German Navy* (2011)

Kennedy, P M, *The Rise and Fall of British Naval Mastery* (1976)

——, *Strategy and Diplomacy 1870–1945* (1983)

Kenworthy, Joseph Montague, *Sailors, Statesmen and Others* (1933)

Keyes, Roger, *The Naval Memoirs of Admiral of the Fleet Sir Roger Keyes* (1934–1936)

——, *The Fight for Gallipoli* (1941)

Kitchen, Martin, *The Silent Dictatorship: The Politics of the High Command under Hindenburg and Ludendorff, 1916–1918* (1976)

Knight, Edward Frederick, *The Harwich Naval Forces: their part in the Great War* (1919)

Koss, Stephen, *Asquith*, (1985)

Lambert, Andrew D (with Marcus Faulkner), *Atlas of the Great War at Sea* (2015)

Lambert, Nicholas A, *Planning Armageddon* (2012)

Larson, Erik, *Dead Wake: The Last Crossing of the Lusitania* (2015)

Lee, John, *The Warlords: Hindenburg and Ludendorff* (2005)

Liddell Hart, Basil, *A History of the World War, 1914–1918* (1934)

——, *The War in Outline* (1936)

Lilley, Terence Dawson, 'Operations of the Tenth Cruiser Squadron; a challenge for the Royal Navy and its reserves' (doctoral thesis, 2012)

Lloyd, N, *Passchendaele: A New History* (2017)

Lloyd George, David, *War Memoirs of David Lloyd George* (1933)

Lowry, Bulitt, *Armistice 1918* (1996)

Ludendorff, Erich, *Concise Ludendorff Memoirs* 1914–1918 (1933)

——, *Ludendorff's Own Story, August 1914–November 1918* (1971)

Macdonald, Lynn, *Somme* (1993)

McLynn, Frank, *Invasion* (1987)

Mace, Martin, *The Royal Navy and the War at Sea, 1914–1919* (2014)

Macksey, Kenneth, *For Want of a Nail* (1989)

Magnus, Philip Montefiore, *Kitchener. Portrait of an Imperialist* (1958)

Mahan, Alfred Thayer, *The Influence of Sea Power upon History, 1660–1783* (1890)

——, *The Influence of Sea Power upon the French Revolution and Empire, 1793–1812* (1892)

Mallet, Bernard, *British Budgets. Second Series, 1913–14 to 1920–21* (1929)

Mallinson, Allan, *Fight the Good Fight: Britain, the army and the coming of the First World* War (2014)

——, *Too Important for Generals; losing and winning the First World War* (2016)

Maltster, Robert, *The North Sea War, 1914–1919* (2015)

Masefield, John, *Gallipoli* (1916)

Massie, Robert K, *Castles of Steel: Britain, Germany, and the Winning of the Great War at Sea* (2004)

——, *Dreadnought: Britain, Germany and the Coming of the Great War* (1991)

Mead, Gary, *The Good Soldier, a biography of Douglas Haig* (2014)

Merridale, Catherine, *Lenin on the Train* (2016)

Mitchell, Brian Redman, *Abstract of British Historical Statistics* (1962)

Monsarrat, Nicholas, *Three Corvette* (1945)

Morgan, Michael Croke, *Lenin* (1971)

Morris, Jan, *Pax Britannica: the Climax of an Empire* (1968)

——, *Heaven's Command: an Imperial Progress* (1973)

——, *Farewell the Trumpets: An Imperial Retreat* (1978)

——, *Fisher's Face* (2007)

Morris, Roger, *Haig* (1982)

Murray, Gilbert, *The Foreign Policy of Sir Edward Grey, 1906–1915* (1915)

Naylor, John F, *A Man and an Institution* (1984)

O'Connell, Robert J, *Sacred Vessels: The Cult of the Battleship and the Rise of the US Navy* (1993)

Osborne, Eric W, *The Battle of Heligoland Bight* (2003)

——, *Britain's Economic Blockade of Germany, 1914–1919* (2004)

Paret, Peter (ed), *Makers of Modern Strategy: from Machiavelli to the Nuclear Age* (1990)

Patterson, A Temple, *Tyrwhitt of the Harwich Force: the life of Admiral of the Fleet Sir Reginald Tyrwhitt* (1973)

Pearson, Michael, *The Sealed Train* (1975)

Pemberton, Max, *Lord Northcliffe. A Memoir* (1922)

Penrose, Barrie, *Stalin's Gold* (1982)

Philpott, W, *Attrition: Fighting the First World War* (2014)

Pollock, John, *Kitchener: Architect of Victory, Artisan of Peace* (2001)

Preston, Diana, *A Higher Form of Killing* (2015)

Price, Emry, *David Lloyd George* (2006)

Purdue, A W, *The First World War* (2015)

Rawson, Andrew, *British Army Handbook, 1914–1918* (2006)

——, *The British Army 1914–1918* (2014)

Reid, Waller, *Douglas Haig* (2006)

Röhl, John C G, *Kaiser Wilhelm, 1859–1941* (2014)

Rose, Kenneth, *King George V* (1984)

Roskill, S W, *Hankey, a man of secrets* (1970–1974)

——, *Admiral of the Fleet Earl Beatty* (1980)

Rowland, Peter, *Lloyd George* (1975)

Ryder, Arthur John, *The German Revolution of 1918* (1967)

Scheer, Reinhard, *Germany's High Seas Fleet in the First World War* (2014)

Sheffield, G, *The Chief: Douglas Haig and the British Army* (2011)

Sheffield, G D, *Command and Morale* (1921)

Sheffield, Gary, *A Short History of the First World War* (2014)

Simkins, Peter, *Kitchener's Army* (1988)

Sims, William Sowden, *The Victory at Sea* (1920)

Staff, Gary, *Skagerrak* (2016)

Stevenson, D, *1914–1918: the History of the First World War* (2004)

——, *With Our Backs to the Wall: victory and defeat in 1918* (2011)

Stevenson, Robert C, *The War with Germany* (2015)

Stone, Norman, *Europe Transformed, 1878–1979* (1983)

Strachan, Hew, *The First World War* (2003)

——, *Masters of the Seas: Naval Power and the First World War* (Rothermere American Institute Inaugural Lecture, 2016)

Swan, Robert, *British Army Transport & Logistics* (1991)

Tait, Ian, *Blockade 1914–1918* (2015)

Taylor, A J P, *Essays in English History* (1976)

——, *English History 1914–1945* (1981)

——, *The First World War: an illustrated history* (1987)

Taylor, Blaine, *Kaiser Bill* (2014)

Terraine, John, *The Great War 1914–1918: a pictorial history* (1965)

——, *Douglas Haig: the educated solider* (1963)

Travers, T, *The Killing Ground: The British Army, the Western Front &
the Emergence of Modern War 1900–1918* (1987)

Tuchman, Barbara W, *The Guns of August* (2000)

Tupper, Reginald, *Reminiscences* (1929)

Van Creveld, Martin, *Supplying War* (1977)

van der Vat, Dan, *Standard of Power: the Royal Navy in the 20th
Century* (2003)

Vincent, C Paul, *The Politics of Hunger*: *the Allied Blockade of
Germany, 1915–1919* (1985).

Wallace, Edgar, *Kitchener's New Army* (2015)

Warth, Robert D, *Lenin* (1973)

Watson, Alexander, *Ring of Steel* (2014)

Weintraube, Stanley, *A Stillness Heard Round the World* (1986)

Wemyss, Rosslyn Erskine, *The Navy in the Dardanelles Campaign*
(1924)

Westlake, Ray, *Kitchener's Army* (1989)

Wettern, Desmond, *The Decline of British Sea-power* (1982)

Wheeler, Harold F B, *Stirring Deeds of Britain's Sea-Dogs in the Great
War* (1916)

——, *The Story of the British Navy* (1922)

Wilhelm II, *The Kaiser's Memoirs* (2005)

Wilson, Ben, *Empire of the Deep: the Rise and Fall of the British Navy*
(2013)

Winter, D, *Haig's Command: A Reassessment* (1991)

Winton, John, *Jellicoe* (1981)

Wolz, Nicolas, *From Imperial Splendour to Internment* (2015)

Wragg, David W, *Fisher* (2009)

Index

ANZAC (Australia and New Zealand Army Corps) 84, 85

Aboukir 75, 153

Admiralty 26, 95, 120, 151, 154, 157: and the blockade 100; Churchill's 1911 move to 27; cryptanalysis section 57; Lloyd George 150, 151, 162–4; Tyrwhitt xx

Alexander III of Russia 145

Alsatian 97, 100

American Expeditionary Force (AEF) 167, 179, 189, 191, 203

Amiens, battle of 187–8

Arabic 80

Arethusa, x, 42, 46, 56, 110

Arlanza, 100

Armistice xiv, xxi, xxiii, 2–11, 126, 178, 191, 199–200: German Armistice Commission 2–5, 199; Ludendorff 190, 192; signing of 5, 9, 11–12; terms 4–5, 6, 194, 200; Wilson's Fourteen Points 4, 190, 194

Arras, battle of 151, 160, 165, 202, 214

Asquith, H H, 1st Earl of Oxford and Asquith 29, 53: Britain's entry to Great War 14, 16; and Churchill xix, 27, 69, 86; the Dardanelles 53; Fisher 53, 70, 87–9; and Kitchener 32; and Lloyd George 86, 145; resignation 127; and Russia 60; as Secretary of State for War 17; and Zeebrugge 69

Aubers Ridge, battle of 82–4, 85, 87

Austerlitz, battle of 58, 201

Australia and New Zealand Army Corps (ANZAC) 84, 85

Austria 24

Austria–Hungary/Austro-Hungarian Empire 6, 14, 25, 37, 62, 118, 130, 135, 170

Austro-Prussian War 15

Bacon, Sir Reginald 90

Bailey, Sir Abraham 205, 209, 210, 216–17

Balfour, Arthur 53, 88, 91, 101

Baltic xvii, 20, 37, 61, 63, 69, 89–91, 153

Barnett, Correlli 110–11, 207

Battenberg, Prince Louis Alexander, Lord Mountbatten 42, 54

Bayano 100

Bayern 147

Beatty, Sir David vii, xvi, xix–xx, 7, 10, 12, 42, 43, 55–6, 67, 106, 215: and the Armistice 7–9, 10–11; and the blockade of Germany 134–5; and Churchill 47, 55, 56, 111, 120; and de

Chair 100, 101; early naval career 55–6; epigraphs 1, 129; and Fisher 56, 57; and the Grand Fleet 137, 155, 183–4; and Jellicoe 56, 106, 119–20; Jutland 12, 56, 106, 108, 111, 113, 119–20; and Kitchener 56; and Tyrwhitt 43, 46

Belgium 14, 15, 18, 20, 37, 39: army 39; German evacuation from 6; and the Schlieffen Plan *see* Schlieffen

Benelux countries 38 *see also specific countries*

Berlin riots 183

Bethmann-Hollweg, Theobald von 129, 136, 140–1, 142, 189

Binyon, Laurence xiii

Bismarck, Otto von 26, 136–7, 138

Bismarck 119

blockade of Germany vi–vii, viii, 51, 93–101, 121, 133–5, 165, 200, 202, 214, 215: boarding blockade-runners 98–9; by Dover Patrol 94, 184; Ministry of Blockade 134; and *Steckrübenwinter* (Turnip Winter) 101; victory through xiv–xv, 13, 51, 215, 216

blockade strategy 20–21: German blockade of Britain vii, 76, 79, 118, 136, 151, 152–6, 157, 170, 203

Blücher 67

Blücher, Operation 180, 181

Boer Wars 24, 32, 103, 104, 144, 166–7

Bolsheviks 142–3, 146–9, 174, 194, 198

Brest-Litovsk, Treaty of 142, 179, 196

Britain: Bismarck and German pre-war detente with 137; Committee of Imperial Defence 17, 88, 212–13; food imports 19; Foreign Office 95, 99, 100, 147, 188; German blockade of vii, 76, 79, 118, 136, 151, 152–6, 157, 170, 203; merchant shipping vii, 19, 56, 79, 136, 151, 152–6, 157, 170, 184; proposals for participation in Great War 'by naval action alone' 14–30; and Triple Entente 14, 37, 142, 146, 151; War Council 17, 29–31, 53–4, 59–60, 62–4, 67–71, 88, 160; War Policy Committee 168, 169

British Army 12, 24–5, 191: 1st Army 82–3, 161; 2nd Army 171; 3rd Army 161; 5th Army 171, 179, 185; British Expeditionary Force (BEF) 14, 17, 30, 31–2, 36, 37, 39, 43–4, 47–8, 52, 58, 59–60, 62, 87, 180, 202, 212, 214; casualties 11, 58, 62, 82–4, 101–2, 105, 109, 116, 151, 160, 162, 166, 174, 179–80, 207, 214; dependence on Royal Navy for transportation and supplies xiii–xiv, 31–2, 167, 203, 215; Kitchener's volunteers 33, 82, 89, 102, 105–6, 114, 122, 176–7, 191, 211; Mediterranean Expeditionary Force 84, 212; protection of troops crossing Channel 31–2

Brittain, Edward Harold 35, 71–2, 128, 145, 162, 171, 177, 199–200

Brittain, Vera 71–2, 104–5, 109, 115, 118, 127, 128, 145, 177, 180, 199–200, 207: *Testament of Youth* 34–5

Brooke, Rupert 35, 133

Brusilov, Aleksei 118, 122–3, 130, 145, 176

Buchan, John xv, xxii, 6, 11, 25, 100, 103, 120, 124, 127, 132–3, 144, 168, 169, 188, 201, 202, 203, 209

Budapest 61–2

Bulgaria 6, 61, 189

Camperdown 65

Carden, Sackville 63, 74, 84, 87, 215

Cardiff 10

Carson, Sir Edward 126–7, 156, 157, 163

Chatfield, Ernle, 1st Baron vi, 43

Childers, Erskine x, 144, 167: *The Riddle of the Sands* xi, xiv, xxii, 25, 26, 28, 212

Churchill, Winston xiii–xiv, xxiv, 36–7, 59, 62, 85, 132, 147, 175, 199, 201, 211–12, 213: in 4th Hussars 18, 33, 56; and Asquith xix, 27, 69, 86; and Beatty 47, 55, 56, 111, 120; and the BEF 30; and the blockade of Germany 95, 101; and Britain as 'the great Amphibian' xiii–xiv, 62, 211; and Britain's entry to Great War 15–17, 30; and the convoy system 164; on cost of victory 11, 34, 49, 115, 207; and the Dardanelles xix, 50, 53, 61, 63–5, 84, 86–7, 123, 125, 211, 212; epigraphs 14, 73, 92, 142, 150, 166; and Fisher xix, 54, 55, 56–7, 63, 67–9, 73, 74, 86, 88, 89–90; and Gallipoli xix; on German navy 40–41; on the Grand Fleet 23; and Haig 12, 176–7, 213–14, 215; and Heligoland 41–2, 46–7; and Jellicoe 33, 66, 67, 86, 120; and Jutland xviii, 111, 118, 120; and Keyes 40, 41, 47, 74; and Kitchener 33, 36–7, 50, 75; and Lanrezac 39–40; and Lloyd George 127, 171; and Louis of Battenberg 54; moved to Admiralty in 1911 27; on naval blockade policy 20, 21; protection of troops crossing Channel 31–2; and *Queen Elizabeth* 64–5, 70, 86; sacked from Admiralty 86; and submarine warfare 74, 75, 76, 77, 79, 129–30, 141, 153, 154, 156, 164; and Third Ypres/Passchendaele 167–8, 169, 171, 175, 176–7; and Tyrwhitt 40, 42, 46–7; *The World Crisis* xvii, 33, 70; and Zeebrugge 69, 185–6

Clemenceau, Georges 4, 126–7, 179, 210

Committee of Imperial Defence 17, 88, 212–13

conscription, British Army 174

Constantinople 61, 64, 70, 87

convoy system vii–viii, xxii, 31–2, 36, 150, 151, 154, 157, 163–4, 170, 174, 184, 202

Cope, Sir Arthur Stockdale: *Naval Officers of World War I* 205, 209–10, 215

Coronel, battle of xvii, 56

Crescent, 95, 96–7

Cressy 75, 153

Curacoa, 9

de Chair, Dudley Rawson Stratford xx, 92–4, 96–7, 100

Dogger Bank, battle of xvii, xx, 9, 67, 119, 137, 210, 215

Dorling, Henry Taprell xviii

Dover Patrol 94, 184

Dreadnought 22, 23, 64, 117

dreadnoughts: German 22–3, 42, 50, 67, 110, 121, 147, 195, 198; RN xv, xvii, 23, 36, 50, 65, 67, 97, 121, 155–6, 195

E11 xx, 87

Earl of Lathom 75, 77, 80

Eastern Front 60, 81, 105, 122–3, 130, 131–2, 146, 176

Ebert, Friedrich 5, 199

Edgar 95

Edgar-class cruisers 95–7, 100

Emden 36

Endymion 95

Engels, Friedrich 143, 196

Enver Pasha, Ismail 81, 85, 87

Erzberger, Matthias 2–3, 4–5, 199

Falkands xvii, 56, 76

Falkenhayn, Erich von 49, 105, 106, 113, 117, 130, 131–2, 139, 176, 196

Faulks, Sebastian xxii

Fearless 42

Ferguson, Niall xxi, 52, 213

fertiliser, German shortages 19, 101, 133–4

Festubert, battle of 82, 85, 87, 101

Firedrake 42

First World War: Britain's entry 16–17, 29–30, 34; British proposals of participation 'by naval action alone' 14–30; Eastern Front 60, 81, 105, 122–3, 130, 131–2, 146, 176; and the fall of empires xii, 145; German 1918 spring offensives 2, 11, 176, 179–81, 192, 202; German August 1914 attack on France 38–9; German home front 132–4, 188–9; 'Great Retreat' of August 1914 39–40, 43–4, 47; Royal Navy's critical importance xiii–xv, 202–4, 215–17; US entry vii, xxi, 124, 138, 147, 215

Fisher, John Arbuthnot 'Jacky', 1st Baron vii, xix, 19, 22, 23, 55, 77, 87, 126, 167, 176, 213, 216: and Asquith 53, 70, 87–9; and the Baltic 63, 69, 89–91; and Beatty 56, 57; and Churchill xix, 54, 55, 56–7, 63, 67–9, 73, 74, 86, 88, 89–90; and the Dardanelles 62–3, 64, 67–71, 86, 89; and Jellicoe 65, 66, 67; and Jutland 108, 118–19, 120, 215; and Kitchener 53–4, 69–70; and *Queen Elizabeth* 64–5, 89; resignation May 1915 86, 89, 145; and Tyrwhitt 91, 120

Flanders xiii, 61, 71, 168–9, 186, 212, 213: and Churchill xii, 59, 61, 108; German naval bases in 170, 184

Foch, Ferdinand xxi, 4, 5, 11, 12, 169, 176, 179, 186, 187, 189, 191

France: and Alsace-Lorraine 25; Britain's commitment to defend 15, 30–1; and Triple Entente 14, 37, 142, 146, 151

Franz Ferdinand, Archduke 14, 143, 145
Franz Joseph of Austria-Hungary 106, 149
French, Sir John xxi, 17, 27, 33, 39, 62, 82, 84, 186, 209: and Churchill 39–40; and Haig 82, 103, 104, 176; and Kitchener 37, 39, 40, 45, 47, 59, 87, 102; and Loos 101–2, 103; and Ypres 58, 172
French army 26, 43, 44, 47, 82, 186: Third Army 161; Fifth Army 37, 39, 47–8; casualties 11, 39, 58, 105, 116, 118, 151, 162, 191; mutinies 162, 165; at the Somme 113–14, 115, 116

Gallipoli and the Dardanelles campaign xvii, xix, xxiv, 53, 57, 61, 62–71, 84–7, 105, 122, 123, 153, 167, 202, 210, 215: and Churchill xix, 50, 53, 61, 63–5, 84, 86–7, 123, 125, 211, 212; and Keyes xx, 47, 74, 84–5, 87
George V 65, 93: and Haig 93, 103, 104
German army (Deutsches Heer) xiv, 26, 131, 138, 139, 146, 188: 6th Army 82, 83, 102; 8th Army 130; and Allied 'Great Retreat' of August 1914 39–40, 43–4, 47; Armistice terms for 6, 194; battle of the Marne 48–9; casualties 11, 58, 115, 118, 130, 151, 181; Operation Blücher 180, 181; Operation Georgette 180; Operation Michael 179–81, 192, 202; prisoners of war 123, 181, 182; and Russian forces 45; storm troopers 181
German Navy, Imperial xvi, xxii, 22, 23–4, 116–17, 137: Armistice terms for 7, 8, 194, 200; arms race and expansion 21–2, 167; and British merchant shipping vii, 56, 79, 136, 151, 152–6, 157, 170, 184; dreadnoughts 22–3, 42, 50, 67, 110, 121, 147, 195, 198; Flanders bases 170, 184; Hochseeflotte (High Seas Fleet) vii, xvi, 5, 8, 10, 27, 40, 50–51, 56, 60, 66, 86, 90, 110–13, 119, 121, 122, 136, 174, 183, 184, 186, 194–6, 197, 202, 210; and the Kaiser x, 21–2, 49–50, 51, 108, 116; Kiel mutiny xxiii, 142, 193, 198; Naval Order of October 1918 193; *Prinzregent Luitpold* mutiny 149, 196; Spee's squadron 56, 76, 137; U-boats *see* U-boats; Wilhelmshaven revolt 5
Germany 15, 25, 37–9: and the Bolsheviks 142–3, 146–9; fertiliser shortages 19, 101, 133–4; food distribution/shortages/prices/riots viii, 133, 134, 149, 181–3, 196; home front 132–4, 188–9; and Lenin's revolutions 142–3, 147–9, 196, 198, 214; November Revolution 193, 198; pre-war detente with Britain 137; Social Democracy/SPD 5, 143, 196, 199; starvation viii, 134, 182–3; *Steckrübenwinter* (Turnip Winter) 101, 134; US discounted as threat to the war by 139–40; US trade 137
Gibraltar 95
Gilbert, Martin xviii, 105, 162, 173, 183, 207
Gneisenau 36, 56, 137, 153
Gough, Sir Hubert 165, 171–2
Grafton, 95
Grey, Sir Edward 53, 144: and Britain's entry to Great War 15; and the Declaration of London 95; on the Navy xiii–xiv
Grigg, John 33, 163–4

Haig, Dorothy Maud, née Vivian 103–4
Haig, Sir Douglas xxi, 4, 12–13, 14, 17, 33, 44, 52, 82, 85, 103–4, 105–6, 114, 150, 179, 186, 190–91, 205–6, 209: and the Armistice 126; and Churchill 12, 176–7, 213–14, 215; and the Council of War 17, 30–1; and French 82, 103, 104, 176; and George V 93, 103, 104; and Jellicoe 166, 167; and Joffre 106, 113; and Jutland 108, 124; and Lloyd George 13, 127, 155, 160, 164–5, 167, 168, 169–70, 171, 175–6, 180, 215; and Nivelle 160, 164–5; and Operation Michael 180; and Robertson 124, 177; and the Somme 106, 108, 109, 113, 115, 122–4, 125, 170, 209, 214; and Third Ypres/Passchendaele 166, 168, 169–71, 173, 175–7, 209, 214; war apologia 12–13
Haldane, Richard, 1st Viscount 22, 104: army reforms 18
Hamilton, Sir Ian 84, 85, 87
Hampshire 108, 109
Hankey, Maurice xxi, 17, 29, 30, 53, 59–60, 64, 109, 126, 155, 158–9, 198, 213: and Grand Duke Nicholas's appeal 61
Harwich Force xvii, 8, 9, 40, 41, 120, 183–4: vs German flotillas north of Heligoland 42–3, 46
Hawke 95
Helgoland-class battleship 22
Heligoland 26–7, 41–2, 170
Heligoland Bight, battle of xvii, xx, 9, 41, 43, 46–7, 49, 50–1, 74, 137, 184, 202, 210, 215
Henderson, R G H 157, 163
Herringen, Josias von 38–9
Hertling, Georg von 178, 186–7, 190
Hickey, Michael 89
Hindenburg, Gertrud von 130
Hindenburg, Paul von 45, 124, 130–1, 132, 138, 146, 161, 175, 178, 181, 195: and Falkenhayn 131–2, 139; and Lenin 146; and Ludendorff 131–2, 138–9, 189–90
Hindenburg line 161, 189
Hipper, Franz von 110, 112, 195, 197
Hitler, Adolf 133
Hogue 75, 153
Holland, Tom 213–14
Holtzendorff, Henning von 135, 136, 140, 152, 153, 193
Hood 119
Hope, George 4, 152
Hopwood, Ronald xviii
Horace 144
Hough, Richard 70, 89, 119, 176, 200
Hundred Days Offensive xxi, 188, 191, 201, 203

Indefatigable 111, 118
India 100
Inflexible 55, 56
influenza epidemic 2, 188
Ingenohl, Friedrich von 40, 46
Invincible 42, 43, 56, 112, 118
Iron Duke 110, 119
Italian army 170, 174

Jackson, Sir Henry 91, 152
Jellicoe, Sir John xv, xix–xx, 50, 65–7, 152, 153,

154, 156, 157, 215: and Beatty 56, 106, 119;
and Churchill 33, 66, 67, 86, 120; and the
convoy system 155, 168; and de Chair 93, 94;
dismissal 176; and Fisher 65, 66, 67; and
Germany's blockade of Britain 170; and Haig
166, 167; and Jutland 66, 111, 112, 119, 120,
125, 155; and Lloyd George 155, 168, 171, 175,
176; and the Northern Patrol 97; and Sims
152, 154; and Third Ypres/Passchendaele 166,
170, 215
Jenkins, Roy 54, 65, 71
Joffre, Joseph 39, 47, 52, 81–2, 102: and Haig
106, 113; Plan XVII 39; and the Somme 106
Jutland, battle of xvi, 108, 109–13, 118–21, 125,
130, 137, 193, 201, 202, 215: and Beatty 12,
56, 106, 108, 111, 113, 119–20; and Churchill
xviii, 111, 118, 120; and Fisher 108, 118–19,
120, 215; and Haig 108, 124; and Jellicoe 66,
111, 112, 119, 120, 125, 155; and Keyes 120–21

Kaiser 198
Keegan, John xvii, xxi, xxiv, 45, 82, 116, 123,
124, 138, 161, 165, 172, 182, 186, 189–90, 206
Kenworthy, Joseph 157–8, 210
Keyes, Roger xx, 40, 41, 42, 74, 84–5, 87 91,
120–1, 156–7, 184–5
Kiel mutiny xxiii, 142, 193, 198
Kipling, Rudyard xviii, 79, 102: on Kitchener
32
Kitchener, Horatio Herbert, 1st Earl xxi, 17, 27,
30, 32–3, 62, 102, 104, 123: and Beatty 56;
and Churchill 33, 36–7, 50, 75; and the
Dardanelles 63, 84; death 108–9; and Fisher
53–4, 69–70; and French 37, 39, 40, 45, 47,
59, 87, 102; Grand Duke Nicholas's appeal to
60–61, 81; and Northcliffe 84; volunteer
armies of 33, 82, 89, 102, 105–6, 114, 122,
176–7, 191, 211
Köln 46
Königin Luise 16
Königsberg 7, 200

Ladysmith, battle of 167
Lambert, Andrew xvii, 90–1, 198
Lambert, Nicholas 20
Lanrezac, Charles 37, 39, 44
Lansdowne, Henry Petty-Fitzmaurice, 5th
  Marquess of 135–6
Lavery, Sir John 54
Law, Andrew Bonar 15, 87, 126–7
Leighton, Roland 35, 71–2, 104–5, 118, 128
Leipzig riots 183
Lenin, Vladimir 142, 143, 145–9, 151, 194, 197,
202, 214
Liddell Hart, Basil xxii, 13, 31, 58–9, 60, 62, 71,
139, 176, 187–8, 203, 208, 209, 214–15
Liège 18, 30, 39, 131
Lilley, Terence 98–9
Lion xvii, 12, 43, 46, 111, 113, 119
Lloyd George, David xiv–xv, xvi, 4, 59–60, 127–
8, 150, 177, 179, 203: and the Admiralty 150,
151, 162–4; and the Armistice 199; and
Asquith 86, 145; and the blockade of
Germany 202, 214; and Britain's entry to
Great War 15, 16, 33; and Churchill 127, 171;

and the convoy system xxii, 150, 151, 154, 155,
163–4, 168, 184, 202; and Germany's 1918
spring offensives 180; and Grand Duke
Nicholas's appeal 61; and Haig 13, 127, 155,
160, 164–5, 167, 168, 169–70, 171, 175–6, 180,
215; and Jellicoe 155, 168, 171, 175, 176; and
Kenworthy 158; and Kitchener 33; and
national coalition government 86, 91, 145;
and naval estimates and expenditure 23; and
Nivelle 159, 160, 168; pessimism about the
war 109, 126; and the press 157; and
Robertson 168, 176; and the Somme 126; and
Third Ypres/Passchendaele 167, 168, 169–70,
172, 175–6; on war prospect and preparations
28; and Wilson's Fourteen Points 190
London, Declaration of (1909) 77, 94, 95
London, Treaty of 14–15
Loos, battle of 89, 101–2, 103, 176, 202, 213–14
Ludendorff, Erich 2, 45, 48, 104, 128, 130, 131,
138, 146, 147, 148, 160, 161, 169, 174, 176, 179,
181, 183, 195: and the Armistice 190, 192; on
battle of Amiens 188; dismissal and flight
197–8; and Lenin 146; nervous breakdown
178; Operation Georgette 180; Operation
Michael/1918 spring offensives 2, 11, 179–81,
192, 202
Lurcher 42
Lusitania 76, 77–80, 97, 107, 137, 153, 202
Lützow 113

Macaulay, Thomas Babington, 1st Baron 205
Magersfontein, battle of 166–7
Mahan, Alfred Thayer xx–xxi, xxii, 33, 117, 216:
  *The Influence of Sea Power upon History, 1660–
  1783*; xv, 20–1
Mainz 46
Mallinson, Allan 52, 120, 124, 167, 173, 192
Maltser, Robert xviii
Marine-Rundschau 117
Markgraf 198
Marne, battle of the 48–9, 52, 201, 202, 203
Marne, river 44, 47, 48
Marriott, Jack 4
Marx, Karl 142, 143, 145, 196
Masurian lakes, second battle of 139, 146
Maubeuge 30, 33
Max-Müller, W G 188–9
Maxim, Hiram 58–9
Maximilian of Baden 3, 5, 190, 192, 194, 199
Maxwell, Sir Herbert xix
Mediterranean Expeditionary Force 84, 212
Menin Gate 173–4
Meurer, Hugo von 7–9, 200
Michael, Operation 179–81, 192, 202
Moltke, Helmuth von 38, 44, 45, 48, 49, 80,
130, 139, 181
Mudros, Armistice of 6

Namur 37, 45
Napoleon I 19, 21
Napoleon III 3
Napoleonic Wars 24
Nasmith, Martin Dunbar- xx
Nassau-class battleship 22

National Portrait Gallery 205–17
Nelson, Horatio xv, 19
Neuve-Chapelle, battle of 82, 87
Nevinson, C R W 128
New York 152
New York Nation 79
New Zealand 42, 43
New Zealand Expeditionary Force 84
Nice 25
Nicholas II of Russia 142, 145: murdered, with
  family 197
Nicholas, Grand Duke 60–1, 63–4, 81
Nicolai, Walther 183
Nivelle, Robert 150, 151, 159–60, 161–2, 168,
  176: and Haig 164–5
Normandy landings xix
Northcliffe, Alfred Harmsworth, 1st Viscount
  17, 84, 157–8, 212
Northern Barrage 184
Northern Patrol (10th Cruiser Squadron) 92–3,
  94, 95–101, 182: AMCs 97, 100; boarding
  blockade-runners 98–9; *Edgar*-class cruisers
  95–7, 100

Oberndorff, Alfred von 4, 199
Oberste Heeresleitung (OHL) 5, 38, 44, 45, 48,
  52, 113, 129, 186–7, 191–2: Dritte OHL 130,
  132, 138–9, 146, 147, 174, 175, 178, 179, 181,
  189, 195, 196 *see also* Hindenburg, Paul von;
  Ludendorff, Erich
Oliver, Henry Francis 85
Ollard, Richard 33
Omdurman, battle of 32, 75
Operation Blücher 180, 181
Operation Georgette 180
Operation Michael 179–81, 192, 202
Opossum 74
Osborne, Eric 50, 51
Ostend 164, 169, 172, 184–5
Ottoman Empire 6, 145: joining Triple Alliance
  60; and Russia 60–2, 81
Owen, Harriet 200
Owen, Wilfred 1–2, 116, 144, 200
Oxford University, Brasenose college 103

Page, Walter 152
Paris 38, 45, 47, 179: and the battle of the
  Marne 52; Commune 143
Parry, Chris vi–viii
Passchendaele, battle of 11, 89, 122, 165, 166,
  171–7, 201–2: early phases *see* Ypres, Third
  battle of
Pathfinder 75
Pax Britannica 18, 166
Pearson, Michael 143
Pershing, John 13, 186, 187
Pétain, Henri 82, 117, 169, 179, 180, 186, 187
Petrograd 148–9
Philip II of Spain 18
Philip of Valois 18
Philipps, Sir Ivor 167
Pless Conference 129, 135, 139–40, 141, 193–4
Plumer, Herbert 171–6
Pohl, Hugo von 50, 51, 109
Poland 25, 105, 118, 122–3: Schloss Pless,

Silesia 129, 135, 139–40, 141, 193–4
Pommern 113
Pravda 147
Princess Royal 43, 111, 118
Prinzregent Luitpold mutiny 149, 196
Prittwitz, Max von 45
Prussia 3, 15, 24, 25, 26, 45, 130–31, 138:
  Austro-Prussian War 15

Queen Elizabeth 7, 10, 64–5, 70, 86, 89, 200
Queen Mary 43, 111, 118
Queen Victoria 148
Queenstown 78

Raeder, Erich viii
Rawlinson, Sir Henry 214
Rennenkampf, Pavel 44–5
Repington, Charles à Court 83–4
Richardson, Victor 128, 162, 165
Robeck, John de 84, 85, 87, 215
Robertson, Sir William 102, 124, 168, 169, 176,
  177: epigraph 107
Roosevelt, Theodore 107–8
Roskill, Stephen 66
Rosyth 7, 8, 10, 57, 137, 183, 200
Royal Air Force (RAF) xvii–xviii: Churchill on
  xvii–xviii; propaganda leaflets dropped by 182
Royal Arthur 95
Royal Flying Corps 39, 186
Royal Naval Air Service 186
Royal Navy: 1st Battle Cruiser Squadron 42, 43,
  46; and the British Army xiii–xiv, 31–2, 166–
  7, 203, 213, 215; Channel Fleet 19; critical
  importance in Great War xiii–xv, 202–4, 215–
  17; Cruiser Squadron, 10th *see* Northern
  Patrol; dreadnoughts xv, xvii, 23, 36, 50, 65,
  67, 97, 121, 155–6, 195; estimates and
  expenditure 23, 50; and Fisher's 'vital
  question' vii, 12, 126, 153, 158, 165, 216;
  Grand Fleet xvi–xvii, xxi, 10, 12, 23–4, 29, 31–
  2, 36, 40, 42, 50, 62, 67, 70, 90, 95, 97,
  110–13, 119–20, 121, 137, 155, 183, 185–6,
  194–5; lack of war plan in 1914 28;
  modernisation under Fisher 57, 65; naval race
  with Germany 21, 167; public expenditure on
  126, 216; ship construction programme under
  Fisher 57
Rupprecht of Bavaria 38, 39, 82, 169
Russia 14, 24, 25, 44–5, 62, 145, 174: 1905
  revolution 144; abdication of the Tsar 142,
  145; appeal to Britain over Turks 60–1, 63–4,
  81; battle of Tannenberg 11, 45, 60, 62, 131,
  139, 146, 201; collapse of Russian empire 145;
  February Revolution 142, 146, 196; Lenin's
  revolutions and Germany 142–3, 147–9, 196,
  198, 214; October Revolution 142, 196; and
  the Ottomans 60–2, 81; and the Treaty of
  Brest-Litovsk 142, 179, 196; and Triple
  Entente 14, 37, 142, 151, 179

St Vincent, John Jervis, 1st Earl 19, 139–40
Salonika, battle of 61, 62, 189, 191
Sassoon, Siegfried xviii, 144, 173–4
Scapa Flow 36, 42, 57, 75, 94, 137
Scharnhorst 36, 56, 137, 153

Scheer, Reinhard von vii, xxi, 90, 109–10, 112, 113, 116, 120, 121, 122, 153, 184, 193–5, 197, 202

Schlieffen, Alfred von 27, 37, 38, 44, 130, 131: plans 27, 44, 45, 52, 57, 146, 180, 201

Schloss Pless, Silesia 129, 135, 139–40, 141, 193–4

Schwieger, Walther 75, 76, 77–8, 79

Seydlitz 119

Signalbuch der Kaiserlichen Marine 57

Skagerrak, battle of 116

Somme offensive xvi, xxi, 11, 89, 106, 108, 113–16, 122–4, 130, 151, 161, 201–2; and Beatty 108; British casualties 109; casualties 115–16, 125, 126, 181; and Haig 108, 109, 113, 115, 122–4, 125, 170, 209, 214

Spee, Maximilian, Admiral von, naval squadron under 56, 76, 137

Stanley, Venetia 16, 70

starvation, German viii, 134, 182–3

Stettin 43, 46

Stevenson, David 182, 191, 199, 203

Strassburg 43, 46

submarines: German *see* U-boats; Royal Navy xx, 73–4, 87, 154, 174, 185

Tannenberg, battle of 11, 45, 60, 62, 131, 139, 146, 201

Taylor, A J P xxii, xxiv, 18, 29, 33, 52, 59, 62, 83, 84, 121, 122, 151, 168–9, 173, 182, 185, 188, 192, 213

Theseus, 95

Tirpitz, Alfred von 22–3, 51, 56, 110

Turkey, 14: and Russia 60–2, 81

Tyrwhitt, Sir Reginald Yorke, 1st Baronet x, xvii, xx, 9, 40, 41, 43, 67, 75, 110, 120, 122, 156–7: and Beatty 43, 46; and Churchill 40, 42, 46–7; and Fisher 91, 120; in Heligoland Bight 43, 46–7; Zeebrugge Raid 184–5

U-boats 74–80, 168, 183, 194–5: Admiralty measures to combat 154, 174, 184 *see also* convoy system; blockade of Britain vii, 76, 79, 118, 136, 151, 152–6, 157, 170, 203; *Lusitania* sinking 77–80, 107, 137, 153, 202; and the RN convoy system vii–viii, xxii, 150, 151, 154, 155, 157, 163–4, 170, 174, 184, 202; unrestricted submarine warfare vii–viii, xvi, 76–80, 121–2,

124, 125, 129–30, 135, 136, 137, 140–41, 146–7, 152–6, 193–4, 202, 215; and the US 80, 137, 140, 141, 152, 215

United States: army/AEF 6, 137, 139, 167, 175, 179, 181, 186, 187, 189, 191, 203; entry into First World War vii, xxi, 124, 138, 147, 215; and U-boat warfare 80, 137, 140, 141, 152, 194, 215

Verdun, battle of 11, 105, 113, 117, 130, 196, 201–2

Versailles, Treaty of 7

Victoria 65

Viknor 100

Vimy Ridge, battle of xxiv, 82, 87, 162

Wemyss, Sir Rosslyn Erskine 4, 5, 157

Western Front xvi, 1–5, 6, 12, 44–6, 49, 60, 71, 81, 87, 101, 105–6, 108, 114, 150, 167

Wilhelm II, Kaiser xvi, 22, 56, 80, 116, 121, 179, 187: abdication xiv, 5, 142–3, 199; and American democracy 141; and Bethmann-Hollweg 136; and Hindenburg 138–9; and the Imperial German Navy x, 21–2, 49–50, 51, 108, 116, 198; indecisiveness 136–7, 138; and Lenin 142, 146, 202; and Ludendorff 131, 138–9, 197; memoirs 22; at Schloss Pless 129, 135, 139–40, 141, 193–4; and unrestricted submarine warfare 122, 124, 129–30, 136–7, 140, 153, 193–4, 202

Wilhelmshaven revolt, Kaiserliche Marine 5

Wilson, Sir Henry 17–18, 27, 30, 37, 172, 209: and Asquith 34

Wilson, Woodrow xxiii, 80, 107, 108, 126, 130, 141, 194: Fourteen Points 4, 190, 194

Ypres, First battle of 58, 62, 82

Ypres, Third battle of 165, 166–77: casualties 174, 181; financial cost 173; and Haig *see* Haig, Sir Douglas: and Third Ypres/Passchendaele; and Jellicoe 166, 170, 215; Passchendaele (final phase of battle) *see* Passchendaele, Battle of

Zeebrugge 62, 69, 164, 172, 184–5: Raid xx, 170, 184–6

Zimmerwald international conference 146